URBAN ITALIAN

URBAN ITALIAN

SIMPLE RECIPES AND TRUE STORIES FROM A LIFE IN FOOD

ANDREW CARMELLINI AND GWEN HYMAN

PHOTOGRAPHS BY QUENTIN BACON

ANDREW

dedicates this book to:

Mom, Dad, and Vince, my first culinary victims, and my grandmothers, Attilia Bertin Carmellini and Victoria Bentowski,

and my aunt, Sylvia Spader, who sent me to Italy for the very first time

GWEN

dedicates this book to:

my family and Mitchell Davis, my great dear friend, who taught me how to play with food,

and the memory of my grandfather Ralph Hyman, who taught me how to play with words

Published by Bloomsbury USA, New York

Distributed to the trade by Macmillan

All papers used by Bloomsbury USA are natural, recyclable products made

from wood grown in well-managed forests. The manufacturing processes

conform to the environmental regulations of the country of origin.

Library of Congress Cataloging-in-Publication Data has been applied for.

ISBN-10: 1-59691-470-X

ISBN-13: 978-1-59691-470-4

First U.S. Edition 2008

1 3 5 7 9 10 8 6 4 2

Design by Level, Calistoga, CA

Printed in China by RR Donnelley, South China Printing Co. Ltd.

{ CONTENTS }

{ TRUE STORIES }

LEARNING TO COOK isn't just about knife skills and timing and technique, and it's not all about that I-am-an-artist thing either. It's about who you are and how you deal with the world: with banging out a meal for six hundred on the fly, for example, or with a crazy restaurateur, or with a pack of starving models, or with three months without a day off. And it's about understanding that cooking is more than just applying heat to food in complicated ways: a good cook brings his or her life to the table, and sucks as much experience as possible from the world to do it. So my education in Italian cooking has happened in kitchens, sure, but also on bucolic hilltops and in train-station cafés in the middle of the night, in Jaguars and in a 1974 Fiat 127, in fancy restaurants and in tents, on the road pursued by the *polizia* and at Park Avenue black-tie events. It's not like a Hollywood movie, where you go into culinary school and come out with a big knife and a hot job; it's more like a bunch of crazy home videos—the kind of stuff that comes out at the end of the night, with old friends, when everyone's had a drink or three. Here are a few of my favorites from the Italian reel.

My grandmother was Italian, in that old-school "if you're not suffering, you're sinning" kind of way. Her family, the Bertins, had drifted into northern Italy from their native France way back when, but she never had a lot of love for the French or their hoity-toity food. This whole "haute cuisine" thing, the idea that France was the cradle of restaurant culture—it was all garbage, Grandma said: if it hadn't been for Catherine de' Medici and her Italian cooks, the Frogs would still be boiling up chunks of meat and fat and calling it dinner. The Italians, they knew what flavor meant!

But she always gave people their props, Grandma—and Auguste Escoffier, he was due his props, French chef though he was. She gave me his books when I was a kid—my first real

cookbooks—and she told me stories about him. The greatest cook of all time, she said. Precision! Integrity! Ingredients! Now that was a chef! Her favorite story about Escoffier went like this:

Once, Escoffier was making a banquet for three hundred people, a wedding. This was no big deal for Escoffier. Three hundred people was like nothing to him. Everything was timed perfectly; every dish went out gorgeous, and the people couldn't believe how great everything tasted. The dessert was soufflé, and it was supposed to go out right after a certain speech was made. It couldn't be served during the speech, because the speaker was the bride's father, a big important guy in Paris, but it had to come out as soon as he was done, or the timing would be off for everything for the rest of the evening. Escoffier knew the guy would talk for twenty minutes, which was exactly how long it would take to make the soufflés. So twenty minutes before the speaker was due to begin, he gave the signal, and all his cooks started cracking shells and separating the yolks and whites of six hundred eggs. And fifteen minutes before the toast started, the great chef and his cooks began beating the egg whites, because the most important thing, with soufflés, is to beat the eggs continuously—fifteen minutes without pause, as fast as you can. As soon as the speaker stepped up to the podium, glass in hand, the beating of eggs ceased, the soufflés went into the oven. Escoffier had a little drink—they all had a little drink—and they waited, quietly, so as not to disturb the soufflés. And at the twenty-minute mark, the soufflés were perfect.

But this father of the bride, even though he was important, he was kind of a nervous guy, and so he'd had a bottleful of wine, more or less, before he got to the podium. When the twenty minutes were up, he was just getting warm, and he was so important that nobody felt like they could tell him to hurry up. Escoffier stuck his head out the kitchen door, and he listened, and it was clear the guy wasn't making any wrapping-up sounds. So he told his cooks to trash all the soufflés—three hundred soufflés!—straight out the back door to feed the beggars in the alley. The cooks didn't dare complain—yeah, precision, ingredients, creativity, the guy had it all, but Escoffier was not known for his patience, was not an easygoing, low-maintenance-type chef. They washed their bowls, went to the pantry, cracked another six hundred eggs. For another quarter of an hour—sweating, grunting, swearing—this kitchen full of men whisked the soufflés, biceps and triceps bulging. Again, the soufflés went into the oven. The cooks collapsed against the counters, dripping with sweat. Precisely twenty minutes later, they raised their shaking arms and—gently, gently—pulled the soufflés from the oven. Once again, each one was a thing of beauty, steamy and high and absolutely ready, right on time. The waiters stood at the door, poised, their smiles ratcheted tight.

And still, the bride's father, drunk, important, more powerful than anyone else in the room, went on talking and talking. He remembered his childhood, the rope swing in his backyard, the time he cracked open his head on a rock hidden in the lake. (The cooks had thoughts, muttered comments.) He told the story of his first true love, of another woman who broke his heart, of the day when he realized that he would be rich. He talked of how the bride was the most headstrong child anyone had ever had to raise, but how she was worth ten of her brother, who seemed somehow to have no interest in money, not even in spending it, except on paint and books and food, fancy food, which he guessed was culture but what good did it do?

Again, the alley door was propped open. Again, the beggars were treated to dessert. The kitchen boys were sent running to all the markets, to their grandmothers' and mothers' and aunties' houses, anywhere, everywhere, for more eggs. Again the eggs were broken, the whites beaten—the cooks shaking now, their arms spasming out of control, whipped egg white flying up, coating their eyebrows, their chins. The beating this time took twenty minutes, they were not so fast, and they tried not

to weep directly into the bowls—the salt being very bad for the flavor. Escoffier, sweating through his chef's jacket, beat his eggs as though his arms were mechanical, magical, glaring out over the bowl, daring anyone else to give up. Again the soufflés went into the oven. The cooks slid to the floor, their backs against the counters, their knees bent up in front of them. Escoffier stood, arms crossed, terrible, serene. In the dining room, the guests, he could see, were slumping over their wine, turning their napkins into folded flowers, playing games with feet and fingers under the table. The father of the bride talked, and talked, and talked, and the cooks lost hope: they would be making soufflés over and over, until their arms fell completely off, until all the eggs in Paris were eaten up by all the beggars in Paris and the chickens were all dead from exhaustion. But just then—just at twenty minutes, just when the soufflés were just done—the father of the bride found that his glass was empty. He hoisted it high above his head. "To the bride!" he shouted. "To the bride!" the crowd replied, deeply grateful, loving the bride, loving the empty glass. And the kitchen door swung open, right on time, and the waiters in their spotless jackets emerged, military, precise, bearing three hundred steaming, high-domed, light-as-air soufflés.

THAT, MY GRANDMOTHER SAID, WAS COOKING.

When I was fifteen, I scored my first real restaurant job, at this Italian place down in the valley. To get there, you drove past a bowling alley, a couple of trucking companies, some warehouses, right down almost to the edge of the canal. This was some time after the Cuyahoga River caught fire, but way before Cleveland started cleaning itself up—so it wasn't exactly the kind of neighborhood where you'd expect to find women in *Dynasty* outfits and big hair or men in fancy Italian suits, but there they were: back in 1987, that restaurant was smokin', packed every night, four hundred covers or more. The front was all done up in greens and mauves and glass block; there was a backyard garden with brick walls, trellises, vines, the whole '80s Hollywood look. It was the place to go for business lunches or fancy dinners, the place everyone made reservations for anniversaries, birthdays, proposals (of all kinds).

I thought I'd learn about food at the Italian restaurant. About the business. I was a kid from the suburbs who played basketball and messed around on the guitar. What did I know?

And I did learn things. I saw all kinds of stuff that fifteen-year-olds don't usually see. Big dudes with nicknames, in good suits, making shady deals at the back tables. Bringing their mistresses one night, their wives another, hookers or strippers from down the street when things were slow. Handing off packages under the table. It was one of those guys—he came in with his wife sometimes, his kids—who offered one of the hostesses four grand to spend the weekend with him. (When she turned him down, her friend stepped up. "I'll do it!" she announced, cheerleader chipper in her big hair. The guy looked her up and down, pulled out a wad of dough. At the end of the shift, there he was, waiting in his Lincoln.)

Women would go into the bathroom in twos and threes, coming out sparkling and sniffing. Cooks disappeared into the walk-in to smoke pot during service, blowing the smoke into the fan intake so it would disappear outside; by the end of the night, you could get stoned just by standing out by the exhaust vent, near the garbage cans in the alley.

I worked every job there was at that restaurant. I started out bussing tables, I hosted, I worked bar-back—and I made good money, up there in the front. But I wanted to cook, and the place had a reputation for serving the best Italian in town, so I asked—asked!—to go work with the mooks in the kitchen. I worked my way up through every station: from salad to fry station to sauté and so forth. On Saturday mornings, I would show up at eight A.M., prep the entire cooking line, and then put together each and every special of the day, all by myself.

The menu wasn't all Italian: no smart restaurateur in that time and place would have gone that way. There was the typical '80s American stuff: burgers at lunchtime, that ubiquitous California chicken salad with fried wonton strips and canned mandarin oranges. I'm pretty sure even Indian restaurants had that California salad on the menu back then. And we did steaks and chops, of course, for all those guys with big shoulders: on Saturday nights, working grill, I could turn out three hundred of those. But mostly it was Italian. That's why I was there. I wanted to learn about authentic European cooking. This, they told me, was the real thing.

(This was way before I went to Italy.)

The menu featured antipasti, lots of pastas, of course. Chicken parmigiana, veal parmigiana. There was always a veal scallopini of the day and a chicken scallopini of the day. This was, in fact, amazing: "of the day" didn't just mean a weekly rotation. It meant that there was a different veal scallopini and a different chicken scallopini every single day of the year, 365 variations. Veal scallopini with tomato-vodka sauce. Chicken scallopini with Marsala and mushrooms. Veal scallopini with sauce picante. Chicken scallopini with Frangelico, cream, and crushed-up hazelnuts. Every single day there was a different chicken scallopini and a different veal scallopini, always served over fettuccini or rice pilaf (your choice!).

Everyone I talked to—the cooks I worked with at the catering place, Pete at the Italian restaurant, my friends' parents—said that the way they were doing things, the way they cooked "I-talian food," was "the way they do it in the old country." So that's what I thought Italian food was: pasta so soft it turned to glue in your mouth; "red sauce" and a large, overspiced ball dumped on the very top of a pile of noodles; cheesecake with canned fruit topping. **THREE HUNDRED AND SIXTY-FIVE FLAVORS OF CHICKEN SCALLOPINI.**

When I was eighteen, I finally made it to Italy for the first time. We went on a huge family trip—aunts, uncles, cousins, crammed carloads of Italian-Americans barreling through the Old Country. My oldest uncles were born in Italy, and they wanted to show us all what it was really like. I was psyched—my first plane trip, my first passport. I knew exactly what it would be like. I'd seen the movies; I'd read the books; I'd heard my uncles' stories. I'd ride a motor scooter fast over the hills, drink espresso in town squares, hang out on Mediterranean beaches crowded with topless European women. Chase curvy Italian girls with long dark hair and sexy smiles. La Dolce Vita.

Well. So.

First of all, my uncles, who were, granted, born in Italy, wanted all of us to pass as gen-u-ine Italianos. Didn't matter that my cousins and I didn't speak a word of Italian that wasn't about food or swearing. We all had to wear long pants and collared shirts every day, in the heat of the Italian summer, jammed into a van without air conditioning, with all our relatives. So I didn't look like an ugly American in a fanny pack and bike shorts, but I didn't exactly look like one of those cool, carefully disheveled Italian dudes either. By the time I crawled out of that thousand-degree van for our first stop of the day, I was wrinkled, sweaty, sodden, and totally pissed off.

Not that it mattered, since there were definitely no beaches to hang on and no girls to chase. Instead, we stopped the car at every church, every monastery, and every castle between Rome and Udine. And at any place that anything historical at all had happened—not just World War I and World War II, but going all the way back to the Peloponnesian wars. Lot of history in Italy. We'd stop, stand around old stone walls or empty fields or town squares, take a picture. I'd kick a rock and stare out in the distance, soulful, sweating. We'd down espresso served by some ancient Italian woman in a headscarf. Then we'd get back in the van, taking a last deep breath of fresh air before crawling back into that smelly oven. We'd get lost, over and over again, driving through the hills past farmhouses and car repair joints and sofa factories on the outskirts of town. "Follow da sun!" my uncle would holler, like we were birds, or eighteenth-century sailors.

We didn't eat in any fancy places on that trip—we couldn't afford ristorantes, and my uncles weren't the type to sit around in a café by a fountain with a guidebook and a pack of cigarettes. So it was trattorias, rest-area espresso joints, osterias, and quick lunches of bread, wine, and cheese in the back of the van. None of it had anything to do with the Italian food I'd eaten in restaurants and at friends' tables all my life. No frozen pasta; no "red sauce"; no cheesecake with canned fruit topping; no scallopini of any kind. Everything was fresh, made five minutes ago, and it had actual, distinct, vibrant flavors. In Friuli, I had white asparagus for the first time—in a risotto, even: not a rice-pilaf-from-a-box-with-cream, like we'd been serving in the restaurant back home, but a whole different thing, a course of its own, soft and comforting and creamy and fresh-tasting. Even the espresso in the rest-stop bars was the best I'd ever tasted. It twisted my head right around. This? This was real Italian? Like they make it in the old country?

THIS WAS *GOOD*.

For my uncles, my re-education was a challenge: like deprogramming a cult member. They were going to beat the midwesterner out of me, no matter how painful the process might be. The very first night in Italy, after we got off the plane at the Malpensa airport in Milan, we stopped at this trattoria my uncle knew for lunch—a very local, very typical kind of place. I'd been awake the whole time on the plane, too psyched to sleep; I'd had two espressos on the way to lunch. I was wired, jumpy. I couldn't focus on the menu, couldn't understand the Italian, and finally I just gave up. "I order for you," says my oldest uncle, and he looks up at the waiter, and he grins, and he says, "Something something *cavallo* something something *per favore*." I'm thinking, "Cabbage? I'm getting cabbage?" (because I've been studying

gastronomic Italian, and I'm pretty good with the vegetables). I'm drinking wine, looking around, listening to all the Italian around us; and I can't believe I'm here—and I'm so tired I'm sort of hallucinating, almost, things spinning and swimming around a bit, like I'm really drunk but totally hopped-up at the same time. And then the waiter appears with this plate, and it's got this pile of ground meat in the center, uncooked, with some olive oil, some arugula, a bowl of crunchy bread on the side. (So I guess it's not cabbage. Right. Cabbage is *cavolo*.) The meat was raw—but that was okay, I was going to be a cook, I knew from French food, it was tartare, it was cool. "What is it?" I asked my uncle. "It's good! You'll like it! Eat!" he answered. I wasn't going to let him think that I was one of those ugly American kids in Europe who asked for soda pop at the table and snuck away to McDonald's first chance I got. So I picked up my fork and I started mixing the meat with the olive oil, piling it onto the bread, tossing the arugula on top. A kind of gamey beef flavor, rich, deep. Local cows, I thought, picturing fields of wandering bovines, muscular, natural. I ate every bite.

"You like it?" asked my uncle. I nodded, wiping my plate with the last of the bread.

"Know what that was? That was *horse!*"

And he laughed and laughed, and my aunts and my uncles, they laughed and laughed, pointing at me, choking on their wine.

My cousins looked a little sick.

Me, I didn't feel the least bit sick. I felt tough. Victorious. Italian.

I'd been at cooking school for three weeks, and I was already bored, stuck up in the middle of friggin' nowhere in upstate New York abandoned-factory country. School had been exciting for the first few days—leaving home, moving into the dorm with my buddy Dante—but it didn't take long to figure out that in the first three months there would be no real cooking, just . . . classes. I am not exactly a big sitting-in-class kind of guy. I was broke too: cooking school was expensive, even back in the day. So I answered an ad on the school job board for a weekend private-chef gig in the area—and I got a call back, on the phone in the dorm hallway, from the Governor's Mansion in Albany.

I GOT IN MY WHITE '73 MAVERICK one cold September Saturday and drove up to the bleak, modernist-brutalist seat of government to do a first interview—with the state troopers. They checked out my background, my criminal history, and my friends and family, fingerprinted and photographed me, and declared me safe to proceed to the governor's kitchen. The next weekend, I went straight to the governor's place, a big Victorian mansion up on a hill. A staffer took me into the kitchen and told me to start cooking: the family would be ready to eat in four hours. I made three courses—a fancy soup, pasta, and some kind of meat, beef maybe. It was the Italian food I'd been cooking for years in C-Town, filtered through that trip to Italy, with some vague ideas about French training and three weeks of classes and books thrown in. But I was fast, and it all looked pretty on the plate, and I must have caught Mrs. Cuomo on a very, very good day. She came back in the kitchen and shook my hand, and that was it. I was the official weekend chef at Governor Mario Cuomo's official residence. State pension, full benefits, the kind of ID card that convinces state troopers to let you go when they catch you speeding on the thruway at three in the morning. I was eighteen years old.

I would drive up on Friday night and cook for the guv through the weekend. The gig didn't include housing at the mansion, so I stayed at one of Albany's finer hostelries: the kind of place where the bikers next door like to slap their hooker girlfriends around loudly at three A.M., between drug sales. (That's the kind of town Albany was.) After a night of gunshots, yelling, creaking bedsprings, and bored, loud *oh, baby*s, I would head up to the mansion to cook a nice dinner for the Cuomos. Sunday night was family night. The governor, Mrs. Cuomo told me, likes to eat lamb shank on Sundays—that's what he grew up with, that's his favorite comfort food. And for dessert? Apple pie. Mario, she told me, loves apple pie. No problem, I said, relieved. I'm from Ohio. Apple pie—check! So the second Sunday of my employment with the governor, I dragged myself out of my cinder block motel room, past the beater cars and the doors behind which the dealers and their hooker girlfriends slept off their Saturday-night crack-induced brawls, and I tied on a clean white apron in the spotless Mansion kitchen, and while the governor and his sons played basketball outside, I made lamb shank and apple pie.

I'd been making lamb shank at home for years, but this was different—this was the Governor's Mansion! So I broke out all my fancy French moves. That lamb shank had a serious, many-hours-reduced veal stock, which became a deep, very French sauce, flavored with some equally serious (and equally French) red wine. I made a bouquet garni; I labored over presentation. I served it with rice pilaf. It was, I thought, a thing of beauty: continental, worthy of Versailles, equal to anything served at any upscale Manhattan restaurant.

The family ate it in the parlor, on trays, while watching TV.

There were no compliments sent back to the chef, but there were no complaints either, and the plates all came back clean—so I figured my lamb shank was a hit. I got back in the Maverick and did 100 all the way back to school, Zeppelin on the radio, and I told everybody about my gig, and how I rocked it.

The next Sunday morning, I rolled out of my cement bed at the motel and washed my face with my sandpaper towel and brushed my teeth and made my way across the crack vials to the Maverick. I walked into the Mansion kitchen and tied on my apron, and I turned around, and there was the man himself, in a sweatshirt, with his arm around this little old Sicilian grandmother. "I brought my mom over," said Mario, in his thick, old-school Queens accent. "She's going to show you how to make the lamb shank." The old lady smiled. The governor wandered off to play basketball.

Mom's lamb shank, it turned out, had natural braising juices, lots of garlic and tomato and herbs and cannellini beans. It was slow-simmered, not "sauced." There was no rice pilaf. It was not continental. It was, in fact, Italian. (I had one just like it in this little town in the mountains of Sicily years later; one bite, and I was back in that Albany kitchen with that old lady from Queens.)

It was the best lesson I ever had about getting to know your customers.

After that, it was lamb shank grandma-style every Sunday night (with apple pie—at least I got that part right. No nonna from Queens does a better apple pie than we do in Ohio).

I had this Italian friend, Sergio, a cook I knew from New York. He was a cool guy, but also sort of a lunatic. On my first visit to Torino, he'd taken me to a soccer game. Nice, right? Some local color. Instead, the afternoon had involved copious amounts of mind-altering substances, illegal stadium entry, explosives, rampaging cops, rampaging fans, car-tipping, and other assorted ultraviolence. Still, when I got back to Torino on my next trip, a scholarship gig involving cooking classes and assorted kitchen slavery, I called up his parents. Maybe I wanted to reaffirm, in my own mind, that the trip to the stadium was an aberration for this guy I'd worked next to on the line, wielding knives and fire. Maybe I wanted to see if psychopathic soccer-hooligan behavior ran in families. Maybe I just needed a day off.

Whatever. Sergio's parents immediately invited me over for dinner. As it turned out, they were perfectly nice people—as far as I could tell, totally unlikely to attack strangers' cars with rocks or bodysurf on extreme inclines. A little bit geeky, even. We sat in the kitchen, drinking coffee and chatting, and suddenly Sergio's dad jumped up, saying, "You're a cook just like my son—you'll appreciate this! Let me show you my cantina!" He opened up a tall kitchen cupboard. Inside, I saw row upon row of small glass jars filled with porcini mushrooms. There was porcini *sott'aceto* (in vinegar), porcini *sott'olio* (in oil), porcini *agrodolce* (sweet and sour)—hundreds, literally hundreds of jars of porcinis. He had, he said, picked all these mushrooms himself.

This is not exactly the kind of thing you see back in Ohio. "Can I go picking with you sometime?" I asked. "Sure," he replied, "come back on Sunday morning and we'll go." Now for a young cook like me, to get invited to go porcini-mushroom-hunting in Italy—that's pretty cool. Most people don't want to show you where they pick their mushrooms; porcinis are nowhere near as valuable as truffles, but they're still worth about twenty dollars a pound, and the competition is fierce. And this guy obviously had a pretty crazy-good spot somewhere, because those mushrooms were huge. I was pumped.

The next Sunday morning—a frost on the ground, snow in the mountains up above us—we headed out in Sergio's dad's Fiat Uno. We drove up toward the foothills of the Alps, through the city's industrial fringe, past old factories, industrial parks, gas stations, everything closed and silent and bleak. By seven thirty or so, we had made it out into the open country, lots of meadows and open fields running up to the mountains. There was no one around—not a building, not a cow. Then, up ahead, I saw smoke rising by the road, and suddenly we came up on traffic, in the middle of nowhere. The cars—Beamers, Mercedes, Mazeratis—are all crawling along, and I'm figuring there must be some kind of fair or show or gathering of rich men, and then we get up to the corner of four cornfields, and suddenly there are fifteen hookers in superhigh heels, fishnets,

short-shorts, and push-up bras with spangles, standing there in the literal actual middle of nowhere, and working it, on Sunday morning at seven thirty.

Most of the women looked North African to me. They also looked like they were freezing, in the way that hookers in fishnets and microminis usually do, and when they weren't actively working the street or climbing into or out of a car (the cars turned off into the cornfields, did their thing, and came right back), they were sitting on milk crates by the side of the road, and each crate had a little open fire built in front of it, burning trash and corn leaves. That, it seemed, was the source of the smoke I'd seen. The scene was hazy, surreal—like something out of *Mad Max*. We crawled along in the little Fiat, and I looked and looked.

Perhaps noticing the shock in my face, Sergio's dad filled me in. This, he explained, was a regular Sunday-morning activity on the outskirts of Italian towns: the women and children go to church, and the men head out to the countryside for a little sumthin' sumthin' in the backseat. He saw these women every week on his way to and from his porcini patch. He felt sorry for them, he told me. **"AH, THE PUTANA..."** he sighed, shaking his head.

The traffic crawled along. The hookers disappeared behind us. The cars vanished, the highway opening out empty, and we headed into the foothills of the Alps near Pinasca. It was beautiful country—mountain lakes, pine forests with little stone houses tucked among the trees, streams cutting through little mountain valleys, amazing early-morning sun. Finally, around nine A.M., we pulled over to the side of the road and parked at the bottom of a pine-covered hill that shot straight up from the road. Sergio's dad handed me a basket made of wire and straw, said something that sounded like "Hup!" and headed up the hill at a brisk clip. There was no path, no easy way up: I swear the man was nearly perpendicular as he swung along, not even breathing hard. He explained to me, as I toiled, sweating, up the hill behind him, that he was bringing me to places where his father brought him to pick porcinis. I was psyched, and I was honored—I really was; he was treating me like a son!—but I was also dying. This guy had to be sixty-five years old, and I was all of twenty-two, and he was just smokin' me, plowing up the hill through the brush and branches as if it were nothing. I gasped for air. I think I twisted an ankle. But I kept going, grim, determined. He seemed, cheerfully, not to notice that I was bathed in sweat.

After what felt like an hour, Sergio's dad called back to me, "Oh, ecco-la"—here they are! I looked at the forest floor, shaded from the sun by a thick pine canopy, and all I saw was sticks and leaves and sticks and leaves. But my eyes adjusted, and there they were: my first wild porcinis. And then suddenly, I could see them everywhere—under every tree, on every rise in the ground, beneath every leaf. "Look," I thought, "it's a thousand-dollar hill!" We picked mushrooms for six solid hours—we'd fill five huge baskets in one area, take the mushrooms down to the car, then head back up the hill with empty baskets to a new spot. Sergio's dad was inexhaustible: he shot up and down that mountain like he had rockets in his hiking boots.

Finally, Sergio's dad pronounced us finished. My legs shaking, I trailed him back to the Fiat. On the way home, we stopped in a little town where there was a mushroom market in progress. This was just like a truffle market—except that instead of a tent, tables, climate-controlled cheese carts, and a car with a huge truffle on top, there was a line of men standing in the street, arms crossed, with wooden crates at their feet. In each crate? Hundreds of dollars' worth of fungi. Sergio's dad walked halfway down the line, checking out the contents of each crate, before he settled on one that seemed to suit him. He sold the owner, a craggy-faced, big-bellied guy like all the other craggy-faced, big-bellied porcini merchants, a couple of baskets of his giant porcini, pocketed the cash, and we were on our way.

There were fewer cars than before when we passed the corner of cornfield and cornfield; in fact, we could almost have cruised right through without stopping. The hookers were still out there, though, hunched over their fires—and Sergio's dad, he drives right up to the middle of the red-light field and pulls the Fiat Uno over. And I think, "This guy's gonna get a quickie!" and I think, "It is like father, like son!" and then I think, "Is he getting me a quickie? Is this a welcome-to-Italy gift? Porcinis and hookers?" (I'm not sure how I feel about that.) But before I can sort out my reactions, he reaches into the backseat and pulls out a basket of porcinis. Then he walks over to one of the women and hands it to her—and she gives him a little kiss on the cheek thank-you. I'm still thinking, "Okay, so he's paying her in porcinis," which, since there's about two hundred dollars' worth in mushrooms in there, is totally reasonable, and maybe even pretty generous—but then he just gets back in the car. And that's when I notice that the women have little makeshift implements and pans and things, and they're actually cooking over those trash fires.

What a good guy.

Nothing like his fuckin' kid.

We drove back to his house and unloaded the porcinis, and he and his wife started this assembly-line thing with the cleaning (they wouldn't let me help, so I sat, quietly massaging my aching calves). They made a quick lunch—eggs and sautéed porcini, with a little glass of vino—and then it was time to can and pickle some more porcini for the cantina. He got out a wire carrier full of glass jars and started cleaning and sterilizing. She busted out the vinegars. It was time to get to work.

I was working at San Domenico in Imola, the sister-restaurant to the place in New York, in Valentino Mercatelli's kitchen. It was New Year's Eve, and we were totally in the weeds, getting ready for the big party that night. I was busy making thousands of miniature ravioli with quail eggs. Suddenly there's commotion. I looked up, and I saw a couple of official-looking Italian gentlemen making their way through the kitchen, stopping to speak to each cook. Some conversations were quick; some were a little more involved. Each conversation included an examination of paperwork.

These guys, I figured, were from the *questura*, the local police headquarters. They'd decided it would be a good idea to do a sweep for illegal workers right then—in a restaurant kitchen, right before New Year's. Guess somebody didn't pay a bribe or something.

I felt bad for the poor suckers who got swept up. And on New Year's Eve too. That totally sucks.

And then the official gentlemen got to me.

"Papers, please!"

I clapped the flour from my hands and I handed them over—everybody in Italy has to carry their papers with them all the time—and I stood, waiting, while they examined my passport and visa.

I'd been in Italy for seven months. Studying. Working. I had crossed the border nine times. My papers had been examined on planes and trains, in cars, in restaurants, once at a movie theater. I was patient, calm, unworried.

Official Gentleman #1—a good half-foot shorter than me—looked up at me. Back at the page. Up at me again. Over at the owner. Over, the other way, at the chef.

He opened his mouth, licked his lips. Actually stuck his tongue out, this guy. Like a snake.

"Not valid," he pronounced.

Seems the student visa I got through the official agency that sponsored my trip—the student visa that had been examined by at least six different official governing bodies—was, according to Mr. Tiny Tim, not quite right. There was, apparently, a special stamp that I did not have. Therefore, my employment was officially terminated.

And, Mr. Snake added, since I was no longer officially employed, I was also officially no longer a legal resident of Torino.

Would I like, Mr. Forked Tongue asked, unctuous, some help in packing up my belongings?

I stood there, covered in flour, my tray of ravioli half-finished. Stunned. Outlawed. Exiled.

Who said Mussolini was dead?

The chef tried to intervene—no dice. The owner had a private word or two—nothing.

I'd stored up quite a rich vocabulary of Italian curses. I think I used all of them. It's possible that this had something to do with the speed of my departure and the ineffectiveness of the owner's intervention. But I don't think so. I think I was fucked from the moment those bastards saw my American passport. My fluency in Italian cursing probably earned me some points, actually.

Whatever. THE TWO *POLIZIA* WERE KIND ENOUGH TO WALK ME BACK TO MY APARTMENT. They watched me pack my bags, and then they very kindly drove me to the train station, where they walked me all the way up to the ticket counter, where I bought a ticket for Milan—only in Milan would I be able to find this mysterious stamp. And then they generously gave of their time to wait with me until my train arrived, and they saw me safely seated aboard, my luggage stowed. They may even have waved as the train pulled out.

I hadn't eaten since breakfast, so by the time I got to Milan, just before midnight, I was starving. I lugged my stuff into one of the twenty-four-hour cafés by the train station and ordered a panino, which I swallowed in about four bites—I don't think I even tasted it. And you know how when you haven't eaten anything all day, and then you eat fast, sometimes you just crash? I was so tired and out of it, and I couldn't believe all this had happened, and I had no idea where I was going to go next, and I had been working since seven A.M., and I hadn't had a day off in about ten days, and so I just sort of put my head down on my bag—just for a second, to rest.

And then I woke up with the waiter tapping me on my shoulder, and I reached into my pocket to pay him, and I discovered that someone had picked my pocket. My wallet was gone. And that stamp I needed? Not so pressing a concern, now that I had no passport.

Happy New Year!

Here's an idea: build a fifty-five-thousand-square-foot replica of an Italian piazza in an armory on Park Avenue in New York City, courtesy of the Italian Trade Commission, and make it the center of a celebration of Italian culture. Keep it open to the public all day long. Serve free cappuccino. Feed ten thousand people a day. Offer displays and exhibits highlighting the best of Italian design, art, and lifestyle. At night, host luxurious, glamorous events in the middle of the piazza, sponsored by Italian high rollers on the cultural scene.

Nice idea! In fact, great idea!

Then hire Italians to run it!

Bad idea!

The place was called Casa Italia, and the first event there was a party for a top Italian designer. The evening would include five hundred guests, a full-on runway show, Lenny Kravitz onstage, tables full of celebrities in the audience, security all the way down the block outside—in other words, it was a very, very big deal. And the upscale Italian restaurant I was working for was catering the whole thing.

I wasn't in charge of anything for this particular event—not even the menu. My job was antipasti, and only antipasti. I should have been relieved. But—maybe it's just the chef control freak in me—I was having issues.

The client had asked for three different antipasti for each guest—1,500 plates at least—some passed, some served at the table. I'd worked for three days on the mise en place alone. My one assistant on this extremely labor-intensive project was an Italian kid, even younger than I was, known in the kitchen mainly for his gift for dating high-end strippers. This was not of much use to me. But whatever. I got the job done—exactly as the chef had asked me to do it, exactly as the menu specified.

I arrived at Casa Italia three hours before the event—accompanied by my trusty assistant—to get the antipasti ready to go and make sure that everything was set up for the dinner. The setup was pretty rough—there was no permanent kitchen at the site, so we were more or less cooking over Bunsen burners—but I got it together, plated everything the way the chef and I had discussed, layered the plates on the tables ready for serving in order of appearance. There was only so much I could do—I could not, for instance, really set up stations for the line cooks without, for instance, the food. Or the implements that the line cooks would be working with. But I was pretty pleased with the whole thing when the chef and the crew—eight cooks—finally showed up with the rest of the food, about half an hour before the party was due to start.

As it happens, our makeshift kitchen was set up right next to the room in which the models were getting dressed and made up. **YOU KNOW THAT THING ABOUT HOW MODELS DON'T EAT? A HUGE LIE.** (Maybe it really is all genetic. Maybe they're all bulimic. I have no idea.) A couple of women came running out from behind the curtain—in heels, hose, underwear and bras, and nothing else—and squealed to the chef, "Ooh! Can you feed us? We're *starving*! There's *nothing* to eat over here!" The chef, being a red-blooded Italian male, immediately abandoned our preparations and started carrying plates of food over to the models, wearing his best I'm-a-seductive-Italian smile. He was trailed by my assistant, and then by half the line cooks. And they didn't just take over a little of this and a little of that. (After all, how much can models eat, really? Even weirdly hungry models?) They took *a lot* of this. And a *whole lot* of that.

Meanwhile the party got underway. Italians and celebrities and Italian celebrities began arriving.

The waitstaff lined up—professionals doing their jobs!—and I started loading them up with antipasti: out went the first round of antipasti plates, or what was left of them after the skinny girls in their underwear next door were finished ravening on them.

In stormed the restaurant's owner.

"Whaddya doing?" he screamed at the top of his lungs, his Italian accent getting thicker by the second. "This is not antipasti! This is French food! This—this—this is *Casa Italia*! Italia! *Italiana*! I want sliced prosciutto! I want chunks of parmesano cheese! I want little panini with buffalo mozzarella!"

Most of this screaming, of course, was directed at me. After all, I had made the antipasti. And anyway, the chef was busy over behind the curtain in Model World.

And it wasn't like I was unaware that the food we were making was not exactly Italian—or, not to put too fine a point on it, not exactly good. Little toast points with smoked salmon. Little baby zucchini stuffed with olives, served cold. Very dainty. Very retro-pretty. Very . . . continental.

But I had assumed—silly me!—that the owner had at least glanced at the menu, which was, after all, put together by his own (Italian) chef.

And I had worked for three days on this.

And the owner was picking up plates and hurling them toward the garbage.

And meanwhile, I was pretty sure that all the Italians and celebrities and Italian celebrities could hear the plates smashing and the owner screaming, and also that it was probably better to send out sucky continental food to a room full of people expecting to be fed than it was to send out nothing at all.

Clearly, however, that wasn't going to happen. I hoped these fashion people liked to drink.

Finally, the chef emerged from behind the curtain, conferred briefly with the owner—much gesturing of hands—and headed out the door with four of the Italian cooks. They got in a cab, went back to the restaurant, picked up all the parmesan and all the prosciutto we had in the kitchen, and brought it back to our little armory field kitchen. They started cutting open the parmesan wheels, breaking them up into chunks, and dumping them into bowls, which they immediately sent out—just like that—to appease the growing (and audible) hunger of the extremely fancy crowd outside. They slammed prosciutto onto trays and sent it out with no plates, no forks—nothing but a handful of napkins for the waiters to pass around with the slices of unaccompanied meat. So professional! So gourmet! So Italian!

The chef did not ask for my help. He was not talking to me. He was acting, in fact, as if all this was my fault.

So I left the kitchen.

Here's how the party was going:

Half-naked models were running around all over the place (some still chewing on our food). Waiters were moving through the crowds with empty trays, looking panicked; a bunch of them tackled me as soon as I showed my face, asking, begging, demanding, "I need more parmesano!" "Where are the toast points? Those ladies want toast points!" "Can't we have some plates for the prosciutto? And can't we have some more prosciutto?" "Aren't we serving the zucchini anymore?"

IT WAS COMPLETE CHAOS.

"I'm just a cook," I insisted. "I know nothing. I have no idea."

Over their shoulders, I watched the crowd. Big white teeth. Skinny little bodies. Fancy outfits. Stars. Stars everywhere, from fashion, from music, from movies. Hungry stars. Drinking stars. Unhappy-looking stars.

I went back to the kitchen.

Finally, an hour behind schedule, it was time to serve the first course—the guests were sitting down, the MC had made his first speech, we were good to go. I helped to plate, hustled the waiters out, wiped the edges of bowls. I had a bad feeling about the whole thing—but who was I? I was just a cook.

And a minute or two after the bowls started going out, in stormed the Big Italian Designer.

"What are you doing?" he screamed, more or less at the owner.

"Do you know who these people are?" he bellowed.

"Why the *fuck* would you serve fashion people *snails* and *polenta*? Do you think they actually want to *eat* snails and polenta?"

Now, mind you, snails and polenta is, unlike toast points with salmon, actually a pretty traditional dish, especially around Emilia-Romagna and Venice—they eat a lot of snails, the Italians. That wasn't the problem.

The problem, as the Big Italian Designer explained in English, in Italian, and in International Swearing, is that, as far as Fashion Stars and other assorted Stars are concerned:

A. *polenta is peasant food;*

B. *polenta is fattening;*

and

C. *snails are disgusting.*

So let's recap. The antipasti were an hour late, seeing as they were in a cab coming uptown when everyone was ready to eat antipasti, seeing as the owner threw the actual prepared, on-time antipasti against the wall. (And okay—so maybe the chef's antipasti menu wasn't Italian, but at least the Stars were eating it, or what they could get of it.)

Then everyone sat down to dinner, pretty much starving, and what they were served was . . . snails.

In yellow gruel.

Fattening, cream-filled yellow gruel.

The Big Italian Designer had a constructive suggestion (more constructive than throwing plates at the wall, anyway). He wanted those guests who declined to eat their snails to be offered a salad.

Of course, when the waiters went out to make this suggestion (quietly, discreetly) to the guests, it quickly became clear that 495 of the 500 people who had been served snails-and-yellow-gruel would prefer a nice green salad.

The owner rushed around, waving his hands; the chef rushed around, waving *his* hands; and magically, out of nowhere, an hour or so later, salad appeared. (To this day, I don't know where it came from. Maybe they ordered in from the deli down the street. Maybe it was from the craft services the models hadn't been able to find.)

In the meantime, the program was running late.

The idea had been that after the first course was served, the Big Italian Designer would show a collection on the runway; after the second course, a second collection; after dessert—Lenny Kravitz.

The producers, apparently, were worried about waiting on the collections. (Maybe the lighting guys were union? Maybe the producers were worried that at midnight the models would turn into pumpkins?) Anyway, they decided they couldn't wait until after the first course was finished—they were an hour late, and they were going to start. So the waiters were running around with salads, and people still had snails on their tables, and now *everyone* wanted salad because they could see that salads were on offer, but the waiters only had enough salads for the 495 people who had asked for them specifically, and now the five people who were stuck with snails were the five wrong people (and some of the people who had taken salads had also eaten the snails, so they were just being little piggies), and of course the five people who had snails and wanted salads were the absolute most important people in the whole crowd of Very Important People, and meanwhile the models were sashaying down the runway in this special one-time-only collection the Big Italian Designer had slaved over just for this event, and the buyers and editors and fashionistas were missing the whole thing because they were busy arguing with the waiters and grabbing each other's plates, and even the people who were trying to actually watch the fashion show couldn't see it unless they stood up because the waiters kept getting in the way.

IT WAS, IN OTHER WORDS, A HUGE FUCKING MESS.

The next course was rack of lamb.

All the racks of lamb were in these rolling portable ovens, back in our camp-kitchen next to the naked models. The portable ovens were a little better than Bunsen burners, but the chef had figured that as long as they started cooking when the antipasti went out, the lamb would be fine: it could slow-cook, no problem. The person in charge of turning on the portable ovens was the sous-chef.

But the thing is, the portable ovens got rolled over into the corner. And then there were the models, and the sous-chef was involved in that. And then there was the antipasti run, and the sous-chef was involved in that. And then there was the thing with the salads, and the sous-chef was very involved in that.

So when we were finally ready to start plating the lamb and sending it out—nearly two hours after it should have left the kitchen—every single rack of lamb was uncooked. Because the sous-chef, he had never turned the portable ovens on.

Shit.

We broke out the pans—every pan, every tray, every flat non-flammable surface we could find. We fired up those Bunsen-burner fires, and we started sautéing the lamb—because there was no way it was ever going to be edible unless we sautéed it. But if you figure everyone gets two lamb chops, and "everyone"

means five hundred guests, that's a thousand lamb chops—and we had maybe five little flames.

So this was taking some time.

Pretty soon the Big Italian Designer decided to come back and start screaming at the owner again.

The owner screamed at the chef.

The chef screamed at the sous-chef.

Guess who the sous-chef screamed at?

I think the second collection went out. I'm not sure. There was some kind of rushing and yelling going on over by the half-naked models, and it didn't seem to involve eating. But I don't know. I was sautéing lamb chops until my arm felt like it had been cooked over the fire till it was well done.

When Lenny Kravitz started playing, that was supposed to be the cue for dessert. After a while, we could hear Lenny Kravitz. But there was no dessert. There was some lamb.

Not all the lamb. But some.

After a long, long time, I handed off my sauté pan and cut out. I went upstairs, got some drinks at the bar, and watched Lenny Kravitz for a while. To this day, I do not know if dessert ever got to the table.

Then there were the Italians who took me to Italy to cook.

I was a sous-chef this time, at a French restaurant run by an Italian, and the event was a party in Montecatini, an ancient spa town in the Tuscan hills. This was the owner's hometown, and he told us the plan was very simple, just a small party.

When we arrived in Montecatini, the owner took me straight to the event site and introduced me to the fine chefs who would be helping me out as I pulled together the dinner he had planned: six courses for six hundred of his closest friends. That's 3,600 plates, if you're counting. The event was in the ancient, still-active spa, all marble and inlay and columns and beautifulness, until you got to the tent that was passing as an outdoor kitchen, which offered a sum total of five portable gas burners and some battered pots and pans. And my crew? The pastry chef from the restaurant back in New York; the owner's nephew, a Montecatini boy, for a sous-chef; and a bunch of retired hack caterers from some *scuola d'albergo* in Florence, wedding guys by the look of them, who'd been dragged away from their TVs to cook for this twenty-six-year-old American kid from whom they clearly didn't want to hear shit. On his way out the door, the owner turned back to give me one more piece of news: "By the way, Rai TV is going to be interviewing you, in Italian, because this dinner is also for this famous designer's birthday"— do you notice a trend here?—"and I've told them you're the chef."

The savory menu was as follows:

The restaurant's signature lobster salad, a straight-out-of-the-early-'80s glory.

Smuggled-in-a-suitcase American foie gras, with peaches.

Paupiette of sea bass. That is, fillets of fish, individually wrapped in potato, cooked in red wine sauce. Over a portable gas burner. In the rain. For six hundred.

Beef with braised vegetables. (Very seasonal, in June.)

In other words, the wedding caterers from Florence were probably the perfect crew to put this meal together.

But I wasn't giving up. I could make this taste great, I figured. We were, after all, in Italy, in June. All sorts of amazing produce must be available! So close to the sea, I'd be able to get beautiful *spigola*—Italian sea bass—for the paupiettes, even if I had to wrap those fillets in potato and cook them over five Bunsen burners.

The spigola my retired wedding caterers had sourced arrived very early in the morning on the day before the party. The moment I cut into the box, I knew we had a problem. **THE SMELL COMING UP FROM BENEATH THE PACKING ICE KNOCKED ME BACK A GOOD FOOT AND A HALF.** This fish hadn't been underneath the waves for at least a week. There was no

way I could serve it. I would be poisoning the entire population of Montecatini. On Rai TV.

I yelled at the caterers. They didn't care. They were busy smoking.

I yelled at the owner's nephew. He wandered away on his Vespa to play video games at a pizzeria.

When there was no one left to yell at, I remembered that a cook I knew named Mario Carbone was doing a stint at a restaurant called La Dogana on the Tuscan coast. I called him up, desperate. I think I probably yelled at him too. So he handed the phone over to his chef.

"There is no problem," the chef told me. "We will take care of this together." It was the most beautiful Italian sentence I'd ever heard.

Early the next morning, I drove down to La Dogana, in the town of Cappezano Pianore, where I met a beefy guy in his fifties with bright eyes, crazy gray curls, and a big gray beard: Vittoriano Pierucci, the chef-owner. We shook hands, drank an espresso over the stoves, and headed off to the fish market. When we got there, it became very clear very fast that none of the purveyors wanted anything to do with me: they didn't know me, I was an American, they didn't have fish for six hundred, it was impossible, what was I asking, what was I thinking?

I gave up. I stopped talking. Screw everyone.

Then Vittoriano took over. Talking loud, fast, emphatically, with highly creative swearing and with his hands, he got me a promise of spigola for six hundred. Cash on delivery.

We drove back to La Dogana. We had some homemade terrines, some local cheese, some fresh bread. We toasted the spigola. By the time I got back to Montecatini, the fish was waiting for me—fresh, glistening, smelling only of the sea. I butchered fish faster than I have ever butchered before or since.

Of course, there were a couple-three other things to do that day.

It being June in Tuscany, I had figured that the season was exactly right for peaches. So, not knowing any more about who to go to when I wanted beautiful peaches for six hundred than I did about who to go to when I wanted beautiful fish for six hundred, I sent the old caterers off to procure 350 beautiful, ripe, luscious Italian peaches.

This they got at least half right. They brought me 350 utterly beautiful, perfectly formed, absolutely tasteless and unripe peach-shaped rocks.

I had approximately ten hours to make these rocks taste like something.

I jumped in the car and drove like hell all the way down to the local Casino supermarket. I bought ten bottles of apricot-peach Fabbri syrup—the stuff they use in espresso bars to flavor coffee—and two huge bunches of overripe bananas. When I got back to our tent, I dumped all the peaches into a garbage bag, and then I squashed up the bananas and put them in the bag too, and then I threw the whole mess outside in the hot summer sun. The bananas would release methane gas, and this little greenhouse-effect thing I'd created in the garbage bag would speed-ripen the peaches.

This went pretty well, until it started to rain.

Six hours later, we were roasting peaches on the five gas burners, deglazing them with syrup, trying to make these slightly softer rocks taste like something—anything, really—as the tent smoked and sagged around us, the corners filling up with rain.

Things began to come together. The peaches softened. The syrup made them taste like . . . peaches in syrup. Which was better than rocks. The fish fillets were all butchered and wrapped in potatoes, ready for the Bunsen burners. The lobster salad had gone out with no problem, and we had begun to cook the six hundred pieces of foie gras for the second course.

Cooking foie gras is messy. You need a superhot pan to do it, so there's a lot of smoke and a lot of splattering fat. It's a challenging dish when you're cooking two or three pieces. The caterers and the nephew and I, with our five burners, were cooking six hundred pieces à la minute.

SO I WAS COVERED HEAD TO TOE IN DUCK FAT, and also in the syrup from the peaches, and I think I smelled a lot like somebody who had been butchering fish all day long, and I turned around, and there was this superhot six-foot-two big-breasted long-haired overtanned supermodel of an Italian reporter, stalking across the tent in seven-inch heels with a microphone pointed at me and a cameraman right behind her. (In Italy, they don't believe in the old-serious-man school of reporting and anchoring. They like to have something interesting to look at, to distract you while they're talking about the economy.) This was the Rai TV interview, and it was live. I thought about what I would say to her, as she came closer and closer, across the tent. What I wanted to say—because I'm a pretty honest guy, and because I'd been cooking in a tent for three days, and because I was serving flavored rocks, and because I'd met the world's oldest dead fish—was, "This country is crazy! All of you goddamn people are crazy! This is the biggest disaster I've ever been involved with. Thank God nobody I know is here in Montecatini; thank God nobody I know will ever see this interview." But before I could say anything, the Rai TV woman held the microphone up to her cleavage and gushed, "This must be such an honor! For you, a young American chef, to come here and cook for such an important designer, and for the owner, who is such an important figure here and in America, and for *six hundred* of his friends! What an opportunity!"

I looked at the microphone, there in her cleavage. I looked at the camera. I nodded and smiled. Yes! I said. An honor! I said. And then the TV cameras went away.

I sent out the foie gras and peaches. I sent out the paupiettes of soggy potato and overcooked fish in cold red wine sauce, or of undercooked potato and al dente fish in hot red wine sauce, depending on when your individual paupiette came off the Bunsen burner. Then it was time for dessert, and I left the tent.

The nephew and I got on his Vespa and went to some pizzeria on the other side of the autostrada. We ate a pizza and got smashed on two bottles of wine and a bottle of limoncello. I was sick for two days.

So my friend Ron was getting married, and I was cooking the wedding dinner. In Italy. In a three-hundred-year-old villa outside Florence. With an open hearth in its hundred-year-old kitchen.

Perhaps this sounds very romantic to you. Well. More on this later.

My wife, Gwen, and I spent the week before the wedding driving around the country, collecting the basic components of dinner for eighty. We bought olive oil outside Sienna, seafood in Viareggio, bread in Carmignano, cured meats in Florence, vegetables at the Florentine market. By the time we got to the villa, the car smelled like we'd been cooking garlic sausage in red wine and tomatoes in there.

The villa was in the rustic, sofa-growing suburbs of Florence. We drove out of Florence, through fields of wildflowers and fields of sofa factories, past worker housing, car repair shops, and shabby, dirty-looking groceries, through another field of flowers or two, and then we were there. The house was a rambling affair on a swath of land, with a big marble-flagged terrace and a pool. The terrace was for the wedding reception. The pool was for every other waking minute.

Ron and Liz's wedding had, unfortunately, landed in the middle of the worst heat wave Italy had seen in a century. The Tuscan plains baked. The villa, without air conditioning, baked on the Tuscan plain. We baked in the villa.

Our cozy little room would, under other circumstances—say, winter—have been a lovely thing: quiet and private, up a back stairway, with its own tiny bathroom, one small, deep-set window. Protected from any stray breezes.

To get to sleep every night, we jumped into the unheated pool and stayed there until we couldn't feel our limbs. Then we drank frozen limoncello in the unheated pool. Then we got under the shower, with the cold tap turned all the way on. Then we got into bed and hoped that we were frozen enough and drunk enough to fall asleep before our bodies realized that **WE WERE BEING COOKED, SLOW-ROASTED, BASTED.**

During the day, when we weren't in the pool with everyone else who wasn't shopping, we drove around collecting more food. With the windows down. The breeze in the car was a beautiful thing.

The last item we needed—the centerpiece for the whole wedding—was the *porchetta*, a whole boneless pig stuffed with herbs and garlic, rolled up into a long cylinder, tied, and cooked. And the best porchetta maker in Tuscany was Dario Cecchini, the famous Dante-spouting, wine-pouring, rubber-boot-wearing, American-foodie-trainee-terrifying butcher of Panzano. So we drove up to Panzano. We ordered porchetta. We drove back to Panzano. We took part in the ritual Dario salon: reciting of *The Inferno*, feeding of hordes of friends and strangers, drinking of good wine, all in the butcher shop amid the hanging meat. Then we got in the car to drive home.

I laid the porchetta carefully in the backseat, and we drove up out of the concrete bunker, inhaling the fragrance of perfectly prepared meat. The burning hills gleamed gold and red in the late-afternoon light. I drove barefoot, with one hand, singing along to the bad Italian pop music: *di mi tre paroles . . . mare, sole, amore . . .* The road bent around the hills, in and out and in again and out and in and then—without warning—in again, a tight turn at the cliff's edge, at an intersection in the middle of nowhere.

There was definitely not enough warning for a person who

had spent the afternoon drinking wine and scarfing down pork in Dario's butcher shop–salon.

Gwen threw her hands over her ears, like that Edvard Munch painting, except not silent: "AND-DREWWWWWW!" she wailed. I hauled the wheel to the right as fast and hard as I could. The passenger-side tires spun out at the edge of the cliff and then, just in time, jumped themselves back on the road—and I barreled right into the side of a little blue Italian truck.

I may be a New Yorker, but I'm still an Ohio boy, and we Ohio boys are serious drivers. I am, I think it's safe to say, a really, really good driver—even when I'm driving barefoot with a map spread over the steering wheel while mainlining coffee. I'd driven all over the world—cross-country in the States three times, on the German autobahn, through the mountains, doing 80 through Paris at three A.M.—but I had never, ever been in a car accident. Not even a fender-bender. Nada. I had no idea what to do.

I sat in the car for a minute, staring; then I started swearing; then I got out of the car, barefoot, to check out the damage. The good news: no one had gone off the cliff. In fact, no one was hurt—not even the porchetta. But the truck was in pretty rough shape, and the driver, a woman in her thirties with long dark hair, was weeping. Glaring at me and gulping down her tears, she explained that she and her husband had saved for five years to buy this truck for their business. She was, in fact, just driving it back from the car lot—still with the new-car smell and the stickers—when I, this unbelievably stupid American, ran into her.

I got on my cell phone and called the rental car company. They were French. They were not helpful.

I called the police. It was Saturday. **IT WAS TUSCANY. NOBODY DEAD? NOBODY WAS INTERESTED.**

The Italian woman was relieved. "The police would only make it worse," she told me, like I was some kind of moron grown only in America.

After a while, when I had apologized twelve or fourteen times and given the angry Italian woman my home phone number and my cell phone number and the villa phone number and my e-mail address and my home address and my work address and my work phone number and all the insurance information I had from the French car company—which was not very much information—she drove away in her wounded, limping, deeply bent truck. And there we were, sitting there in the middle of nowhere in the dark in the mountains on Saturday night at seven o'clock with a front end that was bent all the way in over the front wheels.

I turned on the hazard lights. I got out and pushed the car away from the edge of the road. We drove home at roughly 15 kilometers an hour. There was no cooling breeze. I think we got back to the villa around midnight. "Hey, AC, wussup?" yelled somebody drunk and cold and happy from the pool, as I lugged the porchetta into the hundred-year-old kitchen in the dark.

In daylight, the car looked like one of those cartoon cars from that movie, all curled up on itself, only without the eyes or the cute paint job. I called the rental car company again. They were, if possible, less helpful than they had been before.

Finally, facing another week of Italian driving at 15 kilometers an hour, I decided to get the car fixed myself. I called one of the local body shops, and the owner came out to pick up the car. He was sunburned and grizzled, about seventy. "You drove this down from the mountains like this?" he asked. "You're crazy. You're not driving it anymore." He hauled a rope out of his car, tied it underneath what was left of my bumper, attached it to his beat-up old Fiat, and towed it to off his shop. "I'll pick you up in two days," he said as he drove away, waving.

I heard nothing else from him, but exactly two days later to the hour, there he was, outside the villa, waiting for me. He drove me back to the shop, which was very neat and clean and very quiet—none of the banging and grinding and welding sounds you'd expect to hear in a body shop in the middle of the

morning in the middle of the week. There were some other guys hanging around the shop—all these mechanics with clean hands, very Italian—but nobody seemed to be doing any work (also very Italian). But there was my car, looking perfect—looking as if it had never been in an accident at all. (With any luck, the uninterested French people at the rental car company would forget all about my phone calls.) The owner sat down on the workbench, next to the counter with the espresso machine, and asked me how I knew Italian, where I was from. I told him that my grandfather was from Livorno, and next thing I knew, he'd opened a bottle of wine, and he was telling me about his one trip to New York, and we were sitting on that workbench like old friends, talking soccer and American cars.

About an hour and a half later, I remembered that I had a wedding to cook for, and also that if I drank any more wine I might be right back in the body shop soon. I got up and looked at the car with him for a while. He'd done a really good job: even the paint was perfect, and the car was cleaner than it had been when we picked it up. "How much do I owe you?" I asked, reaching for my wallet. I figured we were talking at least three thousand dollars in bodywork. He didn't say anything—he just gestured me into his office, a tiny, intensely organized space full of papers and memorabilia. The wall behind his desk was covered in American license plates. "You don't owe me anything," he said. "Just send me a license plate from America."

Three thousand bucks in body work, and he was trading it to me for a license plate. I love Italy.

My dad happens to be both a serious old-car aficionado and a collector of midcentury American car memorabilia, not to mention a generous guy. So when we got home, I sent that body-shop owner some of the best from the collection. For the next few years, every Christmas, I got a present from him: a Fiat T-shirt, a Ferrari baseball hat.

And when I got the car back to the rental place, nobody remembered my phone calls, and nobody noticed a thing.

Back in Florence, Gwen and I had this amazing lunch with the American ex-pat food writer Faith Willinger. At the end of our four hours of eating and drinking and talking and laughing and eating and drinking and talking, Faith said, "I'm having dinner with Johnnie Apple next week in Bologna. You should come. He wants to go eat salumi."

"Johnnie" Apple was R. W. Apple, the late, great *New York Times* writer, all-knowing gastronome, and pro-level gourmand. The chef-owner, Faith told us, was the best in the region. The restaurant, Hosteria da Ivan, was closed for the summer but would open, for one night only, for Johnnie's salumi dinner. The dinner, of course, was scheduled for the night before Ron and Liz's wedding, and Fontanelle, the town where the dinner was being held, in the delta of the Po River, was two hours away from Florence, if you drove really fast. But how could we miss it?

I spent the day of the Hosteria da Ivan dinner prepping and chopping and sautéing and marinating and roasting like a crazy man. The kitchen—out in a little brick house behind the pool, where it couldn't heat up the villa—was the original *cucina*, which meant that it looked beautiful to touring couples but was torture when it came to actual cooking. The flat metal roof baked in the sun; the open fires and hundred-year-old stoves smoked and sparked and shot out flames without warning; the overhead fans, pretty much the only innovation in the last century besides running water and a surplus hotel fridge from the '60s, just picked up the heat and moved it around in the almost pitch-black room, since there were no windows. Outside I could hear people yelling in the pool. If I stood very still, I could even, sometimes, hear the chink of ice and liquid in glasses of something cold and alcoholic.

My sous-chef Mikey C. was out there in the pool somewhere. **WITH A GIRL.**

Dinner in Fontanelle was called for nine. Five o'clock went by, then six (I could tell because the face of my watch glowed in the dark). I sliced and diced like a TV ninja, slammed trays

in and out of the oven, ran from stove to fridge. At seven thirty, I jumped in the pool and floated to the top, almost unconscious from the shock. Gwen fished me out and poured me into a pair of jeans, and we were ready to go.

We headed out onto the highway, driving fast through fields and industrial wastelands and an inordinate number of American-style motels. The Po Valley is really flat—like Kansas flat—and the roads are built on top of dikes beside the Po River, so as you drive you get a view over the farms and fields and houses. By 9:20 or so, we were in Fontanelle. We rolled through town slowly. It was beautiful, but eerie. The fields glowed gold in the fading light; the tree-lined streets, dense with dark green, followed the river, winding past grand old houses, restaurants, little local shops. And everything was closed. A small boy walking along the side of the road with a sheepdog turned to look at us, wondering. A head (gray, grizzled) extended from a window as we passed. Otherwise there was no one. Fontanelle was officially closed for the summer.

Hosteria da Ivan was at the far end of town, in a lot on its own, at the top of a little rise. We parked on the street and rushed a bit on the way to the door—we were late, Faith and the Apples would be deep into the salumi by now, stupid rude Americans, and also would there be anything left?—but the door was locked. To keep us out? To stave off the hordes of out-of-season salumi-seekers? We knocked. Waited. Knocked again. Nothing. Finally we headed out back. Up at the top of the driveway, we found a long, bare trestle table and twenty or so chairs set up on the concrete between the restaurant and the garage. Through the open door we heard muttering in Italian. I stuck my head inside the kitchen. There was Ivan, in the earliest stages of starting on his mise en place for the evening. It was just past 9:30.

What was I thinking? This was Italy. Should have had a longer swim.

Over the next hour or so, Ivan yelled, sang, clanged pots, and dispatched a couple of waiters he'd found somewhere to set up the table. Tablecloths appeared, glassware, flowers. We drank white wine and hung around outside; somewhere around 10:15, Faith showed up with the Apples. Johnnie was in the middle of a serious eating tour, and he tossed back the wine, his broad face getting redder and redder, as he told stories, standing on the concrete in the dark. Eventually a waiter wandered outside with some salumi and some bread. We ate it standing beside Ivan's car at the top of the driveway.

By 11, a pack of Italian chefs and their friends had appeared in the driveway, all men with long curly hair and white shirts half-unbuttoned and big teeth, talking loud and fast and laughing a lot. At 11:30 or so, we sat down to dinner. Ivan raised a glass of bright purple lambrusco. This, he explained, was really the *vino da tavolo*—the everyday wine—of the region: you drank it cold, from little juice glasses, and you kept your pinkie finger hooked inside the glass. That way you could keep track of when you needed more: if your finger was dry, you were ready for a refill.

(I grew up with lambrusco: it's my dad's favorite on humid summer nights. It's a dry, frizzy red wine—or pink, or purple. My dad likes to put ice cubes in it. Wine snobs call it soda pop. Personally, I think there's nothing better than a glass of cold lambrusco on a hot day.)

Of course, Ivan made his lambrusco-pinkie toast in Italian. He didn't speak English; neither did any of the Italian chefs or their friends. Johnnie and his wife, Betsy, didn't speak any Italian. I wondered how he would take notes and ask questions for his article. Turns out it didn't matter. Mr. Apple told nonstop stories and jokes, made joyful proclamations about the food, and asked Ivan strings of questions in English, all of which Ivan answered in Italian. No problem. **I THINK IT WAS THE LAMBRUSCO.**

Huge platters came out of the kitchen. We started with fried polenta with whipped lardo and rosemary, served with thick slices of fresh-baked bread. There were what seemed like twelve different kinds of homemade local salumi; then a pasta, pumpkin *lune*. The meat course was duck with mustard fruits. Before the regular cheese course, Ivan served up scraps of freshly made parmesan cheese, a regional specialty, cut up into finger-food-sized bits and fried. By then I had begun to understand why the restaurant closed for the summer: there was, obviously, no light hot-weather menu. Probably everyone in Fontanelle was off at the spa trying to lose the weight they'd gained by eating this stuff all winter long. But man, was it good: the real thing, the kind of Emilian cooking you can't find anywhere else. The night was hot; the asphalt steamed; there wasn't even the ghost of a breeze. Didn't matter. We feasted on the kind of food that makes you feel cozy and well padded in the middle of a snowstorm in February, and we were deeply happy.

By the time the waiters started setting up for the actual cheese course, it was 2 A.M. I had a full day's worth of cooking in the heat ahead of me—the wedding was at 7 P.M.—and I needed to get back to the villa. Ivan couldn't believe it. "Why are you leaving?" he demanded. "We've got three more courses to go! The wedding will be fine—don't worry so much! So you start the dinner a little bit later!" He stood up to block our passage down the driveway, clearly prepared to keep us there by force until we'd finished the dolce and the cafe—until I reminded him that the guests at the wedding were all Americans. "Ah," he said, crestfallen. Clearly, such barbarians would want, inexplicably, to eat dinner on time. He shook my hand and raised a glass to us.

When we got back to the villa, the moon was pale and the sky was going from black to purple. Some of the wedding guests were still in the pool, trying to freeze themselves to sleep. We jumped into the icy water and then headed off to our tiny room, to dream, for an hour or two, about fried *parmesano* and bright purple lambrusco in little juice glasses.

When I left the uptown, upscale French place I'd been cheffing for six years or so, I wanted to do something totally different: to cook in a way that was much more casual, much more down-town, and definitely, absolutely not French. I tried out ideas as I wandered around the city: middle American? pan-European, café-style? a farmer's-market-driven, totally seasonal little boite? No, I was ready to go back to my roots: to do Italian food my way. After years of doing pasta Gallic-style; of dressing Italian food up in fancy clothes to make it ready for its big New York close-up; of cooking my own style of Italian at home and something totally different in my restaurant kitchens, it was time to bring it all together. I wanted to cook food that was Italian and American—but not in that Little Italy, bad-pastries-and-precooked-red-sauce-pastas kind of way; food that was built on tradition but was also totally up-to-date and urban. I was pumped to be cooking Italian food again, because Italian food makes people happy, and making people happy is why I cook. But I wanted to think about Italian food, this time, in a whole different language.

To get in the mood, I went to Italy.

This was to be the granddaddy of all Italian food trips. It was me and Gwen and Luke Ostrom, chef de cuisine in my new place, and later on, Olivier Flosse, our wine guy, and Ron Rosselli, our sous-chef. We would hit markets, lunches, pastry shops, cheesemakers, winemakers, gelaterias, chocalaterias, osterias, trattorias—every "ria" you can imagine, from Rome to Campagna to Palermo to Venice. We had a seriously heavy schedule. For Day 5, for instance, we had booked a run down to Battipaglia to visit the water buffalo and learn about buffalo mozzarella. We would stop for lunch at a Michelin one-star country inn an hour away; then we'd get back in the car and drive four hours back to Massa Lubrense to have dinner at Ristorante Quattro Passi. After that, there was the two-hour drive—twisting, turning, treacherous Amalfi seacliff roads all the way—back to the hotel.

This kind of superfast eating-and-drinking tour could be dangerous. Running from place to place like this, trying to keep to a schedule, scarfing down food and wine on the run and way too much coffee—that's when you can get into trouble. For instance, there was that time Ron and Olivier and I were on our way to the great Ornellaia winery in western Tuscany. We'd been truffle hunting outside Alba, and we'd been up all night, drinking and eating truf-fles and eggs and toast, and we were due at Ornellaia to taste wine and do a tour, and we were late. We were also unshowered, unshaven, uncombed, and otherwise unclean-looking, flying down the A12 in a beat-up black Jaguar (I'd had another Italian car accident), covered in truffle-hunting mud. I saw a cop car up ahead, so I quit speeding, pulled into the right-hand lane behind him, and slowed down. But these cops had already spotted us. Now they turned around and got a good look at us, at the car's bashed-in luxury grill, at the mud, etc. They slowed down a lot, and then the driving cop took out this paddle thing with a big red circle on the top of a stick, something you'd give a little kid to play with, maybe. I'd never seen one of these before, and somehow I didn't think it had anything to do with me. They kept slowing down, till they were way below the speed limit—so finally I just pulled out and passed them. The lights went on, the sirens kicked in, they started following me closely, out in the left lane, signaling me to pull over. And in the middle of this, one of the guys says, "I really need to go to the bathroom. Can we stop at the service station?" "Dude," I said, "these cops are trying to pull us over!" And it was another kilometer to the rest area. But we'd been eating and drinking and eating and drinking for a week solid, and we all had serious food-tourist stomach going on, and by now two of us needed the rest area, maybe three. "I'm not gonna make it, dude!"

somebody said. So what could I do? I went another kilometer. In my rearview mirror, I could see the driving cop had that lollipop thing out again, and he was waving it frantically at me out the window. And then finally we hit the rest area, and I pulled off and stopped.

The cops got out of the car, hands on their weapons, and asked us to show our hands as they came around the side of the car. Somebody actually tried to get out of the car and make a run for the bathroom, but I hit the locks so the cops didn't shoot him. I put down the window and sat very still.

The skinnier of the two cops, the one who had been driving, marched up to my window. "Where are you coming from?" he asked me, the fury barely contained in his voice.

"Piedmonte," I told him.

"And where are you going?"

"Bolgheri."

"Bolgheri?" he asked, and stopped. "You're American? What do you do?"

I told him I was a cook, an American, but my family was from Livorno. Suddenly, everything changed. The cop at my window relaxed, took his hand off his gun. "Hey," he yelled to his partner, "he's Livornese! Ah," he went on, turning back to me, "there's good wine in Bolgheri!" I explained where we were going. That was it: he started joking around, asking about my family, telling us about his favorite winemakers. (Only in Italy do traffic cops tell the civilians they stop about their favorite winemakers.) The occupants of my car, pleased not to be shot or arrested, were still looking with panicked eyes toward the bathrooms, and I still had my hand on the automatic door locks. Finally, the cop asked us for our papers. "Know why I stopped you?" he asked, laughing. "You looked suspicious. **I THOUGHT YOU WERE YUGOSLAVIAN DRUG DEALERS!**"

But the trip started out a little more slowly. On the night we left, I was still fielding e-mails, unpacked, a couple of hours before our flight was due to take off. We made it to JFK airport with an hour to spare, which is not much when you're flying international out of New York. We raced inside, hauling our luggage. "Excuse me," Gwen asked one of the nice women marshaling the lines at Alitalia, "where's the check-in for the six o'clock to Rome?"

Turns out the check-in to Rome is at Newark.

Lucky for us, there were a few extremely expensive seats available on the Milan flight. So we spent the next day driving from Milan to Rome, conveniently reacclimating ourselves to Italian traffic.

Our plan in Rome was to hit the Testaccio Market to see the butchers' stalls and to eat at some of the restaurants around there, famous for rustic Roman dishes: tripe, sweetbreads, brain, oxtail.

We woke up to soldiers marching in formation beneath our windows: miles and miles of soldiers. Helicopters flew overhead. Bands played. It was, it seemed, Italy's biggest martial holiday. The market? Locked up tight. We spent the afternoon wandering desperately from one recommended restaurant to the next, knocking on shuttered doors, desperately seeking foodstuffs. No tripe to be had. No sweetbreads. No nothin'. We ended the evening eating frozen gnocchi in a trendy, overdesigned restaurant.

But as soon as we left Rome, things got better.

We headed down the coast, stopping in Naples to comparison-shop pizza. We hit the great seafood restaurants and trattorias all the way down the Amalfi coast, driving crazy, twisting, stomach-churning roads every night to get to dinner. Every evening, it was total luxury: dinner on a patio somewhere with candles and many courses, our table reserved just for us, course after course of beautiful food. We were serious. We concentrated. We tasted intently. Except for this one dinner, up in the hills of Amalfi above Salerno somewhere. Luke had read about this place: authentic seaside *paesan* food, local gem, not to be missed. So we drove up from our hotel—straight up, on roads that seemed sometimes to be so steep we were about to tip over backward and fall right off. Up near the top of the mountains, in a whole different weather system, we parked our car at the side of the road, and were immediately surrounded by unfriendly locals. Kids kicked at the car tires. Young guys loomed. Older guys stared at us, arms crossed. It was like *Deliverance Goes to Italy*.

We ignored it all. We headed toward dinner.

The place we were headed to was built right into the side of the road, hanging over the cliff at back. It was a house, really: a tiny house. There was a tiny entranceway, and then a step down right into the kitchen, and then you walked sideways past the stove, and then three steep steps up to a porch with a handful of tables. A kid was doing her homework at one table. At another, three local women were arguing about hairdressing. There were cats everywhere, rubbing against people's legs, trying to get at the fish on the tables. (Did I mention I'm allergic to cats? Yeah. Like *really* allergic.) The place was run by these two ancient, toothless women in housedresses who spoke in thick dialect. There was no menu. They asked us what we wanted, and we asked for fish stew—that's what the place was known for. Plus wine. They laughed at us: "You won't want to eat that!" they insisted. "Better to go somewhere else, have some grilled fish! You, you're not going to like our stew!" They cackled and turned their backs on us. But we sat there, and so after a while they brought our dinner.

The stew was made from a local fish, the boniest I've ever seen, fish that maybe starved on the line all the way up from the ocean so by the time it got up to the two sisters there was nothing left to cook. Or maybe the cats had eaten all the meat. It was pretty much bones in overcooked, overgarlicked tomatoes. But there was no way we were not going to eat every bite. So we sat there, drinking our wine from juice glasses, periodically shoving away a cat or two, our elbows sticking to the plastic tablecloth.

From Amalfi, we drove down to Caseificio Venulo to see the water buffalo up close and taste some of the product. We flew to Sicily and did a gelateria, chocolateria, and seafood pasta tour of that amazing island. Back on the mainland, we sampled black-truffle specialties and hit salumerias around Spoleto in Umbria; we went to La Frasca in Castelfranco, Emilia-Romagna; we tasted Parmigiano outside Parma, proscuitto in Langhirano, balsamic vinegar outside Modena. We went to a series of *ombre* (little wine bars that serve snacks) in Padova. We hit the three-Michelin-starred Dal Pescatore, in the farmland near Mantova, and Le Calandre (molecular-gastronomy-influenced "New Italian" cooking) in the industrial suburbs outside Padua. We went to Tartufi Morra for truffles in Piedmonte; we visited the great winemakers Cesare Borgogno, Chiara Boschis, and Elio Altare in the Lange; we had modern Piedmontese cooking at Borgo Antico in Barolo and Ligurian seaside fare at Buca di Bacco.

IT WAS A GASTRONOMIC MARATHON.

Then we came home, raring to go, to launch a whole new kind of Italian restaurant. Well. So...

Opening up a restaurant in New York City, I learned, takes time. You're dealing, for starters, with egomaniacal designers, difficult real estate brokers, impossible licensing bodies, disappearing general contractors, subcontractors who walk off the job at the slightest excuse, and sub-subcontractors who fix the mistakes made by the subcontractors. So the six-month reno we'd planned on? A full year. Which left me six months of extra time. For the first time in my adult life, I didn't have much to do. So I did something I'd never done, in my fifteen years in New York City: I cooked at home on a regular basis.

I'm not saying I'd never turned on the stove in my apartment before. Every once in a while, I would bust out a meal on my day off: a Christmas dinner, a birthday treat for my wife, supper for friends. But it wasn't any kind of regular thing. Those stories about chefs who spend all their free time shopping for groceries and cooking up homey twelve-course meals for twenty in photo-ready loft kitchens in New York City? Myth, as far as I was concerned. After a long week of eighteen-hour days in a restaurant kitchen, the last thing I wanted to do was apply heat to food. When people congratulated my wife on landing a man who surely cooked the most amazing meals for her at home, she liked to tell them an old story about a shoemaker whose children had no shoes. We ordered in, or we ate out. **MY MAJOR PIECE OF HOME KITCHEN EQUIPMENT? THE COFFEEMAKER.**

But after a couple of weeks of meetings, meetings, and more meetings, I really missed cooking. So I made my way past the coffeemaker and turned on the stove. Once I got started, I couldn't stop. I repaid years of dinner invitations from friends; I made a meal for my wife nearly every night. And most of this time, I was cooking Italian.

I had always thought that home cooking would be ridiculously easy for me: somebody who turned out polished multi-course meals for a couple of hundred people every night could definitely make dinner for six or so without breaking a sweat, I figured. I was wrong. It's not that the cooking part was harder—it was the logistics. In a restaurant kitchen, I work with a team of ten cooks and five dishwashers. One person does nothing but make pasta all day. Somebody else spends all morning chopping vegetables. We get the best ingredients delivered fresh to our door every day; we have great equipment, and there's space to cook and store everything.

My kitchen at home, on the other hand, measured three feet by nine, and there was nobody in it but me. When I wanted great ingredients, I had to schlep them home on the subway.

So I got out and foraged. I took the N train to Fort Hamilton Parkway in Bensonhurst, one of the great New York Italian culinary neighborhoods. I went to Coluccio's, the legendary Italian market on Sixtieth Street, one of my favorite suppliers, and bought sun-dried Calabrian peppers and provolone picante. I stopped at Royal Crown Pastry Shop on Fourteenth Avenue for broccoli rabe bread; I ate cassata cake at Villabate on Eighteenth Avenue. I went to the Bronx: I took the Metro North train up to the zoo, then walked across Tremont to Arthur Avenue, that other great old Italian food strip. I bought sopressata and spicy anchovies at Calabria Pork Store; at Biancardi Meats, I got veal osso bucco and liver sausage. Back in Manhattan, I hit DiPaolo's Dairy, one of the last bastions of the old Little Italy, on Grand Street, for homemade ricotta. And every Monday, Wednesday, and Friday morning all summer, I went to the Union Square Greenmarket. I hauled home bags of just-picked, local fruit and vegetables. It all got me thinking about new ways to bridge the gap between Italy, American-Italian food, and my own brand of Italian cooking, American-style.

(It also made me realize what a pain in the ass it is to carry home all your own groceries. I still wake up sweating from nightmares of being stranded on a street corner somewhere, miles from home, at rush hour, utterly unable to get a cab, surrounded by bags and bags and bags of groceries.)

Back at home, I discovered what happens when you use a different pot or pan for everything and you don't have somebody standing behind you washing the pots (or, for that matter, anywhere to put the pots). I learned to cut down on cooking steps so that I could actually sit down and eat dinner with the people I'd invited to eat with me. And I found out that some dishes that, for instance, work beautifully in a professionally vented restaurant kitchen, lead to smoke-alarm trauma and complaints from the neighbors in a poorly ventilated New York City apartment. There was the time I drove all of my dinner guests into the bedroom by trying to reduce balsamic vinegar. There was the time I threw a sheet tray full of smoking lamb leg onto the top of the air conditioner outside my living room window before the alarm went off. There were the many, many times Gwen stood with the door open to the hall, shivering as the wind swept through the apartment from all the open windows, while I jabbed at the smoke alarm, yelling, "Shit! Shit! Shit!" and the neighbors opened their doors to glare at us. I learned that even when the smoke alarm stops going off, when your only kitchen vent is the little baby recirculator on the microwave, you can pretty much count on your house smelling like that roasted veal you made for about a week after you cook dinner. I learned that you can't just leave the gas stove on without any pots on it when you're cooking at home, because, for instance, your wife's hair might catch fire on the leaping flames.

But still, I loved it. I cooked multicourse dinners for no good reason almost every night. On a slow Saturday at home, I might throw together gnocchi, spinach with crispy chickpeas and ricotta salata, and almond granita, just for the two of us. I'd pop open a bottle of old Barolo that I'd gotten as a gift, and then we'd sit and eat it all on the couch while watching *Family Guy*.

My home kitchen turned into a culinary lab: my Italian travels, my French cooking background, my New York City sensibility all combined in new ways when I was cooking just because I wanted to. I didn't want to spend my time remaking dishes that I already knew. I wanted to cook Italian food that was all about New York. And it was here that many of the dishes that ended up on the restaurant menu took shape. The cooking I did, during that strange in-between-restaurants time? That's the heart of what I call Urban Italian cooking.

Meanwhile, work on the restaurant went on. And on. And on.

We were supposed to be open by November: that was the revised revised plan. But November came around, and then December, and there was still no restaurant. And then it was Christmas. I'd told my parents I wasn't coming home because we were opening the restaurant—and everyone else had told their parents too. By the time it became clear that we weren't opening

anything anytime soon, we were all stuck. One good friend of mine couldn't get to Hawaii to see his family; another restaurant orphan couldn't get home to Texas, and so on. I had to keep morale up. So that's when we had everyone over for Christmas dinner.

It was one of those New York City winter nights that is not in the least bit Christmas-storybook pretty: the snow was turning into gray sludge as soon as it hit the ground; the wind whipped up the garbage on Avenue A. The city felt deserted: everyone but us had gone home to Mom and Dad.

SO WE HUNKERED DOWN AND ATE.

Luke brought the antipasti, some foraged and some home-made: smoked fish from Russ & Daughters and cheese from Murray's (this was one of those old-fashioned New York Jewish-Catholic-Baptist-generic-Christian Christmases), sopressata from Arthur Avenue, Marcona almonds—plus tuna-stuffed peppers and eggplant agrodolce. I made roast veal tenderloin wrapped in pancetta, polenta, my grandma's ravioli, potatoes alla montagna, and escarole calabrese. We drank champagne and red wine from Montepulciano. For dessert we had pecan pie with homemade ice cream and Nero cookies and passito. It was our last chance, we figured, to kick back, before the craziness of opening the restaurant kicked in. So we sat around the big wooden table in my crowded, steamy New York City apartment, and we ate, drank, and generally made merry deep into the night.

{ A NOTE ON THE RECIPES }

HI. WELCOME TO THE RECIPE SECTION. BEFORE YOU GET STARTED COOKING, HERE ARE SOME THOUGHTS AND TIPS:

FIRST OF ALL: Do not stress out.
Cooking should be fun. If you get into it, it can even be a stress-relieving therapy: it engages your senses, takes your mind off your day-to-day problems, and makes both cook and diner happy. Don't let the number of steps in these recipes intimidate you. I've broken everything down really thoroughly here; the numbers are there just to make life easier. Don't be afraid of the length of the ingredient lists, either: salt, black pepper, olive oil, onions, garlic, and other stuff are constants in these recipes because they're crucial to bringing out flavor. You've probably got a lot of this in your pantry already—and if you don't, it's a good idea to stock up if you want to do any kind of cooking.

Don't be afraid to taste, touch, smell, feel, and make a mess.
This is how you make great food. Get into what you're making. That's why it's called cooking, not chemistry.

Measure, but don't be a slave.
I tested every one of these recipes at home, in my New York City apartment, using ordinary cup and spoon measures, so that I could be sure you'd be able to make them work in your kitchen. But don't be a slave to the measuring cup. There are, I think, two kinds of cooks: those who measure everything exactly, no matter what; and those who, like Obi Wan Kenobi, "use the force" a little more—who improvise, taste, put in a little of this and a little of that. Cooking is definitely more art than science. Like every pro cook, when asked how much of something I put in a particular dish, I answer, "a little," or "as much as it needs," and think I'm being exact. (Trust me when I say that it killed me to measure things. As we tested recipes, Gwen kept asking me, "How much was that you just put in?" "A little bit," I would say, vaguely, busted again. "Wait!" she'd yell. "Stop! Remeasure it!")

Don't be afraid to adjust to taste . . .
Everybody's taste is a little bit different, so if you're not liking my seasonings, change it up. I tend to season pretty aggressively with salt, acidity, and herbs—but if you're the guy who always orders his wings "volcanic," you're probably going to want to spice things up, since the heat here is Italian-style, and Italians don't do spicy. (I do use a lot of crushed red pepper, like the stuff you sprinkle on your pizza at your local joint. It doesn't make food especially hot, but it does bring the flavors together.)

. . . but don't leave out the salt or the fat.

Salt gives food flavor. If you're afraid of it, your food will be shy and retiring, too. And fat is important for mouth-feel. My food isn't very heavy, but it does involve butter, cheese, and olive oil. Skip the trans fats in the prepackaged food aisle and eat this stuff instead.

Time things out, but be a time-tester.

I tested all these recipes on an ordinary gas-powered home stove, and in an ordinary oven—nothing high-powered or fancy. That's what all the timing is geared to. But when I tried out a few recipes on my mom's electric stove, I discovered that everything went a little slower. So if you're using an electric stove, you will definitely need to allow more time for cooking. And every oven, gas or electric, has its own thing going on. I've given you descriptions of what things should look or taste like at every stage, so you don't have to rely only on timing to know when something's ready.

Every recipe has a timing estimate at the top. If you chop really slowly, or just like to be really leisurely, add some time in.

Work with what you've got . . .

These recipes are best-case-scenario joints. In a perfect world, you can always find all the ingredients you need, and you always have enough time to make everything from scratch, and you're never too tired to get started. But real life doesn't work like that. So if, for instance, it's Tuesday night, and you're making Chicken Leg Cacciatore, and the recipe calls for you to roast peppers, and it's just one step too much after a long day at work? Buy a jar of roasted peppers. *Basta.* It won't be exactly the same—but it'll still be pretty damn good. Don't want to soak your beans overnight? No problem: canned ones work just fine. Fresh pasta rocks, but if you don't have a pasta machine and a lot of time, just pick up a box of the dried stuff (or fresh-frozen, from your local specialty store) and follow the directions on the box, subtracting one minute from the cooking time. And if you can't find Calabrian oregano on the branch, the regular dried stuff will still make you happy. Don't have red chili flakes? A couple shots of Tabasco will do the trick.

. . . but when it comes to dessert, follow the rules.

Pastry is a whole different animal. If you're making desserts, you need to be exact, because pastry is as much science as art. So don't substitute, and make sure you measure carefully. When I first started cooking as a kid, I baked—but all that rule-following is the reason I didn't become a pastry chef. I'm more of a let's-just-bang-it-out kind of guy.

Plan ahead.

If you're having people over for a party or a big holiday dinner, do as much as you can ahead of time—even the day before. Some recipes in this book are designed to be done in steps; everywhere possible, I've told you how long things will hold in the fridge at various stages. Nothing's worse than being stuck in the kitchen, sweating your butt off, when everyone else is having a good time and getting drunk.

1

{ ANTIPASTI }

TOMATO AND BUFFALO MOZZARELLA ARANCINI

Arancini are sort of a Sicilian cross between a Chinese soup dumpling and a hush puppy: they're risotto balls stuffed with ragu, cheese, or just about any other rich filling designed to ooze out a bit when the arancino is bitten into. They're served in Sicilian sandwich shops and *tavola calda* ("hot tables," places to get a little baccalà, a piece of pizza, a little this or that—an Italian deli). They're usually fried ahead of time and served at room temperature, but I like them hot, in bite-sized form for antipasti or bigger for appetizers. I've given you the straightforward tomato-cheese recipe here, but these are also great stuffed with Lamb Ragu (page 100) or Pesto (page 288).

TIMING: These are a project, but you can do them in stages: make the rice the day before, and then roll the rice balls and stuff them. The breaded, unfried arancini balls are actually better if you leave them in the fridge overnight. Unfried arancini will hold in the freezer for up to 2 weeks—just be sure to let them defrost thoroughly before frying.

MAKES 30 TO 35 ARANCINI; SERVES 6 TO IO AS AN APPETIZER

INGREDIENTS

For the rice:

1 tablespoon extra-virgin olive oil

2 tablespoons butter

1 small onion, minced (about ½ cup)

2 cups Arborio rice

4 cups low-sodium chicken broth or water

1 cup white wine

1½ tablespoons tomato paste

¼ cup Parmigiano-Reggiano

1½ teaspoons salt

¼ teaspoon coarse-ground black pepper

For the stuffing:

2 balls of mozzarella di bufala cheese
   (about 2 pounds)

>>>

METHOD

TO PREPARE THE RICE:

1. Heat the olive oil and 1 tablespoon of butter in a large pot on medium heat. Add the onion and cook until it's soft.

2. Add the rice, stir to combine, and sweat together for a minute or 2, until the rice is coated with onion, olive oil, and butter. Meanwhile, heat the chicken stock or water in the microwave on high for 3 to 5 minutes, until it's hot but not boiling. (Basically you're making stuffed risotto, so you want to heat the stock first; I use the microwave to save on time and pot-washing.)

3. Add the white wine, turn the heat to high, and cook till the wine is evaporated, stirring constantly to keep the rice from sticking. Add 2 cups of the chicken stock or water and continue to cook, stirring regularly, until all the liquid is absorbed and the rice has puffed up. Add the remaining 2 cups of chicken stock or water and keep cooking and stirring. When the liquid has been absorbed again, turn off the heat. (For good arancini, you need to cook the rice a little longer than you would for regular risotto, so the rice releases a lot of starch, making it good and sticky. The whole cooking process should take approximately 25 minutes.)

4. Add the tomato paste and stir it in well. Grate the parmesan into the mixture and stir well. Add the other tablespoon of butter and stir well. Add the salt and pepper.

5 Pour the rice onto a baking sheet and spread into a thin layer using a rubber spatula. Use the spatula to chop open areas into the layer of rice so it cools better. Place the rice in the refrigerator for approximately 20 minutes, until it has cooled to maximum stickiness.

TO PREPARE THE ARANCINI BALLS:

1 When the rice is completely cold—almost icy-feeling and very sticky—remove it from the fridge and make golf-ball-sized rice spheres with your fingers. Pack each ball together tightly and then use your thumbs to create a well in the center. Place the arancini well-side up on a baking sheet. (They should look sort of like ceramics-class candle holders, only made of rice.)

2 Cut the mozzarella into bite-sized pieces (about 20 pieces per mozzarella ball; each piece should fit snugly inside the well of an arancini ball). Put a piece in each arancino well, then close up each ball, packing it the way you would a snowball.

You can bread the arancini now, but it's better to put them back in the fridge, covered in plastic wrap, to cool down again. Leave them overnight if possible.

TO BREAD AND FINISH THE ARANCINI:

1 Preheat the oven to 200°.

2 Heat the oil in a large pot on the stove to about 375° (when you drop an arancino in, it should crackle).

3 Make an egg wash: crack the eggs in a large bowl, add ½ cup water, and whip them together. Place the flour in a separate bowl. Place the breadcrumbs in a separate large bowl.

4 Remove the arancini from the fridge only when you're ready to actually start the breading process, so they stay as cold (and sticky) as possible. Roll each cold arancino in the flour (holding it lightly with two fingers so as not to crush it) and then put it in the bowl with the egg wash.

>>>

For the breading:

6 cups corn oil or grapeseed oil
(for frying)

6 eggs

3 to 4 cups dried breadcrumbs

2 cups all-purpose flour

5 When you have a batch that fills the bowl without crowding it, remove the arancini from the egg wash (making sure that each ball is thoroughly coated with flour and egg wash) and put them in the breadcrumb bowl. Coat the arancini thoroughly with breadcrumbs, then drop them in the hot oil. Let the arancini fry in the hot oil for about 2 minutes, until they turn hush-puppy golden brown.

6 With a slotted spoon or spider, remove the arancini and place them on a plate or baking tray covered with a paper towel. Salt them while they're still hot, then put them in the oven for about 10 minutes to temper. When they come out, they should have a hush-puppy-like texture: a bit crisp on the outside, soft and warm and gooey on the inside. Sprinkle a bit more salt over the arancini to bring out the flavor before serving.

ARTICHOKE FRITTO WITH YOGURT AND MINT

This is my version of one of my favorite Roman foods: *carciofi alla giuda*, whole fried artichokes in olive oil. They're served at out-door cafés in the spring, on brown parchment, with a bit of lemon on the side—perfect with a glass of Frascati wine. But they're also a big mess—fatal to your manners and dangerous to your clothing, not to mention that worn by passersby—and they require a gallon or so of expensive olive oil. So in this version, I cut out the outer leaves and cook down the artichokes before I fry them, to make them less greasy. And to balance them out, I add a sauce with cool mint, heat, spice, and sweetness, plus a little bit of tart-ness from the yogurt.

The precooking definitely makes this recipe a little labor-intensive, but it's worth the work: it's total impress-the-guests stuff that's fun to eat. You can serve this at a fancy dinner, or just as high-concept Superbowl or Oscar food; the sauce is great with wings, too.

TIMING: This one is a project, so give yourself lots of time. The best thing to do is to cook the artichokes in advance. They'll hold in the fridge for up to 2 days, but they should be fried immediately before serving. If you're in a rush (or just looking for instant grat-ification), you can skip the whole artichoke-prep thing: pick up some good artichokes in oil or in water at your local Italian grocer or gourmet shop. Drain them well, dry them thoroughly on a paper towel, and go straight to sauce-making and frying.

SERVES 3 TO 4

INGREDIENTS

For the artichokes:

2 cups white wine

1 teaspoon red pepper flakes

1 teaspoon whole fennel seed

3 bay leaves

2 teaspoons salt

6 large artichokes

For the yogurt-mint sauce:

1 cup plain yogurt

1 teaspoon extra-virgin olive oil

¼ teaspoon hot pepper flakes or
  harissa juice and zest of 1 lemon

a pinch of salt

1 tablespoon sugar

¼ cup mint leaves, rough-chopped
  lightly to avoid bruising

>>>

METHOD

TO PREPARE THE ARTICHOKES:

1. Combine the wine, red pepper flakes, fennel seed, bay leaves, and salt with 12 cups of water in a large pot. Set aside.

2. Clean the artichokes: Cut off the bottom of each stem, leaving about half the stem intact. Pull off the tough outer leaves, revealing the closely packed, tender leaves in the center; they will be tight around the bud, and should be a soft pale-green springtime color. Use a small paring knife to peel off the remnants of the outer leaves from around the base of the bud, and then peel the base and the stem with the knife until you reach the inside, which is the same light color as the bud. Cut off the top of the bud so the purple heart inside is exposed. Once each artichoke is cleaned, put it in the pot with the wine-water mixture.

3. Put the pot on the stove on high heat and bring the liquid to a rolling boil, then turn the heat down to low and cook at a slow simmer for about 30 minutes, until a sharp knife easily penetrates the artichokes. The outer leaves of the artichoke will turn green-brown as they cook. (At the restaurant, we use Vitamin C powder and a whole lot of white wine to keep the artichokes white; at home, this is way too much

>>>

trouble, so I just let mine go khaki-colored.) Allow the pot to cool down until you can handle it comfortably, and then cool the whole thing in the fridge, uncovered, for at least 1 hour.

For frying and finishing:

6 cups corn oil or grapeseed oil

2 heaping teaspoons flour

a generous pinch of salt

1 tablespoon Parmigiano-Reggiano

4 When the artichokes have cooled, remove them from the pot and slice each one in half lengthwise. Using a spoon, scoop out the fibrous, furry bit at the center of the bulb—the bit that looks like the stamens of a flower, or the interesting part of a Georgia O'Keeffe painting—and the purple leaves that are attached to it. Leave the rest of the leaves, the stem, and the choke (the meaty top part of the artichoke below the stem) intact.

TO PREPARE THE YOGURT-MINT SAUCE:

1 Combine the yogurt, ¼ cup of water, olive oil, crushed hot pepper or harissa, lemon juice and zest, salt, sugar, and mint leaves, in that order, whisking them together as you go until the sauce is well combined.

TO FRY THE ARTICHOKES AND FINISH THE DISH:

1 Heat the oil in a fryer or a large pot with high sides on high heat on the stove.

2 Place the flour in a large bowl. Dry the artichokes a bit on paper towels. Toss each artichoke in the flour with your hands, being sure to coat it thoroughly. Don't worry if some of the artichoke leaves come off: you can fry those, too, and they'll make crispy and delicious additions.

3 When the oil reaches about 375° (that is, when you put in a test artichoke and it crackles), put the artichokes in to fry in batches of 3 or 4, so they're not crowded. Fry for about 1 minute, until the leaves are brown and crispy (they should look a bit like a dried flower—they're really beautiful).

4 Remove with a spider or slotted spoon to a paper-towel-lined plate and sprinkle immediately with salt, so that the salt adheres to the oil on the artichokes. Spread a thick coating of the yogurt sauce on a plate or serving platter. Put the artichokes on top and sprinkle the Parmigiano cheese over them. If there's sauce left over, use it for dipping.

ASPARAGUS A LA PARMIGIANA

In America, the phrase "alla Parmigiana" gets attached to anything with parmesan cheese in it. Italians, in my experience, feel the need to correct this all the time: as they'll tell you (even if you don't ask!), "alla Parmigiana" just means "in the style of the city of Parma." This isn't completely without debate, of course (we're talking about Italy, after all): eggplant Parmigiana is from the south, not from Parma, so the Sicilians claim that "Parmigiana" is a bastardization of a phrase meaning "from Palermo."

Whatever. Guess what? Food from Parma—that is, cuisine "alla Parmigiana"—features lots of prosciutto and ... Parmigiano-Reggiano.

So. This Parma-style dish is best in the springtime, when asparagus is in season and it's tender and delicious. But don't go for the little baby stalks; you want the thick, meaty jumbo-sized asparagus here. I've put this recipe in antipasti because that's the standard restaurant way, but it could really go anywhere: it makes a great contorni, and it also rocks as a breakfast dish.

TIMING: Fast; this takes about 30 minutes, tops. And you can hurry things up by using the microwave instead of boiling a pot of water; take a look at Asparagus with Citrus and Oregano (page 210) for my technique. If you don't have any Crumbs Yo! (page 291) on hand, you can use panko breadcrumbs instead.

SERVES 4

INGREDIENTS

1 bunch jumbo-sized asparagus
 (about 16 stalks)

1 teaspoon melted butter or extra-virgin
 olive oil, plus more to coat the pan

a generous pinch of salt and coarse-
 ground black pepper

2 teaspoons fresh thyme leaves

2 teaspoons fresh rosemary leaves,
 roughly chopped

4 eggs

2 tablespoons grated Parmigiano-
 Reggiano

1 tablespoon Crumbs Yo! (page 291) or
 panko breadcrumbs

a generous drizzle of vin cotto (or good
 balsamic vinegar)

Optional:

6 slices bacon, diced (¼ cup); see
 method at end of recipe

METHOD

1. Put a large pot of salted water on to boil.

2. Trim about 2 inches off the bottoms of the asparagus. (If you really want to be fancy, you can peel the stalks with a carrot peeler.) Blanch the asparagus in the boiling water for 2 to 3 minutes, until the color intensifies. Remove it and place it in a bowl of ice water to immediately stop the cooking process. (Or see asparagus-in-the-microwave technique on page 210.)

3. Set an oven rack one notch below the top (checking to make sure your casserole will fit), and turn the oven on to broil.

4. Coat the bottom of a long Pyrex or earthenware oven-friendly casserole with melted butter or olive oil, using a pastry brush or your fingers. Lay the asparagus in the casserole, making sure the pieces are placed tightly together with no spaces in between. (Otherwise, the egg will run through instead of browning over the asparagus.)

5. Use a pastry brush or your fingers to glaze the asparagus in melted butter or olive oil. Season with salt and pepper, and sprinkle the thyme and rosemary on top. Be generous with the herbs and seasonings: they're important to the dish's flavor, so make sure every piece of asparagus gets its share.

6 Crack the eggs directly over the asparagus; each egg should be positioned over its own 4 pieces or so. Grate the parmesan cheese over the whole shebang.

7 Put the casserole in the oven and broil for 2 minutes. The egg whites should be fluffy white with brown flecks, but the yolks should still be runny when cut. The asparagus should retain some snap between the teeth and some freshness of color and flavor.

8 Remove the asparagus from the oven and sprinkle with toasted breadcrumbs and drizzle the vin cotto over the top. (If you've got a really good balsamic vinegar on hand—sweet and thick—you can use that instead.) Serve immediately in the baking dish.

OPTIONAL:

At the restaurant, we do this dish with pancetta, but it's a crazy two-day process that begins with curing the meat. If you have some bacon lying around in the fridge, you can get a bit of that flavor: fry the bacon up really crispy, let it cool, crunch it up into little bits with your hands, and sprinkle it over the asparagus just before you add the vin cotto.

CALAMARI MARINATO WITH HARISSA, CHICKPEAS, AND CELERY

Some people think they don't like calamari, but that's because they've only had the beer-bar version—the kind that tastes like a chew toy. This marinated salad is different: it's light and, believe it or not, fresh-tasting. The calamari on top has some spice to it, while the vegetables underneath are cooler. Harissa is really important here: it gives the dish a lot of depth, not to mention olives and a fistful of different spices. (It may not be Italian, but those Mediterraneans, they've got a lot in common.)

You can avoid the horrors of rubberiness by doing a few simple things: buy smaller calamari (they're more tender); don't let your water come to a boil; and, above all, cook the calamari really, really quickly. This cold dish is easy to do ahead of time, so it's great to serve as part of a range of antipasti, but it also makes a delicious starter course on its own.

TIMING: About 1 hour, depending on how long you let the calamari marinate

SERVES 4

INGREDIENTS

For the calamari:

1½ pounds calamari (ask the fishmonger to clean them for you)

¼ cup olive oil

1 to 2 teaspoons harissa

½ teaspoon salt

juice of 1 lemon

For the salad:

1 15-ounce can chickpeas

½ cup celery, thinly sliced on the diagonal

½ small red onion (about ½ cup), sliced thin

¼ cup parsley leaves, roughly cut

zest and juice of 2 lemons

zest and juice of 1 orange

¼ cup extra-virgin olive oil

½ teaspoon salt

½ teaspoon coarse-ground black pepper

METHOD

TO PREPARE THE CALAMARI:

1. Bring a medium-sized pot of water to just below a simmer—*not* a boil; you never want to boil calamari.

2. Rinse the calamari well in cold water in a colander.

3. Separate the heads (the purple parts with the arms) and the bodies (the white triangular bits). Slice the heads in half unless they're bite-sized. Slice the bodies into thin rings.

4. Drop the heads in the simmering water, and let them cook for about 15 seconds—just until the arms start to stiffen up. Remove them with a spider, put them on a plate, and immediately place them in the fridge to cool down. Repeat the process with the rings; again, the pieces are ready when they stiffen up a bit, about 15 seconds.

5. When the calamari have cooled, drain off all the excess water. On the plate or in a bowl, add the olive oil, harissa, salt, and lemon juice to the calamari and mix well to coat. Refrigerate the calamari in this marinade until the salad is ready.

TO PREPARE THE SALAD:

1. Combine the chickpeas, celery, red onion, and parsley in a bowl. Grate the lemon and orange zest over the salad and squeeze in the juice. Stir in the olive oil, salt, and pepper. Taste and adjust the seasonings as needed.

2   Marinate the chickpea salad in the fridge. This is a quick marinade—
15 minutes to an hour will allow the flavors to set in—but if you're in
a serious rush, you can just mix the calamari with the salad and serve
it right away, as long as you've already marinated the calamari.

3   Arrange the salad on a broad plate (I like to spread it out so it's a flat
base), and pile the calamari on top of the salad. Serve immediately,
with all the ingredients cold.

CRISPY CALAMARI SALAD WITH ARUGULA, FENNEL, AND LEMON SAUCE

On my first trip to Tokyo, I had this great fried calamari over seaweed with a spicy mayonnaise-based sauce. Later that year, I was sitting in a café in Rome, drinking limoncello, a liquor that tastes like really, really good lemonade with a kick. (We keep a bottle of it in our freezer all summer long.) Suddenly—eureka!—I got this great idea: calamari salad, based on the one I had in Tokyo, but with a lemonade-flavored sauce! Tokyo calamari with greens plus Roman streetside limoncello in one dish? That, my friends, is truly Urban Italian.

This salad's got everything: it's leafy, crunchy, sweet, and sour all in the same bite. The acid of the lemon sauce is great with the fried calamari—like lemon juice on steroids, it breaks down the fried flavor and brightens everything up.

TIMING: 1 hour

SERVES 6

INGREDIENTS

For the lemon sauce:

4 medium-sized lemons

1 tablespoon sugar

¼ teaspoon cayenne pepper or Tabasco

1 egg yolk

1 teaspoon salt

½ cup extra-virgin olive oil

½ cup corn oil

For the calamari:

6 cups corn oil or grapeseed oil

1½ pounds calamari (cleaned by
　　your fishmonger)

10 ounces club soda

2 cups all-purpose flour

2 teaspoons salt, plus a pinch for
　　sprinkling at the end

½ teaspoon coarse-ground black pepper

¼ teaspoon cayenne pepper or paprika

>>>

METHOD

TO PREPARE THE LEMON SAUCE:

1. Put a small pot of water on to boil.

2. Peel the lemons with a vegetable peeler. If there's any excess white stuff inside the peel, scrape it off with a paring knife and discard it. Reserve the outer peel.

3. Juice the lemons; you should have about ⅓ cup of lemon juice. Reserve the juice.

4. When the water has boiled, add the lemon peel and cook until the pieces of peel are soft: about 7 minutes. Drain the peels and rinse them under cold water to cool.

5. Combine the lemon peel, sugar, cayenne or Tabasco, egg yolk, salt, and 2 tablespoons of water in the blender. Purée to combine the ingredients thoroughly, then add the olive and corn oils slowly, one at a time, as you continue to blend. When it's done, the sauce should be yellow-white and frothy, and it should taste like really good lemonade with a tiny kick.

TO PREPARE THE CALAMARI:

1. Heat the corn oil or grapeseed oil over high heat in a large pot on the stove.

2. Rinse the calamari well under cold water in a colander. Separate the

>>>

For the salad:

1 fennel bulb, thinly sliced

1 head arugula, washed and with
    stems removed

10 fresh, ripe cherry tomatoes, halved

1 cup Peppadew peppers
    (or peperoncini), quartered, plus 2
    tablespoons juice

2 tablespoons extra-virgin olive oil

juice of ½ lemon

salt and coarse-ground
    black pepper to taste

heads (the purple parts with the arms) and the bodies (the white bits). Keep the heads whole. Slice the calamari bodies into ½-inch-wide rounds. Place the calamari pieces in a bowl and pour the club soda over them.

3 Combine the flour, salt, pepper, and paprika or cayenne in a large metal bowl. Drain the calamari in a fine sieve and dump them into the flour mixture. Mix well to coat every piece.

4 When the oil reaches about 375° (that is, when you put a piece of calamari in and it crackles), put the calamari in to fry in 3 or 4 batches, so they're not crowded. Fry each batch for about 2 minutes, until the pieces are really crispy (but don't fry 'em till they're brown like they do it at your favorite beer bar—the pieces should retain their color). Remove the calamari with a spider, place them on a paper-towel-lined plate, and immediately sprinkle them with salt, so the salt adheres to the oil on the calamari.

TO PREPARE THE SALAD AND FINISH THE DISH:

1 In a mixing bowl, combine the fennel, arugula, cherry tomatoes, and Peppadew peppers with their juice. Add the olive oil, lemon juice, and salt and pepper to taste. Mix well.

2 Divide the salad mixture onto 6 plates. Top with calamari and drizzle with the lemon sauce. Serve immediately.

CAPONATA MODO MIO

Caponata is the traditional Sicilian sweet-and-sour eggplant stew—more of a relish than a dish—that you see on antipasti platters and in jars in specialty stores. This dish is a bit different: it is, like the name says, caponata "my way," a hearty, savory cross between ratatouille and caponata with peppers and zucchini, all stewed together for extra soul. I serve it at the restaurant with grilled bread. It's spicy, crunchy, sweet, and lively. (If you're using Italian eggplant for this, salt the diced eggplant in a colander for a half hour to draw out the bitterness.)

TIMING: You can bang this out pretty quickly, especially if you're fast with a knife

SERVES 8
(OR 4, WITH LEFTOVERS FOR SOME PRETTY DAMN GOOD SANDWICHES THE NEXT DAY)

INGREDIENTS

⅓ cup extra-virgin olive oil

1 medium onion, diced large

1 red pepper, diced large

1 yellow pepper, diced large

2 Japanese eggplants or 1 Italian eggplant, diced large

3 stalks celery, sliced large

1 large or 2 small zucchini, diced large

½ teaspoon salt

¼ teaspoon coarse-ground black pepper

½ teaspoon red pepper flakes

2 cloves garlic, sliced Goodfellas thin

½ cup white raisins, rehydrated in 1 cup water

1 cup Basic Tomato Sauce (page 285)

2 tablespoons fresh oregano leaves

¼ cup red wine vinegar

½ cup pine nuts, toasted and rough-chopped

METHOD

1. Heat the olive oil in a large saucepot over high heat. Add the onion, peppers, and eggplant. When the vegetables have softened a bit (about 5 minutes), add the celery and zucchini. Season liberally with half the salt and pepper. Mix the ingredients together and continue to cook.

2. After 10 minutes, add the red pepper flakes and garlic. Cover, reduce the heat to medium, and let the steam roast the vegetables for 5 minutes.

3. Add the rehydrated raisins, without the water, and the tomato sauce. Reduce the heat to low and simmer for 10 minutes, until the vegetables are soft but not falling apart and the sauce is well incorporated.

4. Remove the saucepot from the heat. Add the fresh oregano and season with the remaining salt and pepper. Mix in the vinegar. Serve in a large bowl with the pine nuts sprinkled on top.

I like this at room temperature, but it can be served hot or cold as well, depending on timing and taste. It will keep in the fridge for up to a week.

CHILLED TOMATO SOUP

Okay, I admit it: there are a lot of frickin' tomatoes in this book. But come on—tomatoes are just about the most iconic ingredient in Italian cooking next to pasta, right? Which is sort of amazing, since they came from the New World to Italy, so they've only been part of the cuisine for the last two hundred years or so. That's nineteenth-century globalization in action, I guess.

I love great tomatoes—the kind you can only get in summer, meaty and deep-tasting and sweet—and I love chilled soups, so the combo is a no-brainer for me. I did some in-depth experimentation with non-gazpacho chilled tomato soups, and after working my way through three different finalist versions, I can tell you for sure that the best tomato soup involves a half-and-half mixture: half the puréed tomatoes are raw, to give the soup that fresh summer taste, and the other half are puréed after oven-roasting, for intensity and depth.

TIMING: About 15 minutes' worth of prep and blending, plus 30 minutes to bake the tomatoes and 30 minutes to cool the soup

SERVES 4 TO 6

INGREDIENTS

For the soup:

2 pounds (about 8 medium) ripe
    beefsteak tomatoes, cored

4 tablespoons extra-virgin olive oil

1 clove garlic, sliced

¼ teaspoon salt for baking, plus ½
    teaspoon for blending the dish

¼ teaspoon coarse-ground black pepper

¼ teaspoon Dried Herbs (page 292)

1 tablespoon red wine vinegar

1 teaspoon red pepper flakes

1 tablespoon sugar

For the garnish:

Lots of options: 1 medium avocado, chopped; or sprinkle Dried Herbs; or 8 leaves basil, chopped; or 1 cup assorted diced summer vegetables: zucchini, peppers, yellow squash, wax beans, cherry tomatoes

METHOD

1. Preheat the oven to 350°.

2. Separate out half the tomatoes, remove the ends, and slice each one in half widthwise. Place the sliced tomatoes in a baking dish and pour 2 tablespoons of the olive oil over the top. Distribute the garlic on the tops of the tomato slices. Sprinkle with the salt, pepper, and Dried Herbs.

3. Place the tomatoes in the oven on the middle rack and bake for about 30 minutes, until the garlic is browned and fragrant and the tomatoes have wrinkled up.

4. Meanwhile, quarter the remaining uncooked tomatoes.

5. When the baking process is finished, put all the tomatoes together in the blender (if you need to do this in batches, be sure to combine fresh and baked tomatoes in each batch). Blend on high until everything is combined and smooth. Add 2 tablespoons of olive oil, the vinegar, the red pepper flakes, and the sugar, and continue blending until all ingredients are combined and smooth.

6. Strain the soup through a fine sieve, using the back of a wooden spoon to push it through, so that the soup has a cream-of-tomato consistency. Put the strained soup in a covered container in the fridge to cool.

You can garnish this with just about anything summery and vegetable: chopped basil, chopped avocado, a drizzle of olive oil, maybe some diced summer vegetables. Consult your inner chef.

MEATBALLS MODO MIO WITH CHERRIES

Okay: so this isn't the most authentic Italian meatball you've ever tripped over. But Urban Italian? Definitely.

This dish was born one long afternoon when I was sitting around in my home office with Luke Ostrom, my partner in crime. We were drinking coffee and listening to tunes as we hashed out menu ideas. I tend to develop new recipes in a stream-of-consciousness kind of method: I'll write down every idea I can come up with, then boil them down, do some research (on ingredients, history, whatever), and start to really put things together so I see how the menu looks as a whole. (This is all way before I get in the kitchen and start playing with ingredients.) That's what we were doing with our menu that day. *What's the most iconic Italian-American food?* we asked ourselves. The answer was clear: meatballs. *Well, how can we sex up meatballs?* (Which are pretty unsexy, in their pure form: all Mama-in-Queens, right?) We came up with a long list of ideas—but duck and foie gras were the first ingredients we brainstormed, and that's what we ended up using. I based the cherry sauce on a purée I used to serve with duck, a pretty French thing, but with the traditional Italian mustard flavor added. So these are Italian-American-French New York meatballs. Totally Urban Italian.

Well-ground meat is absolutely key to this dish. If you're doing it yourself, you'll need a good meat grinder or a KitchenAid mixer with the grinding attachment. If you don't have grinding technology in your kitchen, you'll need to have a really copacetic butcher who will grind the duck, the pork shoulder, and the fatback for you—this ain't your local Stop 'N Save job.

TIMING: This one's a project: it takes about 6 hours, over a day or two

MAKES APPROXIMATELY 30 MEATBALLS; SERVES 6

INGREDIENTS

For the meatballs:

1 pound boneless duck legs (or 2 pounds if bought on the bone)—about 5 legs, cut into 1-inch pieces (about 2¾ cups)

¾ pound pork shoulder (about 1¼ cups)

½ pound fatback, cut into 1-inch pieces (about ½ cup)

1 cup fresh foie gras or foie gras paté, at room temperature

1½ teaspoons salt

½ teaspoon coarse-ground black pepper

1 teaspoon ground red pepper flakes

½ teaspoon ground fennel seed

1 teaspoon ground coriander seed

2 tablespoons milk

>>>

METHOD

TO PREPARE THE MEAT:

1. Trim the excess skin from the outsides of the duck legs. If you purchased the legs with the bone in, remove the meat using a boning knife, being sure to cut away any pieces of hard sinew.

2. Cut the duck meat into 1-inch pieces and place it on a plate.

3. Do the same with the pork shoulder and the fatback.

4. Cover all the meat with plastic wrap, place it in the freezer, and allow it to freeze thoroughly—at least 2 hours. (This step can be done up to 2 weeks in advance.)

TO PREPARE THE FOIE GRAS:

If you are working with foie gras paté, let the paté come to room temperature.

IF YOU ARE WORKING WITH FRESH FOIE GRAS:

1. Let the foie gras sit out at room temperature so that it becomes very soft—almost like butter.

>>>

¼ cup fresh bread, chopped small

¼ cup dried breadcrumbs

2 eggs

a pinch of chopped chives

For the cherry mostarda:

1 cup dried cherries, rehydrated in
    1 cup hot tap water

½ cup red wine vinegar, reduced by
    half on the stove

2 teaspoons Japanese mustard paste

2 tablespoons grappa or brandy

a pinch of salt

2 Clean the foie gras by removing any veins with a small knife.

3 Press the foie gras through a fine strainer or chinois into a bowl with your hands or the back of a spoon. You want the foie gras that comes through to look more or less like thick peanut butter, or very expensive Play-Doh.

TO GRIND THE MEAT:

1 Attach the grinding attachment and the medium die on a KitchenAid mixer, if using.

2 Remove the meat from the freezer just before grinding. This is very important: you want the meat to go through the grinder frozen so that it comes through easily. If the meat is frozen going in, it'll come out looking like those meat-grinder cartoons in Pink Floyd's *The Wall*. If it's not frozen, you'll just end up with mush.

3 Grind the duck and the pork shoulder, alternating bits of each in order to help the meats emulsify.

4 Remove the ground duck and pork from the bowl and put it through the grinder again, alternating it with pieces of the frozen fatback. This will help emulsify and blend the meats so that the meatballs end up tasting really well mixed.

5 As you go, use the plunger to push everything through the grinder as thoroughly as possible. You want the meat to be well ground and well mixed, and you don't want to leave it all on the inside of the grinder.

TO PREPARE THE MEATBALL MIXTURE:

1 Combine the ground meat, foie gras, salt, pepper, red pepper flakes, fennel, and coriander in a large bowl, and mix together well with your hands.

2 In another bowl, combine the milk and the chopped bread. Add this to the meat mixture.

3 Add the eggs and the dried breadcrumbs to the meat mixture and mix together well with your hands, as though you're working with bread dough, until everything is thoroughly emulsified.

4   Cover the mixture with plastic wrap and refrigerate for 1 hour. The mixture will keep in the fridge for up to two days.

TO PREPARE THE CHERRY MOSTARDA:

1   In a blender, combine the cherries and their rehydrating water, the reduced red wine vinegar, the mustard paste, the grappa or brandy, and the salt, and blend on high until smooth. The flavor should be smooth, mustardy, with a sweet dark undertone—really sweet-and-sour. (If you're making the meatballs in stages, the mostarda can be prepared up to a week in advance and held in the fridge in an airtight container.)

TO MAKE THE MEATBALLS:

1   Preheat the oven to 425° on the convection setting.

2   To make each meatball, form about 1 heaping tablespoon of the meat mixture into a ball, rolling it between your hands like a snowball.

>>>

3   Place the meatballs on a baking sheet or sheet tray with high sides (there will be a lot of fat; you don't want it to fall to the bottom of the oven and produce a lot of smoke).

4   Bake the meatballs for 3 minutes, until they begin to brown on top.

5   Rotate the pan and flip each meatball over. Bake for another 3 minutes, until the meatballs are dark brown all over. Remove them from the pan and discard the excess fat.

TO FINISH THE DISH:

1   Heat the mostarda in a large sauté pan over medium heat until it reaches a simmer.

2   Add the meatballs and cook together, coating the meatballs thoroughly with the mostarda until they're shiny with the glaze and the sauce has worked its way into the outer layer of the meatball, about 2 minutes.

3   Garnish with chopped chives and serve immediately.

LAMB MEATBALLS STUFFED WITH GOAT CHEESE

This dish is kind of Middle East–meets–Little Italy: it's totally spaghetti-and-meatballs-style when it comes to the sauce, but then there's the lamb, not to mention the goat-cheese center, which oozes out of the meatballs—surprise!—when you cut into them. The method here is a little different from the one I use for the Meatballs Modo Mio with Cherries (page 55): while those are baked and then sauced, these are cooked right in the sauce, so that the flavors meld. Serve these on their own as antipasti, or toss them with some penne or rigatoni as a main course, a great Sunday-night dish for family and friends.

TIMING: About 1 hour, depending on whether or not you have Crumbs Yo! (page 291) on hand. If you don't have any and don't have time to make them, you can leave them out: you'll just be missing a little crunch on the outside of the final product.

MAKES ABOUT 30 MEATBALLS; SERVES 6 FOR ANTIPASTI

INGREDIENTS

For the meatballs:

3 tablespoons extra-virgin olive oil

1 small onion, chopped (about ½ cup)

1 clove garlic, finely chopped

½ teaspoon ground coriander seed

1 teaspoon ground fennel seed

1 tablespoon rosemary, finely chopped

¼ cup fresh goat cheese

½ pound merguez sausage, about 8 links (or 2 links hot Italian sausage, if you prefer), with casings cut away

1 pound ground lamb

½ cup dried breadcrumbs

2 eggs

½ teaspoon salt

>>>

METHOD

TO MAKE THE MEATBALLS:

1. Heat the olive oil in a sauté pan over medium heat. Add the onion and sweat for 3 minutes. Add the garlic and cook for 1 minute, stirring constantly.

2. Add the coriander, fennel, and rosemary. Cook together 1 minute, so that the aromas of the spices and herbs are released. Remove to a bowl and place in the fridge to cool (about 5 minutes), so that you're not combining hot onions with cold meat.

3. Meanwhile, roll the goat cheese between your palms to form ½-inch balls (the size of a pebble). Place them on a plate and reserve.

4. When the onion-herb mixture has cooled, combine it in a large bowl with the sausage, lamb, breadcrumbs, eggs, and salt. Mix well with your hands.

5. Form the meatballs: for each meatball, scoop up about 2 tablespoons of lamb mixture and roll and press it into an oval, about the size of a distended Ping-Pong ball. Use your thumb to create a goat-cheese-ball-sized dent in the middle, and drop a goat-cheese ball inside. Pinch the lamb mixture up around the goat cheese to close the hole, and roll the meatball between your hands till it's round and smooth. Repeat until you've used up all the goat cheese and the lamb mixture.

>>>

TO MAKE THE SAUCE:

1 Heat the olive oil in a large pot over medium-high heat. Add the onion and cook until it starts to soften, about 1 minute.

2 Crush the tomatoes in a bowl with the heel of your hand. Add them to the pot, then add the tomato juice, red pepper flakes, salt, sugar, and oregano. Mix to combine. Cook over medium-high heat for 10 minutes, until the flavors combine and the sauce is reduced.

3 Add the meatballs, being careful not to break them. Reduce the heat to low, so the sauce is at a very low simmer, and cover. It's very important that the liquid never come to a boil. You want as slow a simmer as possible, so the flavors really come together, the cheese melts, and the meat becomes rich and tender. Cook for 5 minutes, turn the meatballs with a spoon, and simmer another 5 minutes, until the meat is cooked and the sauce takes on the flavor of the meatballs. (Some goat cheese may find its way out during the cooking process—it depends on how tightly you've made your meatballs—but don't worry about this: the meatballs will still taste good.)

TO FINISH THE DISH:

Ladle the meatballs and sauce into 6 bowls. Sprinkle with the Crumbs Yo! and the grated cheese. Serve immediately.

For the sauce:

¼ cup extra-virgin olive oil

1 medium onion, diced (about 1 cup)

1 28-ounce can Italian tomatoes
  (San Marzano, if possible) plus
  their juice

¼ teaspoon red pepper flakes

½ teaspoon salt

½ teaspoon sugar

½ teaspoon dried oregano,
  preferably on the branch

To finish the dish:

¼ cup Crumbs Yo! (page 291)

¼ cup grated pecorino cheese

SHRIMP MEATBALLS

This is true Urban Italian stuff: Italy meets Asia, by way of Mulberry Street. In my favorite Vietnamese and Cambodian restaurants (down below Canal Street, in what New Yorkers still call Chinatown), little fish balls in soup are a menu staple, the best way to start a meal. Here I've taken them out of the soup and done them Italian-style. These make great antipasti, but you can also serve them with pasta—braised in Basic Tomato Sauce (page 285), for instance—or as a garnish for fish, or whatever way appeals to you; there are definitely no rules with this one. If you really want to get fancy, you could even substitute lobster meat for the shrimp. (Use the same amounts.)

TIMING: This one will take you a couple of hours, including cooling-down time. You can do it in two stages if that's easier; the unrolled meatball mixture will keep in the fridge overnight.

MAKES 30 MEATBALLS; SERVES 5 TO 7 AS ANTIPASTI

INGREDIENTS

For the meatballs:

½ cup diced dried chorizo (about ½ a sausage)

1 small onion, chopped (about ½ cup)

1 teaspoon red pepper flakes

1 pound scallops (about 2 cups)

¾ cup cream

1 egg yolk

1½ tablespoons chopped parsley

1½ tablespoons chopped chives

½ tablespoon salt

½ tablespoon coarse-ground black pepper

¾ cup dry breadcrumbs

zest of 1 lemon

1 pound shrimp, diced

>>>

METHOD

TO PREPARE THE MEATBALL MIXTURE:

1. Sweat the chorizo in a dry pan over medium heat to release its oil. When there's a fair amount of red oil in the pan, add the onion, reduce the heat to low, and sweat the onion until it's soft and colored by the oil. Add the red pepper flakes and continue cooking on low heat about another minute to combine the flavors. Put the mixture on a flat plate in the refrigerator to cool (about 15 minutes).

2. Put the scallops in a food processor. Add the cream and blend into a smooth paste. Add the egg yolk and blend together. The result should look like very wet pasta dough (or melted ice cream). Turn the mixture into a bowl and add the parsley, chives, salt, pepper, breadcrumbs, and lemon zest.

3. Blot the diced shrimp well with a cloth or paper towel to make sure that they're as dry as possible (excess moisture will make your meatballs fall apart). Add them to the scallop mixture.

4. When the chorizo mixture has cooled completely, add it to the scallop-shrimp mixture and mix everything together well with your hands. The mix should be sticky, like tacky spackling. Cover the mixture with plastic wrap, and put it in the fridge to cool for at least 1 hour. It's very important to make sure the mixture is cold, so that you can work with it effectively. (If you'd like, you can hold the mixture in the fridge for up to 24 hours at this point.)

TO PREPARE THE MEATBALLS AND THE SAUCE:

1 Remove the mixture from the fridge and begin rolling the meatballs immediately; for each meatball, roll a heaping-tablespoon-sized chunk of the mixture between both hands until it forms a tight ball. (You can make the meatballs bigger or smaller if you prefer—just remember to adjust the cooking time.)

2 Over medium heat, warm the butter and olive oil in a large sauté pan (pick a pan big enough to fit all the meatballs at once). When the butter starts to melt, add the red pepper flakes, garlic, and bay leaves. Cook for a few seconds, shaking the pan to keep the garlic from burning.

3 When the aroma of the garlic comes up, add the white wine and turn the heat up to high. When the wine has evaporated completely, leaving only olive oil and butter bubbling in the pan, add the clam juice, then immediately place the meatballs in the pan by hand, one by one (it's easiest if you can cook them all in one batch; don't worry if the meatballs are close together, or even touching).

4 Let the liquid come up to a simmer, then cover the pan and lower the heat to medium. Cook the meatballs for 2 minutes at a low bubble. Remove the lid, turn the meatballs over with a spoon, and then cover and continue cooking for about 2½ more minutes. The meatballs are done when they have some bounce to them when you poke them with a finger. (When you bite into them, they should be cooked through, and you should get a bit of that bounce between your teeth.)

5 Remove the pan from the heat and add the parsley. Serve the meatballs immediately, in a large bowl, covered with the sauce. Be sure to put some toasted bread on the table for dipping in the extra sauce.

For the sauce:

1 tablespoon butter

2 tablespoons extra-virgin olive oil

1 teaspoon red pepper flakes

2 cloves garlic, sliced Goodfellas thin

3 bay leaves (preferably fresh, though dried will work too)

½ cup white wine

½ cup clam juice

⅓ cup chopped parsley

Optional:

toasted bread for dipping in extra sauce

THREE ANTIPASTI: EGGPLANT AGRODOLCE (PAGE 65),
PEPERONATA MODO MIO (PAGE 76), AND RON'S EGGPLANT PICKLES (PAGE 66)

EGGPLANT AGRODOLCE

This antipasti spread gets its name from that classic Italian sweet-and-sour combo, vinegar and honey. And I do mean classic: the combination goes back at least to the Renaissance. I prefer to use Japanese eggplant—the long, skinny purple kind—because you don't need to salt them to pull the bitter liquid out, as you do with the larger Italian variety. If your local grocer only stocks the Italian kind, make sure you salt the sliced eggplant in a colander for a half hour before you start working with it; otherwise, your sweet-and-sour combo will be sweet-and-sour-and-bitter, and nobody wants that.

I like to serve this at room temperature, with grilled bread, but it works well chilled, too—or as a hot side dish.

TIMING: Quick; less than 30 minutes

SERVES 6

INGREDIENTS

⅓ cup extra-virgin olive oil

2 Japanese eggplants, sliced on the
diagonal (each slice about ½ inch
wide), or 1 large Italian eggplant,
sliced and salted for 30 minutes

1 small red onion, cut in halves
and then sliced

2 tablespoons honey

½ cup red wine vinegar

1 cup Basic Tomato Sauce (page 285)

12 large fresh mint leaves, sliced or
snipped widthwise into narrow
ribbons

salt and pepper to taste

1 tablespoon grated Parmigiano-
Reggiano

METHOD

1. Heat half of the olive oil on medium-high heat in a wide saucepan. Add the eggplant slices to the pan and brown them evenly on both sides. If you can't fit all the eggplant in at once, don't squish 'em; do two batches instead. It's important that each slice get properly golden-brown. As the eggplant cooks, it will soak up the oil, so add the other half of the olive oil when you turn the slices. (If it seems like the oil is really disappearing, you can always add more—up to another ¼ cup.) Set aside the finished slices on a plate, but don't discard the cooking oil!

2. Add the onion to the oil in which you've just cooked the eggplant and sauté for 2 minutes. Try not to let the pieces color, but don't worry too much if they color up a little bit.

3. Add the honey to the onions and stir together so the honey bubbles and caramelizes. Deglaze with the vinegar, and let the mixture reduce by half. Add the Basic Tomato Sauce.

4. Return the eggplant to the saucepan and mix it in. Simmer on low heat for 5 minutes, so that the eggplant slices absorb the flavor of the sauce; they should soften but mostly retain their shape. Remove the pan from the heat.

5. Once the eggplant has cooled slightly, add the mint and mix together. Season with salt and pepper to taste. If you want a slightly more sour taste, add a little more vinegar. Place in a serving bowl, shake the Parmigiano-Reggiano over the top, and serve—with Grilled Country Bread (page 81) if you want.

RON'S EGGPLANT PICKLES

Ron Rosselli and I have been cooking together since back in the day. He's a great sous-chef and a serious guy. Lately, Ron's become a sort of scholar of preserved foods, reading old recipes and researching old curing techniques—the forerunners of modern cooking, he calls 'em. Plus they remind him of cooking with his mom.

This dish is a quickie preserve: you're preserving the eggplant *sott' olio*, under oil. It's an old Italian technique, and the result of Ron's scholarship here is a dish that's like the sweet-and-sour Chinese eggplant of your dreams (without the MSG): really tender eggplant and lots of well-balanced flavor, with freshness from the herbs and a tiny kick from the red pepper flakes. Most of our test batch disappeared way before the dish made it to the table.

If you can't find small Japanese eggplant, you can use 2 large Italian ones, though the dish won't be quite as good—in this case, be sure to peel and salt them before using, and cut the oil down to 1 cup.

TIMING: About 30 minutes

SERVES 10 AS ANTIPASTI

INGREDIENTS

1 cup rice wine vinegar

2 tablespoons honey

2 cups extra-virgin olive oil

7 small Japanese eggplants or
     2 Italian eggplants (about 2 pounds),
     cut into ¼-inch slices

1½ teaspoons salt

1½ teaspoons coarse-ground
     black pepper

3 cloves garlic, sliced Goodfellas thin

1 teaspoon fresh rosemary, chopped fine

1 tablespoon fresh thyme leaves

1 tablespoon fresh mint, rough-chopped

½ teaspoon red pepper flakes

METHOD

1. Combine the vinegar and honey and stir so the honey dissolves. Reserve.

2. Heat a large sauté pan over medium-high heat and add ½ cup of the olive oil. When the oil smokes, add ⅓ of the eggplant, laying the pieces flat and making sure they don't overlap. Season with ¼ teaspoon of the salt and pepper. (If the pieces start to stick anywhere in the process, add more oil.)

3. When the eggplant has turned yellow all over from the olive oil and has browned slightly in places, about 2½ to 3 minutes, flip the pieces over, season with another ¼ teaspoon of the salt and pepper, and continue cooking for another 1½ minutes. (Don't overcook the eggplant by trying to brown it completely—you want it to stay firm).

4. Pour ⅓ of the honey-vinegar mixture over the eggplant. Allow the eggplant to absorb half the liquid (about a minute), and then remove the eggplant to a bowl. Repeat with the 2 remaining batches of eggplant.

5. Put ½ cup of the olive oil and the garlic in a small pot and allow to cook for about a minute on low heat, so that it comes to a simmer and the garlic is just tender. Remove the pan from the heat and add the rosemary, thyme, mint, and red pepper flakes. Stir to combine.

6. Pour the mixture over the eggplant, and stir to make sure all the pieces are covered. Set the eggplant in the refrigerator to cool.

Serve at room temperature, as an antipasti or as a great accompaniment to lamb.

FALL INSALATA WITH GREEN APPLE, MARCONA ALMONDS, AND FENNEL

A chef I know and admire was once quoted in a national magazine as saying, "I hate salads—they're so predictable." Much as I like the man, I thought this was crazy talk. Good salads, like good pastas, are the opposite of predictable.

I love salads—and as it happens, my wife and cowriter, Gwen, is the queen of salads. Her secret is to make sure there are lots of little surprises in every bite: something crunchy, something sweet, a little bite of cheese ... so that's what's happening in this one.

I use Marcona almonds here, but if you can't find them in your neighborhood—or if they cost a small fortune—you can substitute regular roasted, salted almonds.

TIMING: Supereasy; 15 minutes plus raisin-soaking time

MAKES 4 SMALL SALADS

INGREDIENTS

¾ cup white raisins

1 bunch arugula, leaves picked
    and washed

1 bunch watercress, washed and with
    bottom stems removed

1 fennel bulb, thinly sliced lengthwise

1 green apple, quartered and sliced thin

3 celery stalks, sliced

8 basil leaves, washed

¼ cup roasted, salted almonds
    (preferably Marcona)

¼ cup extra-virgin olive oil

zest and juice of 1 to 2 lemons

salt and pepper to taste

2 tablespoons grated pecorino or
    Parmigiano-Reggiano

1 tablespoon Crumbs Yo! (page 291)
    or panko breadcrumbs

METHOD

1   Soak the raisins in warm water for 20 minutes to rehydrate them.

2   Combine all the ingredients except the oil, lemon, cheese, and bread-crumbs in a bowl.

3   Drizzle the olive oil over the salad and mix with your hands to make sure it's evenly distributed. Squeeze the juice from each lemon half over the salad and mix, tasting as you go to determine your preferred level of lemoniness; then zest the lemon over the salad with a hand grater. Season with salt and cracked pepper.

4   Divide the salad into 4 salad bowls. Top each portion with cheese and breadcrumbs and serve immediately.

MARCONA ALMONDS

Even though almonds are found all over Italian cookery, Marcona almonds are not technically Italian—they're from Spain. But who cares? They're the best eating almonds in the world. They're widely available around the country now, and even if your local grocery doesn't have them, they're worth tracking down. You can get them roasted or unroasted; I prefer the roasted ones, because they're greasy and salty and delicious. They're especially good in salads, though they're pretty great in front of the TV with a beer too—if I know I'm going to make a dish with Marconas, I make a point of buying an extra box so I've got some to snack on.

GUFFANTI AFFINATORI

I love cheese almost as much as I love dessert. I've probably tasted thousands of French cheeses and hundreds of American artisanal varieties; but I didn't know much about Italian cheeses beyond the basics (mozzarella, gorgonzola, parmigiano) until I stumbled on the Guffanti cheese warehouse in Arona, just south of Lago Maggiore. The Guffantis are *affinatori*: for three generations, they've used traditional techniques in their work as artisanal cheese ripeners. And they take their calling as seriously as any winemaker: for instance, they actually bought an old silver mine near Varese to age gorgonzola cheese in the proper conditions. You can't just walk into the cave, of course—that's the serious inner sanctum, and I've never had the chance to put on a miner's cap and descend into the cheesy depths. But I did get to float in a sea of Guffanti cheese nevertheless: I was lucky enough to have a friend who's a friend of the Guffanti family's, and so I was invited into the ripening rooms in town, in an old warehouse that's been turned into a rough-and-ready cheese palace. The place is amazing. The best, richest, most flavorful cheeses from every single region of Italy are here: Asiago d'Allevo from the Veneto, Fiore Sardo from Sardinia, the superstinky Lombardian Bagos—you name it.

The Guffanti warehouse is not a place for the gastronomically faint of heart; even the most dedicated cheese lover needs a moment or two of preparation before stepping inside. When I walked into the warehouse on my first visit, I was hit by a wave of ripening-cheese smell so strong it pretty much knocked me out the door and flat on my back—you could almost see the cheese odor traveling through the air. I got right back up and started tasting. (I've been back twice since, and I always remember to take a big gulp of air before I open that door.) Guffantis junior and senior (the elder in his midsixties back then) were so excited to see an American cook who was actually interested in Italian cheese that they sat me down right in the ripening rooms and started pulling things from the shelves. We spent the whole afternoon talking cheese, smelling cheese, eating cheese. When I left, I smelled as though I had been ripening for at least a year.

MARINATED BEETS WITH GRAPEFRUIT, PISTACHIOS, AND GOAT CHEESE

I grew up on beets—and I hated them. But at some point: taste revolution! I discovered that beets are maybe the best vegetable ever. I've done a million salads with beets over the years, a whole United Nations' worth of purple vegetables: French, Russian, Polish, American-style. So I couldn't resist trying an Italianized version of the classic beet-and-goat-cheese salad. Turns out this one's my favorite. I've used mixed beets in this version, but it's just as good with the standard red variety. You do, on the other hand, need a really good red wine vinegar. Here I use Barolo vinegar, aged and with a very deep color and flavor, but any good aged red wine vinegar will do.

TIMING: About 2 hours, but an hour of this is beet-roasting time, and you can prep everything else while the beets are marinating. If you know you're going to be rushed, roast the beets in advance; they'll keep in the fridge for up to 3 days.

SERVES 4 TO 6
INGREDIENTS

For the beets:

5 to 7 medium-sized mixed beets: red, yellow, and candy cane (Chioggia)

3 shallots, peeled and diced

3 tablespoons extra-virgin olive oil

1 tablespoon Barolo vinegar (or other good aged red wine vinegar)

¼ teaspoon salt

¼ teaspoon coarse-ground black pepper

¼ cup shelled pistachios

2 Ruby Red or other pink grapefruits

For the goat-cheese mixture:

¼ cup soft goat cheese

1 tablespoon olive oil

½ teaspoon Barolo vinegar (or other good aged red wine vinegar)

2 tablespoons whole milk

a pinch of salt

½ teaspoon coarse-ground black pepper

>>>

METHOD
TO PREPARE THE BEETS:

1. Preheat the oven to 400°, with the rack on the middle setting.

2. If the beets are wearing their greens, remove them and discard (or use them for something else); remove all of the top and bottom stems, and wash the beets thoroughly. Wrap each beet individually in foil (so they roast more evenly and don't dry out). Place the beets directly on the rack in the oven, and bake them until a fork or knife goes in easily (they should resemble a well-baked potato in texture)— about 1 hour. Remove the beets from the oven and allow them to cool on the countertop in their foil wrappers—about ½ hour.

3. Once the beets have cooled, peel off the skins and remove any hard or overly brown bits. Cut the beets into medium bite-sized pieces.

4. Place the pieces in a bowl and add the shallots, olive oil, vinegar, salt, and pepper. Let the mixture marinate for at least 1 hour in the fridge. (Beets are like sponges: they'll soak up everything, so be sure to taste them while they're marinating, and be prepared to adjust the seasonings before you serve them.)

5. While the beet mixture is marinating, reduce the oven temperature to 350° (or use a toaster oven). Roast the pistachios in a dry pan over very low heat for about 10 minutes, until they're golden brown (and delicious to the testing tongue). If the pistachios are unsalted, season them liberally with salt.

>>>

For the greens:

1 bunch arugula, stems removed
and washed

1 bunch chicory, stems removed
and washed

3 tablespoons extra-virgin olive oil

1 tablespoon red wine vinegar

a pinch each of salt and pepper

6 Meanwhile, peel the grapefruit with a sharp knife to remove all the skin and the white, and then segment them with a knife to get rid of seeds and skeleton (the membrane around the meat). Put these aside.

TO PREPARE THE GOAT-CHEESE MIXTURE:

1 In a small bowl, mix the goat cheese, olive oil, vinegar, milk, salt, and pepper until smooth.

TO PREPARE THE GREENS AND FINISH THE DISH:

1 Tear the arugula into small bits and mix it with the chicory.

2 Drizzle the 3 tablespoons of olive oil and 1 tablespoon of red wine vinegar over the arugula and chicory, and season with the salt and pepper.

3 Pile the beets on a large platter or on individual serving plates. Arrange the grapefruit segments on top of and around the pile of beets. Distribute dollops of goat cheese around the plate. Pile the greens on top of everything, and sprinkle with the pistachios. Serve immediately.

FIG SALAD WITH ARUGULA, PARMIGIANO-REGGIANO, AND PROSCIUTTO

Unless you grew up in California, Israel, Sicily, or Greece—or in certain Greek neighborhoods in Queens—you probably didn't eat a lot of figs as a kid. (We didn't exactly have a fig tree in my backyard in Ohio, either.) And if you did happen to taste one, it was probably green and unripe, with the texture and flavor of a racquetball. But it only takes one taste of a luscious, soft, deeply flavored ripe fig to turn a fig loather into a fig lover—they're totally sexy (so sexy the word *fichi* is Italian slang that will get your face slapped in a lot of places). This dish needs beautiful ripe figs, so if you can only find hard, unripe ones, leave them out for a couple of days to soften.

TIMING: Couldn't be easier; about 10 minutes, 30 if you need to make the dressing

SERVES 6

INGREDIENTS

1 pint (10 to 12) ripe figs, preferably
 Black Mission
½ cup Garlic Dressing (page 293)
1 large bunch arugula, stems removed
 and washed
4 thin prosciutto slices, cut into
 1-inch strips
salt and pepper for seasoning
¼ pound Parmigiano-Reggiano
 (you won't use all of it, but you'll
 need this much to get nice slices)

OR

**If you don't have any garlic dressing
on hand:**
½ cup olive oil
juice of 2 lemons

METHOD

1. Trim the tops and the stems off the figs and cut each fig in half. Arrange 5 or 6 halves in a circle around the outside of each plate. (You can also serve this family-style: arrange all the figs around the outside of a large plate and proceed accordingly.)

2. Drizzle the Garlic Dressing over the upturned halves with a spoon (2 to 3 tablespoons per plate). Or, if you're using the olive oil-and-lemon alternative, whisk the ingredients together in a bowl and drizzle over the figs.

3. Put the arugula and prosciutto in a bowl. Add ¼ cup of dressing, a couple of cracks of pepper, and a large pinch of salt. Toss lightly.

4. Place a generous pile of arugula in the center of the each plate so it's surrounded by figs. Using a vegetable peeler, shave the cheese on top—5 or 6 good-sized curls per portion. (You can also grate the cheese if you prefer). Serve immediately.

PASTA E FAGIOLI

Growing up, "pasta e fagioli" was a term I heard a lot—except that I heard it in dialect, so until I went to cooking school, I thought this soup was called "past fajool." The name means "pasta and beans," and that's what it is: a type of *minestra*, a hearty, stewy, wintery kind of soup-pasta hybrid, thick and hearty, usually flavored with pork, sausage, and vegetables. In my version, I substitute farro for the pasta, because this is one of those cases where tradition can definitely be improved on: farro holds its texture in the soup, while pasta turns into a mushy baby-food-like substance. I make it fancy here by blending the soup, so it gets super-super-silky, creating a contrast between the rustic flavors and the sophisticated texture. If you'd rather serve it countrified, dice the ingredients instead of cubing, chopping, or peeling them, and don't blend the soup at all. Whichever way you do it, serve this soup with some toasted bread, and drizzle a little bit of extra-virgin olive oil over the top before you serve it.

I think that *fagioli del babi* (dialect for "frog's beans") are the best-tasting Italian beans you can get in America. Mine come from the Cascina del Cornale co-op outside Alba. I found them through my good friend John Magazino, who imports them through his company, Primizie Fine Foods. But you don't have to do this with fancy imported dried beans: it's good with your basic supermarket variety, and canned beans are totally okay too, as long as you drain them well before putting them in the soup.

TIMING: If you're using large dried beans, this recipe could take about 3½ hours (not counting the 2 days' bean-soaking time), though most of this is simmering time, so you can go do something else while the soup cooks itself. If you're using canned beans, figure on about 1 hour or a bit more.

SERVES 4 TO 6
INGREDIENTS

For the soup:

¼ cup extra-virgin olive oil

¼ cup pancetta, cubed (about 3 ounces)

1 medium onion, rough-chopped

2 stalks celery, rough-chopped

2 cloves garlic, whole, peeled, and
   crushed with the side of a knife

¼ teaspoon red pepper flakes

1½ cups dried Corona or other white
   beans, soaked in 5 cups of water for
   2 days (this'll be about 4 cups after
   soaking); or 2 16-ounce cans
   cannellini or navy beans

2 cups chicken broth

2 stalks thyme

>>>

METHOD

TO PREPARE THE SOUP:

1. Heat the olive oil in a medium soup pot over medium heat. Add the pancetta and render it in the olive oil, so that some of the pork fat is released.

2. Add the onion and celery and mix to combine. Cook until the onions are slightly soft, about 2 minutes, then add the garlic. Stir until the garlic releases its aroma, then add the red pepper flakes and the beans. Add the chicken broth and 5 cups of water.

3. Tie the herbs together in a bundle with butcher string (this makes the herbs easier to remove later—if you don't have string, just be prepared to pick out lots of bits). Add them to the soup.

4. Bring the soup up to a simmer and cook, covered, until the beans pretty much fall apart when smashed by a fork—3 hours for dried beans, or 30 to 40 minutes for canned beans. Check the soup periodically; if the level of liquid falls below the beans, add more broth or water so the beans stay covered.

TO MAKE THE FARRO:

1. In a small pot over medium heat, combine the farro with ¾ cups of water, the sage, olive oil, tomatoes, salt, and pepper. Bring the mixture to a low boil. Cook for 20 minutes, uncovered, until nearly all the water has been absorbed (there will be a little bit at the bottom, but the top will look dry) and the farro is soft. Season with salt and pepper to taste. Reserve.

TO FINISH THE DISH:

1. When the soup is ready, remove the herb bundle. Remove the soup to a blender in batches and blend on high until it's smooth. (Make sure the lid is on very tight—I hold mine down with a towel, just in case—and pulse first to get everything mixed. I learned the hard way about hot-soup blender geysers.) If the mixture is too thick when you blend it (i.e., if it comes out looking like thick, smooth oatmeal, and it seems to be straining your blender), add another cup of water and blend again. Season with more salt and pepper. (If you want a very elegant and smooth soup, you can strain it through a strainer or china cap at this point, but when I make this at home I never bother.)

2. Ladle the soup into bowls and place a large spoonful of farro in the middle of each. Drizzle with olive oil and sprinkle with grated Parmigiano-Reggiano. Serve hot.

5 sprigs rosemary

2 bay leaves

For the farro:

½ cup farro

2 sage leaves

2 tablespoons extra-virgin olive oil plus some for drizzling

5 canned Italian plum tomatoes, chopped (about 1 14-ounce can)

¼ teaspoon salt

¼ teaspoon coarse-ground black pepper

2 to 3 tablespoons grated Parmigiano-Reggiano

PEPERONATA MODO MIO

I'm a sucker for antipasti: I love making a meal of small plates of food. On long, lazy Sunday afternoons, sitting around a table with friends having a beer or two, peperonata, paired with thick, crusty grilled bread, is exactly the kind of food I want to eat. I use vinegar and Peppadews—spicy-sweet little South African peppers—to give this classic laid-back dish some bite. If you can't find Peppadews, you can substitute peperoncini, the little sweet-spicy pickled green peppers you find in every antipasti platter and I-talian salad across America.

TIMING: Superquick; once the peppers are roasted, about 20 minutes. There's no need to prepare this à la minute: peperonata is one of those recipes that actually tastes better when everything marinates together in the fridge for a couple of days.

SERVES 6 TO 8

INGREDIENTS

1 medium onion, sliced (about 1 cup)

¼ cup extra-virgin olive oil

1 clove garlic, sliced Goodfellas thin

⅛ teaspoon red pepper flakes

6 roasted peppers, 3 yellow and 3 red,
    sliced into ½-inch strips,
    plus ¼ cup of their roasting juice
    (see How to Roast Peppers the
    Easy Way, page 294)

2 bay leaves

1 whole sprig rosemary

1 whole sprig thyme

¼ cup Taggiasca or Gaeta olives

½ cup Peppadew peppers, quartered,
    with their juice

2 to 3 tablespoons red wine vinegar

METHOD

1. Sweat the onion in the olive oil in a medium-sized saucepot over medium heat until it softens; then add the garlic. Cook together, stirring constantly so the garlic does not brown. As the garlic begins to open and give off its aroma, add the red pepper flakes. Add the roasted peppers and their juice. (If you don't have the roasting juice left over for some reason, just use water.) Add the bay leaves, rosemary, and thyme.

2. Bring the peppers up to a light simmering boil, then cover and reduce the heat to low. Let the peppers simmer, stirring occasionally. After 15 minutes, add the olives and the Peppadew peppers and their juice. (By this time, the stock will be darkish and the aroma of the herbs strong.)

3. Cook the mixture uncovered on low heat for 5 more minutes. Remove the saucepot from the heat and add the vinegar.

4. Cool in the fridge with the herbs—for two days if possible (the mixture will keep in the fridge for up to a week), but at least till it's completely cool. The flavors will continue to meld and strengthen as the peppers sit.

5. Remove the herbs before serving the peperonata in a large bowl, accompanied by grilled bread.

PRIMAVERA SALAD

This is my take on that great American classic, Caesar salad, but this ain't the overdressed version you get at the local diner. When you do a Caesar right, it's delicious—but you need crunch to stand up to that dressing. So that's what we've got here: lots of different vegetables, raw and cooked, drizzled with (not bathed in) Caesar dressing, and topped with cheese and breadcrumbs. You can use any or all of the vegetables I've listed below, or others that are delicious, fresh, and seasonal. Amounts are a bit arbitrary, because it really depends on which veggies you've got around.

I've given you the classic raw-egg-yolk version of the dressing, with an alternative if you're skeeved out by that idea. But there's no alternative for anchovies here: nothing else will give you that great flavor.

TIMING: About 30 minutes

SERVES 4 TO 6
INGREDIENTS

For the Caesar dressing:

1 egg yolk

1 clove garlic, peeled

10 salted anchovy fillets
   (don't be scared: it's delicious)

1 tablespoon capers

2 lemons

½ cup extra-virgin olive oil

½ cup corn oil

OR

For the alternate, egg-free Caesar dressing:

1 clove garlic, peeled

10 salted anchovy fillets

1 tablespoon capers

2 lemons

¾ cup prepared mayonnaise

For the salad:

Any or all of the following:

10 yellow wax beans, blanched

1 cup sliced English cucumber

>>>

METHOD
TO PREPARE THE DRESSING:

1. Put the egg yolk, garlic clove, anchovies, capers, and ¼ cup of water in the blender. Zest the lemons into the mixture with a microplane or the side of a cheese grater, and then squeeze in their juice. Purée the whole thing for about 15 seconds, until you have a frothy white mixture in which all the flavors are blended. Purée again, adding the olive oil and corn oil slowly through the small blender opening until the mixture is emulsified. When it's finished, the dressing should be tangy but smooth-tasting.

FOR THE ALTERNATE, EGG-FREE DRESSING:

Follow the method above, omitting the egg yolk and oils, and increase the water to ½ cup. Once the mixture is puréed, add the prepared mayonnaise and blend 10 seconds longer.

The dressing will keep for up to 24 hours in the fridge if you're using the raw egg yolk, longer if you're using the mayonnaise—but be sure to keep it cold.

TO PREPARE THE SALAD:

1. Combine all the vegetables in a bowl. Squeeze the lemon juice over the top and drizzle on the olive oil. Add salt and pepper to taste and the grated Parmigiano-Reggiano. Mix it all in well with the vegetables.

2 Arrange the vegetables on individual serving plates (I like to use long, narrow plates for this) or, if you prefer, on a serving platter. Drizzle the Caesar dressing over the top. Sprinkle the breadcrumbs on top and, if you like, add more Parmigiano. Serve immediately.

ANCHOVIES

People think they hate anchovies, but that's because they have no idea how often they're eating—and loving—something with anchovies in it. If you're going to cook great Italian food (or any Mediterranean food, for that matter), you can't do without them. For me, anchovies are as basic and as essential as salt, pepper, and water. At my place, we add anchovies to sauces and dressings all the time, not because we want them to taste like salty fish but because anchovies deepen the flavor and make everything taste like there's more there, somehow.

When you buy anchovies at the store, look for the fillets in oil; they come in cans and in glass. Whatever you do, don't make the mistake of buying the salted whole variety. Nothing's worse than getting your anchovies home to discover that they're whole, packed in salt, and still wearing their bones and their heads. And don't be afraid of anchovy haters—after all, you don't have to tell anybody about your secret ingredient.

1 fennel bulb, sliced

12 cherry tomatoes, halved

1 head baby romaine lettuce, cleaned and torn

8 radishes, quartered

1 red pepper, sliced thin

1 yellow pepper, sliced thin

2 stalks celery, sliced thin

2 baby zucchinis, sliced thin

8 asparagus stalks, blanched and cut in half widthwise

any other fresh, delicious vegetables you have on hand

Make sure you don't overcook the asparagus (or any other vegetables you may be blanching): no matter what you're including, there should be some significant crunch so that the veggies stand up to the dressing.

To top off the salad:

juice of 1 lemon

2 tablespoons extra-virgin olive oil

salt and pepper to taste

1 tablespoon grated Parmigiano-Reggiano

1 tablespoon Crumbs Yo! (page 291) or panko breadcrumbs

ROCK SHRIMP WITH CANNELLINI BEANS

Scampi, scampi, scampi! That's what we're talking here. Outside the world of Red Lobster, scampi is just a sautéed sweet shrimp dish. This one is very fresh and citrusy, with the room-temperature bean salad offsetting the richness of the shrimp. It's ridiculously easy too. If you want to get all complicated, you can buy dried cannellini beans and soak them overnight, but the canned ones work perfectly well.

TIMING: Super-super-quick; 15 minutes at most

SERVES 6

INGREDIENTS

For the bean salad:

1 15-ounce can cannellini beans

¼ cup red onion, minced

¼ cup extra-virgin olive oil

juice of 1 lemon

10 drops Tabasco sauce

¼ cup parsley, rough-chopped

¼ teaspoon coarse-ground black pepper

¼ teaspoon salt

Optional:

2 tablespoons Pesto (page 288)

For the shrimp:

1 pound rock shrimp (or tiger shrimp, peeled, deveined, and split in half, head to tail)

4 tablespoons olive oil

1 garlic clove, chopped

½ teaspoon red pepper flakes

1 tablespoon fresh thyme leaves

1 tablespoon fresh rosemary, chopped

juice of 1 lemon

2 tablespoons parsley, rough-chopped

¼ teaspoon salt

¼ teaspoon coarse-ground black pepper

METHOD

TO MAKE THE BEANS:

1. Drain and rinse the beans in cold water.

2. Combine the beans, onion, olive oil, lemon juice, Tabasco, and parsley in a bowl. Season with salt and pepper. If you have some Pesto around, add that too; it will give the dish a nice herby flavor. Allow the mixture to marinate on the countertop while you prepare the shrimp.

TO MAKE THE SHRIMP AND FINISH THE DISH:

1. Rinse the shrimp and blot dry on a paper towel.

2. In a nonstick skillet, heat 2 tablespoons of the olive oil over medium-low heat. Add the shrimp, turn the heat to low, and cook until the shrimp begin to turn white—about 1 minute.

3. Add the garlic and the red pepper flakes. Continue cooking for 1 minute, until the fragrance of the garlic is released. Turn off the heat and add the remaining 2 tablespoons of olive oil and the thyme, rosemary, lemon juice, parsley, salt, and pepper.

4. Arrange the beans on a serving plate and pile the shrimp mixture over the top. Serve hot or cold.

GRILLED COUNTRY BREAD

The key to a great antipasti course is simple: great grilled bread, the perfect vehicle for all kinds of little tastes. And if you do it right, this grilled country bread is addictive all on its own. The crunchy, blackened bread rocks with whatever you dip it in, but it's especially irresistible as an edible scoop for Sheep's Milk Ricotta (page 83) or Peperonata Modo Mio (page 76). Grill it up right before you need it, so it comes to the table warm, luscious, and crunchy.

This recipe is easy, but hygiene is important here: make sure your grill is clean. You don't want this bread to taste like last July's steak, that salmon your buddy brought back from his fishing trip last October, etcetera. (I can't tell you how many times I've gone over to someone's house for a summer meal, and they say, "Hey, AC, can you grill up these steaks?" and I say, "No problem!" And then I get over to the grill, and it hasn't been cleaned in four summers, and the thing looks like Pompeii.) If you're in an apartment without a grill (or if firing the monster up just for bread seems crazy), you can use the oven broiler, but it won't be the same.

TIMING: Superquick; 20 minutes, from preheating the grill to serving

SERVES 6

INGREDIENTS

1 loaf Italian bread (ciabatta or
    semolina)
about 1 tablespoon of olive oil per slice
    of bread, with extra for bigger loaves
salt and pepper for sprinkling
2 garlic cloves, crushed

METHOD

1 Preheat your grill to the highest setting, or put your oven on broil and set the rack on the highest level.

2 Cut the bread into inch-thick slices. Drizzle both sides of each slice with olive oil and season with salt and pepper.

3 Grill the bread (on the grill or under the broiler) until it's charcoal-colored on the edges. Turn it and do the same on the other side.

4 Pull the bread off the grill and rub it on both sides with a fresh garlic clove. Serve warm.

SHEEP'S MILK RICOTTA

Ricotta cheese is one of those Italian specialties you can find everywhere, in one form or another. It's usually made from cow's milk, which gives it the mild, rich, creamy flavor it's known for. Some of the best cow's milk ricotta in the U.S. is made fresh every day at DiPaolo's Dairy, an ancient, crowded, old-country-style Italian cheese shop on Grand Street in Little Italy. But the ricotta I like to serve up is a little bit different. It's sheep's milk ricotta, from Sardinia, the rocky, sheep-ridden island off the coast of Tuscany. This stuff is more expensive than the cow's milk variety, but its rich tanginess makes it worth the price. It's the primary ingredient in one of our most requested "signature" dishes— probably one of the simplest things I've ever made.

I get my ricotta from the Pinna brothers, amazing artisanal cheesemakers in Sardinia. We buy every ounce of ricotta they export to America. In fact, we buy so much of it that one day, one of the brothers walked into the restaurant, announcing that he had come all the way to New York just to check out who was buying all his cheese. When he sat down to dinner, we sent him the ricotta— on the house, of course.

SHEEP'S MILK RICOTTA

Every chef loves playing with complex flavors and textures, but this dish is a great reminder that straightforward, delicious food, made with the best ingredients, always makes people happy. This simple dish is possibly my most popular antipasto ever. Texture is key here: I whip the ricotta with a splash of milk to make it airy and fluffy—a great contrast with the depth and weight of the flavor. I like to add a fair bit of olive oil, so that the rich cheese emerges from the nutty oil like an island in a sea. I like to pair the ricotta with grilled chunky bread rubbed with garlic and send this out as a "first taste," but I always have a hard time getting it off the table; people keep eating it all the way through dinner.

TIMING: Superfast and supereasy; about 10 minutes to put the cheese together, plus bread-grilling time if you're serving this up with Grilled Country Bread

SERVES 6

INGREDIENTS

2 cups Sardinian sheep's milk ricotta
    (if you can't find this, use the regular
    cow's milk ricotta)
1 cup whole milk
1 teaspoon table salt
1 teaspoon fleur de sel or coarse sea salt
1 teaspoon coarse-ground black pepper
1 teaspoon fresh thyme leaves
1 tablespoon dried oregano, on the
    branch if possible (I use Calabrian
    or Sicilian)
2 to 3 tablespoons extra-virgin olive oil

Optional:
Grilled Country Bread (page 81)

METHOD

1   Beat the ricotta and the milk together until the mixture is light and fluffy, using a KitchenAid with the paddle attachment if you've got one, or a whisk and a medium-sized bowl if you don't. Add the table salt and mix well.

2   Place the mixture in a serving bowl. Sprinkle the fleur de sel, pepper, thyme, and oregano generously across the top.

3   Top with the olive oil, which will settle on and around the cheese. Serve this with a board full of Grilled Country Bread. I guarantee you won't be able to stop eating it.

SUMMER MELON WITH FETA, BASIL, AND CUCUMBER

I love summer melons. When they appear at the Greenmarket around the end of July, I have a bad habit of buying an armful—and then getting home and realizing I can't fit them all in the fridge. So I came up with a quick and easy salad. It's delicious—and it takes up much less space.

I use Bulgarian feta cheese to give the dish a sharp Mediterranean feel, but if you can't find the good stuff, you can also use ricotta salata or a sharp soft goat cheese.

TIMING: Super-super-fast; 20 minutes including refrigeration time

SERVES 6 TO 8

INGREDIENTS

Melons vary wildly in size, so adjust the ingredients up or down, depending on what you've got: the ratio is 1 pound of melon to ½ of an English cucumber.

1 1-pound melon, cut in chunks ½ inch
    by 2 to 3 inches
8 basil leaves, cut into strips
½ English cucumber, halved lengthwise
    and sliced into ½-inch pieces
¼ teaspoon salt
¾ cup Bulgarian feta cheese
2 tablespoons extra-virgin olive oil
¼ teaspoon coarse-ground black pepper

Optional:
½ teaspoon crushed red pepper flakes
    or harissa

METHOD

1. Combine the melon and basil in a bowl and refrigerate for at least 10 minutes.

2. Combine the cucumber slices and salt and refrigerate until they are very cold.

3. Arrange the melon on a platter, and lay the cucumber over the top. Sprinkle on the feta cheese, pour on the olive oil, and crack the black pepper on top. Serve immediately.

Alternative: You can also give this recipe a bit of heat and spice—great in the heat of summer, when, as the Italians say, hot things on a hot day cool you down—by whisking crushed red pepper flakes or harissa with the olive oil before drizzling it.

TUNA-STUFFED PEPPERS

These little antipasti definitely have that kitschy, 1950s Entertaining-at-Home look going—but there's nothing kitschy about the taste. These are Peppadew peppers: tiny, round South African products, crunchy and spicy and sweet, sold packed in their pickling liquid. (You can get these all over the country now: when I make this dish at home, I get mine at Whole Foods, where they're stocked next to the olives.) Combined with the tuna, they're totally addictive: once you start eating 'em, you can't stop. The mayonnaise in this recipe may seem like a big Americanization, but it's actually totally authentic Italian: in *vitello tonnato*, for instance, the famous sauce is basically tuna and mayo.

I can't overemphasize how easy this dish is; you don't even need to turn on the stove. If you're short on time and you've got people to impress, this is the antipasti for you. Serve it with prosecco or champagne—and maybe put some Sinatra on the hi-fi.

TIMING: Super-super-fast; about 10 minutes

MAKES 30 STUFFED PEPPADEWS; SERVES 5 TO 7

INGREDIENTS

1 6-ounce can tuna in oil (preferably Italian; definitely good tuna)

2 scallions, white part, minced

2 tablespoons mayonnaise

1 tablespoon extra-virgin olive oil

salt and pepper to taste

1 tablespoon juice from the Peppadew peppers

juice of 1 lemon

6 basil leaves, chopped (about 2 tablespoons)

30 Peppadew peppers

Optional:

½ bunch chives, chopped (about 2 tablespoons)

METHOD

1. Drain the oil from the tuna. Combine the tuna and scallions in a bowl.

2. Add the mayonnaise and olive oil to the tuna and mix well (exactly as if you were making tuna salad). Season with the salt and pepper, adjusting the flavor to your taste. Add the juice from the Peppadew peppers, lemon juice, and basil. Mix well.

3. Using your fingers, stuff each Peppadew pepper with the tuna mixture, letting some of it burst over the top. If you're really feeling fancy (1950s-style), you can dust the tops with chopped chives.

WINTER INSALATA OF RADICCHIO, PEARS, AND HAZELNUTS

Italians love bitter: think broccoli rabe, or espresso. Or vermouth, that all-important martini ingredient. When I was in Italy, I learned to drink the stuff on its own, on the rocks—no gin or vodka to get in the way of all that bittersweet flavor.

This dish is more like a martini than a glassful of vermouth: the fresh sweetness of the pears and the meatiness of the hazelnuts are a great contrast to the bitter depth of the winter greens, and the Parmigiano-Reggiano brings the whole thing together. The trick is to mix the grated cheese *into* the salad instead of sprinkling it on top, so you get that great savory cheesiness right in there with the pears and hazelnuts.

TIMING: Superquick; 20 minutes, plus a few to prep the lettuces and the pears. This is an easy dish to throw together.

SERVES 4 TO 6

INGREDIENTS

¾ cup hazelnuts, roughly chopped

1 cup chicken stock

3 tablespoons red wine vinegar or
    walnut vinegar

¼ cup extra-virgin olive oil

2 tablespoons hazelnut oil or
    other nut oil

a pinch each of salt and pepper,
    plus another pinch of each for
    seasoning

1 tablespoon fresh thyme leaves

4 big handfuls mixed winter lettuces
    (radicchio, castelfranco, hearts of
    escarole), washed and roughly torn

2 ripe, beautiful, sexy pears
    (preferably red ones, if you can find
    them; I like to use Red Crimsons),
    thinly sliced

2 tablespoons grated Parmigiano-
    Reggiano

¼ cup Crumbs Yo! (page 291) or
    panko breadcrumbs

METHOD

1. Roast the hazelnuts over very low heat in a dry pan on the stove until golden brown: this'll take about 5 minutes, longer on an electric stove. Be sure to shake the pan regularly to avoid burning the nuts.

2. Meanwhile, reduce the chicken stock in a small pot until you have approximately 3 tablespoons—about 3 to 5 minutes.

3. Combine the chicken stock, ½ cup of the hazelnuts, the vinegar, and 2 tablespoons of water in a blender. Cover and blend on medium until the mixture becomes chunky, about 15 seconds. Add both oils and a pinch each of salt and pepper, and blend until everything is combined and the mixture is relatively smooth, about 30 seconds. Add the thyme and mix briefly to combine.

4. Put the lettuces, the remaining toasted hazelnuts, and the sliced pears in a large bowl. Add about half the dressing and the Parmigiano-Reggiano and toss the salad, mixing with your hands to be sure that all the ingredients are coated but not soggy. Taste and add more dressing as necessary. I've given you a generous measure for the dressing here, because the amount of greens will vary; be sure not to just dump all the dressing over the salad. You don't want to end up with a soggy mess. Season to taste with more salt and pepper. Serve topped with the breadcrumbs.

{ PRIMI }

FETTUCCINI WITH SUMMER CORN, BACON, AND SHIITAKE MUSHROOMS

I may have Italian roots, but I'm a midwestern boy at heart, and I love my corn. So I do a bunch of different corn pastas at the restaurant (and a lot of dishes using corn in unexpected ways: gelati, custards, fillings, sauces ...). But this dish, featuring bacon, cream, and corn, is really a little piece of the heartland, Italian-style. The bacon gives the dish a smoky, substantial flavor; the mushrooms bring earthiness, contrasted with the crunch from the corn. I don't know what the Italians would think about it, but in America, we call that good eating.

TIMING: Superquick; about 20 minutes

SERVES 4 TO 6

INGREDIENTS

1½ cups diced bacon

6 cups fresh summer corn kernels
(about 8 ears' worth)

2 pounds shiitake (or oyster or wild)
mushrooms, each one cut in half

½ cup whole milk

½ cup heavy cream

¼ teaspoon coarse-ground black pepper,
plus more to taste

a pinch of cayenne pepper

1 pound fresh fettuccini (see Pasta
Dough for Long Pasta, page 295)

½ cup grated Parmigiano-Reggiano

½ cup chopped fresh parsley

a pinch of salt

METHOD

ORDER OF OPERATIONS: Your aim here is to get the pasta and the sauce finished at the same time—but if something has to sit around, make it the sauce.

1. Put a large pot of salted water on to boil.

2. Sweat the bacon in a medium pot at medium-high heat, without any oil, until the fat is rendered and the bacon begins to crisp, about 3 minutes.

3. Add 3 cups of corn and the mushrooms to the bacon pot and cook together until the flavors blend and the mushrooms caramelize slightly, about 2 minutes.

4. In a blender, blend the remaining 3 cups of corn, the milk, and the cream together on high speed until the mixture is all liquid, about 1 minute.

5. Strain the corn-cream mixture through a chinois or a fine strainer into the bacon-mushroom pot, pushing the mixture down with a heavy spoon so all the liquid ends up in the pot. Simmer all the ingredients together until the corn mixture heats through and starts to thicken, about 2 minutes.

6. Add the black pepper and cayenne pepper. If the pasta isn't finished yet, remove the sauce from the heat and reserve.

7. Meanwhile, when the water comes to a rolling boil, add the fresh fettuccini and cook until it is just al dente, 1½ to 2 minutes.

8. Remove the pasta with a pair of tongs and add it to the bacon-mushroom-corn mixture in the pot. (Do not rinse the pasta—you want all that

>>>

stickiness so the sauce will adhere.) Mix well to thoroughly coat the pasta.

9. Turn off the heat and mix in the parsley and Parmigiano-Reggiano. Season with salt and more pepper.

10. Plate the pasta, covering each serving with the sauce that remains in the pot. Make sure that you get all the good bits of bacon, corn, and mushrooms at the bottom.

FARFALLE WITH SHRIMP, ZUCCHINI, AND LEMON

Rock shrimp are a chef's secret weapon. You can get them year-round; they're from Florida, so you can always find 'em; and they're impossible to overcook, so you never end up with rubbery little nuggets. They are, in other words, the easiest seafood ever.

This one-pot dish is also pretty much the easiest ever. I've put it on lots of restaurant menus: people love it, especially at lunch, because it's so light and sharp and fresh-tasting and has such a great mouth-feel.

If you're putting this together at the last minute and don't have any Basic Tomato Sauce on hand, use the jarred stuff if you must, but get the most basic tomato-and-basil sauce you can find. No Ragu or Your Mama's Sauce—none of that. That junk is full of sugar, second-rate spices, and crappy tomatoes. And no matter what, make sure you use fresh herbs, otherwise you won't get the fresh taste that's key for this recipe.

TIMING: Supereasy; about 30 minutes

SERVES 4 TO 6

INGREDIENTS

1½ pounds rock shrimp (or peeled and deveined tiger shrimp, split in half from head to tail)

3 tablespoons extra-virgin olive oil

a pinch of salt and coarse-ground pepper

¼ teaspoon red pepper flakes

2 tablespoons fresh thyme leaves

2 tablespoons chopped fresh rosemary

2 medium zucchini, halved and thinly sliced (about 3 cups)

1 clove garlic, minced

2 cups Basic Tomato Sauce (page 285)

1 pound dried farfalle pasta

juice of 1 lemon

2 tablespoons butter

2 tablespoons roughly chopped fresh parsley

2 tablespoons Crumbs Yo! (page 291) or panko breadcrumbs

METHOD

1   Put a large pot of salted water on to boil for the pasta.

2   Pat the shrimp with a paper towel to remove excess liquid.

3   Heat the olive oil in a saucepan over high heat. Throw in the shrimp and cook for 1 minute, flipping the shrimp in the pan or stirring occasionally to keep them from sticking. Season with the salt and pepper.

4   Add the red pepper flakes, thyme, rosemary, zucchini, and garlic. Sauté everything together for about 1 minute, until the zucchini has just started to cook.

5   Add the Basic Tomato Sauce and cook together another 3 minutes or so. At this point, the flavors should be combined, the zucchini should be a bit translucent but still have some crunch to it, and the shrimp should be opaque and should pop between your teeth. Remove the saucepan from the heat.

6   Meanwhile, cook the pasta until al dente. (Follow the directions on the box, subtracting 1 minute from the cooking time; be sure to test a couple of pieces in the last 2 minutes of cooking to avoid mushiness.)

7   Drain the pasta well and return it to the pot, with the heat off. Add the shrimp and sauce, straight from the saucepan, and combine well.

8   Squeeze the lemon juice over the pasta, and add the butter and the parsley.

9   Sprinkle the Crumbs Yo! or panko breadcrumbs over the top. Serve immediately.

THE BEST GNOCCHI

Gnocchi is the reason I went to Italy; gnocchi is the reason I became a chef; gnocchi is the reason I'm writing this book. I love gnocchi! Gnocchi would be my last meal if I got to pick; it's the food I'd want to have if I could only have one.

I've spent a lifetime searching for the perfect gnocchi technique, the one that makes the lightest, fluffiest gnocchi. I've been working on it ever since I first made gnocchi with my aunt, when I was twelve. In the local Italian restaurant I worked in as a teenager, they were flavorless lead sinkers, and that's how I thought they were supposed to be. I was pretty sure my aunt's version was just some weirdly delicious home-cooking thing she'd come up with herself. When I went to Italy and had them at the source for the first time, I realized that my aunt had just been cooking Italian-style: gnocchi, done correctly, are actually sublime, melt-in-your-mouth morsels. Unless they're made of semolina, gnocchi should be light, airy, smooth, and luxurious.

Not that everybody agrees with me. Not long ago, a cook who had worked with me took a chef's job in his hometown. He put my gnocchi recipe on the menu—and the owner complained that they were "bad" and "inauthentic" because they weren't dense and heavy enough. He wouldn't like this version much, either.

The sauce I'm using here is my version of *pom d'oro*, which means, in some dialects, "tomato of gold" (a play on the Italian *pomodoro*, tomato). It's just my Basic Tomato Sauce with a generous extra dose of olive oil, parmesan cheese, butter, and basil.

TIMING: The potatoes take 1 hour or so, but once that's done, it's pretty quick—about ½ hour

SERVES 4
INGREDIENTS

For the gnocchi:

4 large Idaho potatoes
    (about 2 pounds), scrubbed

1 egg, beaten

2 tablespoons grated Parmigiano-
    Reggiano

1 tablespoon extra-virgin olive oil

1 tablespoon unsalted butter, melted

1 teaspoon salt

¼ teaspoon coarse-ground black pepper

1½ cups all-purpose flour

For the sauce:

3 cups Basic Tomato Sauce (page 285)

½ cup fresh basil leaves

2 tablespoons extra-virgin olive oil

2 tablespoons butter

½ cup grated Parmigiano-Reggiano

METHOD
TO PREPARE THE GNOCCHI:

1. Center a rack in the oven and preheat it to 425°.

2. Prick each potato several times with a fork; place them on a baking sheet or in a roasting pan large enough to hold them all in a single layer. Bake in the oven until the potatoes are tender enough to be easily pierced with a small knife, about 1 hour.

3. Remove the potatoes from the oven and let them cool just enough so that you can handle them, about 6 to 10 minutes. They should still be steaming when you cut them open. (If you let the potatoes get too cool, the proteins in the egg won't bind with them, and your gnocchi will fall apart, or you'll have to add too much flour and you'll end up with chewy potato bullets.)

4. Cut each potato in half lengthwise and scoop out the flesh with a spoon. Discard the skins. Pass the potato flesh through a food mill or press through a ricer set over a medium bowl.

5. Using your hands, gently stir the beaten egg, Parmigiano-Reggiano, olive oil, melted butter, salt, pepper, and 1 cup of the flour in with the

>>>

potato. Stir only enough to combine: anything more will overwork the dough, and your gnocchi will come out tough (like the frozen-in-a-bag variety). Work the mixture into a smooth ball; if the dough seems a little too moist for this, add a touch of flour (the moisture level in every potato is different, so every batch of gnocchi will be a bit different too). The dough should feel soft and slightly tacky but not sticky—sort of warm and sexy.

6. Turn the dough out onto a lightly floured work surface. Working quickly, cut the ball of dough into inch-thick slices, using a dough cutter if you've got one, or a regular butter knife if you don't.

7. Roll each slice between your hands to form a ball.

8 Using the palms of your hands, roll each ball back and forth on your work surface until it extends into a long "snake," 14 to 16 inches long and about ¾ inch thick. (This isn't a precise measurement. You can make your gnocchi whatever size you want—this is just how I like 'em.) Keep adding more flour to the work surface as you go to help as you roll the dough.

9 Cut each snake in half and roll it out again, thinner, to the same length. Sprinkle the rolled-out snakes with flour to keep them from sticking.

10 Cut each snake into gnocchi-sized pieces (I like mine to be about 1 inch long), and place the pieces on a lightly floured baking sheet. Cover this with a cloth or plastic wrap until you're ready to cook the gnocchi, so they don't dry out.

>>>

Gnocchi are delicate little things; fresh ones should be cooked the day they are made, or at the very latest, the next day. Frozen and stored in an airtight container, they'll keep for up to a month.

TO COOK THE GNOCCHI:

This step is just as important as the preparation: tender gnocchi require careful attention.

1. Bring a large pot of salted water to a rolling boil.

2. Add the gnocchi all at once. Stir around once gently, so that the water is aerated and the dough doesn't become glued together like one big gnoccho.

3 Let the gnocchi cook until they bob to the surface (about 1 to 2 minutes); wait 1 more minute and then, using a slotted spoon or spider, remove the gnocchi. (Don't dump the gnocchi out into a colander the way you would spaghetti. All the gnocchi will crash onto each other and break.)

TO PREPARE THE SAUCE AND FINISH THE DISH:

1 While the water is boiling for the gnocchi, heat the Basic Tomato Sauce in a pan over medium heat and roughly chop the basil.

2 Remove the tomato sauce from the heat. Put the gnocchi right into the sauce when you remove them from the boiling water.

3 Toss the gnocchi in the sauce so every piece is thoroughly coated. Add the olive oil, butter, Parmigiano-Reggiano, and basil and mix well. Serve as quickly as possible.

SALT

The Italians have a saying: "The pasta water's salted enough when it tastes like the sea." I know some people—including members of my family, who will remain nameless here—don't want to salt their pasta water because they're worried about the sodium. Now, I've heard all kinds of arguments, pro and con, about the medical implications of salt. I'm no doctor, but I am a specialist in flavor, and I can tell you for sure that if you don't salt your water, your pasta will taste like plain wet cardboard. Salt is what gives food that elusive quality known as "taste": it brings out the sweetness in carrots and the acidity in tomatoes. Me, I'd rather skip that bag of chips or those movie-theater nachos and salt my pasta water instead.

Salt's water-drawing abilities make it useful for a lot of bonus culinary tricks. In the Basic Tomato Sauce recipe (page 285), for instance, I put the salt in right at the beginning of the cooking process, so that the water comes out of the fruit and the sauce begins to thicken and cook right away—preserving that crucial fresh-tomato taste. On the other hand, when I roast vegetables, I want strong flavor, but I also want good caramelization, so I add the salt later; otherwise, the salt will pull the liquid out of the vegetables so they steam instead of caramelizing.

LAMB RAGU

Traditional ragu is made with beef, veal, pork, or a combination of the three, but you know I'm not afraid to mess with tradition in the interest of great food. Lamb is just more flavorful in this kind of dish. And the Italians love their lamb; they just haven't put it together with pasta very often, an oversight I thought I'd correct for them. I add a little cumin here too—think Bologna by way of the Sicilian beaches, just about a rock's skip from North Africa—but only enough to enhance the meat, not enough to really taste.

I like to use canned cherry tomatoes in this recipe because they're packed full of sweetness. If your grocery has these, grab 'em, but if not, good Italian canned whole tomatoes will do. If you're having the butcher grind the lamb for you, ask for the shoulder: it's got the best meat-to-fat ratio for tender meat. In any case, you want 25 to 30 percent fat. If the meat is too lean, it won't be tender no matter how long you cook it.

I like to put this ragu together with gnocchi, rigatoni, or papardelle, and top it with sheep's milk ricotta (the same stuff I use in the antipasti; page 83). I haven't included a pasta choice here: that's up to you.

TIMING: About 15 minutes of prep time and another 2 hours to cook. This sauce will hold in the fridge for up to 2 days, or you can stick it in the freezer for up to 1 month.

SERVES 6

INGREDIENTS

For the ragu:

¼ cup olive oil

1½ pounds ground lamb (shoulder if possible)

½ cup finely diced carrot

½ cup finely diced onion

½ cup finely diced celery

1 tablespoon tomato paste

1½ cups dry red wine

1 cup canned cherry tomatoes or good quality Italian canned whole tomatoes

3 cups low-sodium chicken broth (or water)

2 bay leaves

½ teaspoon ground cumin

½ teaspoon ground coriander

½ teaspoon ground fennel

¼ teaspoon red pepper flakes

>>>

METHOD

TO PREPARE THE RAGU:

1. Heat the olive oil in a large stewpot over medium-high heat. (You need a pot with a very large bottom in order to brown the meat all at once. If you haven't got one, brown the meat in a large saucepan first and then add it to the stewpot.)

2. Add the ground lamb, breaking it apart into small bits as you drop it into the oil, and brown it over high heat, about 5 minutes. If the lamb releases a lot of liquid, so that the meat begins to steam instead of browning, just drain off the juice and put the pot back on the heat to start the browning process again.

3. Add the carrots, onion, and celery and mix well. Cook together over high heat until the vegetables start to soften, about 2 minutes.

4. Add the tomato paste and stir to incorporate. Cook together until the mixture becomes a thick reddish mix, about 1 minute.

5. Add the red wine and stir to incorporate, making sure that no bits of meat or vegetable are sticking to the bottom. Use a wooden spoon or rubber spatula to scrape down the sides; you don't want bits of sauce to burn and flavor the whole ragu. Cook until the wine evaporates completely: about 2 minutes.

>>>

1 tablespoon fresh thyme leaves

1 tablespoon fresh rosemary leaves

½ teaspoon salt

¼ teaspoon coarse-ground black
pepper

To finish the dish:

1 pound The Best Gnocchi (page 95) or
pasta of your choice

2 tablespoons extra-virgin olive oil

2 tablespoons butter

¼ cup grated pecorino cheese

¼ cup chopped fresh mint

6 Add the canned tomatoes and the broth (or water). Then add the bay leaves, cumin, coriander, fennel, red pepper flakes, thyme, rosemary, salt, and pepper. Scrape down the sides of the pot again.

7 Bring the mixture to a low boil, and then reduce the heat to medium-low to keep the ragu cooking at a simmer. Cook the lamb, uncovered, until the liquid evaporates and the flavors meld, about 1½ hours. Continue scraping the sides of the pot at regular intervals to avoid burnt bits. The meat will turn dark brown and the liquid will turn a dark orange color as it cooks. When it's done, all the flavors will be melded, and the sauce (if you've broken the meat up enough) will look like a sauce: dark brown, rich, thick, and textured.

TO FINISH THE DISH:

1 Cook the gnocchi (page 95) or the pasta of your choice.

2 Drain the pasta, add it to the sauce, and stir together over the heat, adding the olive oil, butter, and mint to make it smooth and rich-tasting on the tongue.

3 Remove the pot from the heat, ladle the pasta and sauce into individual bowls, and top with the pecorino.

LINGUINI WITH BROCCOLI RABE PESTO, OREGANO, AND PEPPERS

Like most chefs, I don't have any dietary restrictions whatsoever: if it tastes good, I eat it. But when I met my wife, she was a vegetarian, and she stayed that way for the first six years we were together. So I learned a whole lot about cooking vegetarian food. The real challenge is hitting a balance so the flavors and textures pop but also have some depth, dimension, and—that elusive thing in vegetarian cooking—mouth-feel. This pasta is one meaty meat-free dish.

Though they're added last, the roasted peppers are key here: their sweetness and texture contrast really well with the sharpness of the broccoli rabe and the toastiness of the browned garlic. The peppers are pretty quick to do (see How to Roast Peppers the Easy Way, page 294), but if you have time to make it, Peperonata Modo Mio (page 76) is great with this dish.

TIMING: Superfast; about ½ hour. You can make the pesto ahead of time; it will hold in the fridge for 1 or 2 days, or in the freezer for 2 weeks.

SERVES 4 TO 6
INGREDIENTS

For the pasta:

1 pound dried linguini

For the pesto:

1 bunch broccoli rabe

½ cup extra-virgin olive oil

¼ cup pine nuts

½ teaspoon salt

2 tablespoons grated Parmigiano-Reggiano or pecorino

To finish the dish:

2 tablespoons extra-virgin olive oil

2 cloves garlic, sliced Goodfellas thin

¼ teaspoon red pepper flakes

½ cup grated Parmigiano-Reggiano or pecorino, plus extra for sprinkling

1 tablespoon fresh oregano leaves

3 roasted peppers, julienned (see How to Roast Peppers the Easy Way, page 294); or 1 cup Peperonata Modo Mio (page 76)

2 tablespoons Crumbs Yo! (page 291) or panko breadcrumbs

METHOD

ORDER OF OPERATIONS: Your aim here is to finish everything at once; I've given you pasta directions not because I think you don't know how to boil pasta, but to help you out with timing. If something has to get finished first, make it the sauce: you don't want the pasta getting clumpy and cold, because it won't combine well with the sauce.

TO MAKE THE PASTA:

1 Put a large pot of salted water on to boil.

2 When the water comes to a boil, add the linguini and cook until it is just al dente. (Follow the timing on the box, subtracting 1 minute from the cooking time. Be sure to test a couple of pieces in the last 2 minutes of cooking to avoid mushiness.)

TO MAKE THE PESTO:

1 Put a medium-sized pot of salted water on to boil to blanch the broccoli rabe.

2 Remove the leaves from the broccoli rabe, cutting them off right at the stem. Reserve the leaves. Trim the broccoli rabe stems so that 2 to 3 inches of stem remain below each floret. Cut these into thirds.

>>>

3 Blanch the stems and florets in the boiling water for 30 seconds, until the color has intensified. Remove with a slotted spoon to a bowl of ice water to stop the cooking process. Set aside.

4 Blanch the broccoli rabe leaves in the boiling water until they're tender, 60 to 90 seconds. Remove with a slotted spoon to a separate bowl of ice water to stop the cooking process.

5 When the leaves are cold, remove them from the water and squeeze out the excess water with your hands.

6 Combine the olive oil and the broccoli rabe leaves in a blender and blend on medium until a smooth paste forms, about 30 seconds. Add ½ cup water and blend until the leaves are completely puréed, about 30 seconds. Add the pine nuts and blend on medium-low until smooth, about 15 seconds. Add the salt and the cheese and blend very briefly, about 5 seconds, to bring everything together.

TO FINISH THE DISH:

1 Heat the 2 tablespoons of olive oil in a large pot over medium-high heat; then add the garlic and brown slightly for a minute.

2 Add the broccoli stems and florets and the red pepper flakes and mix to combine.

3 Remove the pot from the heat and add the linguini and pesto. Blend well.

4 Add the grated cheese and fresh oregano, and mix well to blend everything to a rich smoothness.

5 Distribute the pasta into individual low bowls or onto medium-sized plates, and top each serving with an equal measure of the julienned roasted peppers or peperonata. Sprinkle more cheese to taste and the Crumbs Yo! or panko breadcrumbs over the pasta. Serve immediately.

LINGUINI WITH CLAMS CASINO

One family vacation when I was a kid, we were driving around Italy in a big old van, and, as usual, we were lost. My uncle, who believed not in maps and road signs but in solar navigation ("Follow the sun, dammit!" he yelled regularly), finally bellowed, "Where the hell are we?"

My cousin Ray yelled right back, "We're at the corner of linguini and clam sauce!"

This was true, but not very helpful. Every inch of Italy within a hundred miles of the sea, pretty much, is the corner of linguini and clam sauce, and every town has its own proprietary recipe for the stuff. America has its own version: that Continental classic, Clams Casino. This recipe makes things interesting by combining the two. Very cross-cultural, huh?

At first, I bowed to both traditions and made this dish with spaghetti. But Rich Torrisi, one of my sous-chefs (see Rich's Spicy Linguini and Crab, page 109), insisted that linguini was definitely the superior clam-sauce pasta. He was right. Linguini tastes better and gives superior mouth-feel. We have no scientific or culinary reason for this. It just is. Trust me.

It's nice to use yellow, red, and green bell peppers to give the dish some visual pop, but if you don't have all three, you can just use one or two colors. I serve this with the clam shells in the pasta (it's prettier that way), but if you don't want to deal with shell removal at the table, you can shell the clams after cooking and put the meat into the sauce before you mix in the pasta.

There's no added salt in this recipe. Between the bacon, the clam juice, and the clams, you're covered in the salt department.

TIMING: Superquick; about ½ hour, depending on your knife speed with the peppers

SERVES 4 TO 6
INGREDIENTS

1 pound dried linguini

1 tablespoon extra-virgin olive oil

⅓ cup finely chopped bacon

2 cloves garlic, sliced Goodfellas thin

1 medium onion, finely chopped (about 1 cup)

1½ cups diced bell pepper—use equal parts red, yellow, and green peppers, or any combination thereof

⅛ teaspoon red pepper flakes

1 tablespoon all-purpose flour

⅓ cup white wine

1 cup clam juice

½ cup heavy cream

>>>

METHOD

ORDER OF OPERATIONS: Your aim here is to finish everything at once; I've given you pasta directions not because I think you don't know how to boil pasta, but to help you out with timing. If something has to get finished first, make it the sauce: you don't want the pasta getting clumpy and cold, because it won't combine well with the sauce.

TO MAKE THE PASTA:

1. Put a large pot of salted water on to boil for the pasta.

2. When the water comes to a boil, add the linguini and cook until it is just al dente. (Follow the timing on the box, subtracting 1 minute. Be sure to test a couple of pieces in the last 2 minutes of cooking to avoid mushiness.)

3. Drain the pasta, but don't rinse it: you want as much stickiness as possible, so the sauce adheres.

>>>

1½ teaspoons dried oregano, on the
   branch if possible (I use Sicilian or
   Calabrian)
½ teaspoon coarse-ground black pepper
2 pounds fresh small clams
   (e.g., Manilas or Littlenecks),
   well washed
¼ cup roughly chopped fresh parsley

TO MAKE THE CLAM SAUCE:

1. Heat the olive oil in a large pot over medium-high heat. Add the bacon, then the garlic, and cook until the scent of the garlic is released and the garlic slices just begin to brown, about 1 minute.

2. Add the onion, bell peppers, and red pepper flakes and cook, stirring frequently, until the bell peppers are soft, about 4 minutes.

3. Stir the flour into the sauce and cook together until it is smoothly incorporated, about 1 minute.

4. Add the wine and cook until the alcohol has evaporated, about 30 seconds.

5. Add the clam juice, cream, oregano, and black pepper. Stir to combine. Bring the mixture up to a low boil and allow the liquid to reduce by half, about 5 minutes.

6. Add the clams. Cover the pot and continue cooking until all the clams are completely open—about 5 minutes total, depending on the size of the clams. After about 2½ minutes (at the halfway mark for your clams), open the cover and mix everything around a bit, then cover again. (If you're removing the clam shells, this is where you take the clams out of the sauce, pull the meat out of the shells, and put it back in the sauce by itself.)

7. Turn off the heat under the clam sauce. Add the pasta to the sauce-pot and stir well to combine. Add the parsley and mix well. Serve immediately.

RICH'S SPICY LINGUINI AND CRAB

I've worked with Rich Torrisi for six years, uptown and downtown. He's a talented guy—he came up with this pasta dish out of total frustration. We had a stuffed-zucchini-flower thing on the menu at my last, uptown restaurant—and stuffed zucchini flowers are delicious, but they aren't easy to work with. The dish was, as Rich put it, "a pain in the ass to make." So he went to work to come up with a dish that had all the same flavors but didn't require so much haute cuisine labor. He ended up with a great summer pasta that feels American and Italian at the same time, with a spicy kick from the chilies and fresh lemon to pump up the flavors. It's always a hit: uptown, downtown, everywhere.

If you can't find fresh long, red Holland chili peppers, you can substitute red pepper flakes or chili paste—just make sure that whatever you use is good and spicy. The zucchini flowers are absolutely not a pain in the ass here, but they're sometimes tough to find, so they're optional.

TIMING: Superfast; about 20 minutes

SERVES 4 TO 6

INGREDIENTS

¼ cup extra-virgin olive oil

1 tablespoon butter

3 cloves garlic, sliced Goodfellas thin

¼ cup thinly sliced red Holland chilies
(about 2 peppers); or ½ teaspoon red
pepper flakes or chili paste

3 bunches scallions, whites only,
chopped (1 cup)

a healthy pinch of saffron

½ teaspoon salt

1½ cups clam juice

1 pound dried linguini

12 ounces fresh jumbo lump crab meat
(about 2 cups)

⅓ cup chopped fresh parsley

juice of 1 lemon

Optional:

12 zucchini flowers, cut into wide strips
lengthwise

METHOD

1. Put a large pot of salted water on to boil for the pasta.

2. Heat a large saucepan over medium-low heat. Add the olive oil and butter and stir to combine for a few seconds.

3. Add the garlic, chilies, scallions, and saffron (it's important to add the saffron immediately so that it has a chance to bloom). Stir everything well to combine and reduce the heat to low.

4. Add the salt and cook the mixture, stirring frequently, until the scallions are translucent and everything is soft and cooked through—about 3 to 4 minutes—but don't allow the garlic or scallions to color.

5. Add 1 cup of the clam juice and turn the heat to high. Let the clam juice come just to a boil—about 1 minute—and then immediately remove the pan from the heat. (If you allow the clam juice to reduce, you'll end up with nothing but an overwhelming salt flavor.)

6. Meanwhile, cook the linguini until just al dente, about 7 minutes. Drain very well—if there's too much liquid on the pasta, it won't combine well with the sauce—reserving about 1 cup of the pasta water.

7. Add the pasta to the sauce and return the pan to low heat. Mix very well, so that the clam juice adheres to the strands of pasta. If the juice is all sucked up immediately, add the remaining ½ cup of clam juice or an equal amount of the pasta water—whichever you prefer.

>>>

8   Add the crab meat and mix well.

9   Add the parsley. If you're using the zucchini flowers, throw them in here. Toss everything together very quickly, just for a few seconds—if you're using the zucchini flowers, you want them just barely wilted.

10   Remove the pan from the heat and squeeze the lemon juice over the top. Mix well to combine.

11   Taste the pasta and adjust seasoning as needed. If the flavor needs a bump, add up to ½ teaspoon of salt. If the pasta seems a bit dry, add a splash of the pasta water (2 to 4 tablespoons) and toss the mixture on low heat for a second or two. Serve immediately.

RIGATONI PUGLIESE

Like all Italians—pretty much like all humans—I love the mouth-feel of rich pasta. But I don't like the old-fashioned heaviness of food cooked with a lot of cream and butter. The chickpea purée in this pasta dish creates a smooth, rich texture and a full-bodied, earthy flavor without a lot of fat. The combination of legumes and pasta may seem unusual, but in Puglia, in the heel of Italy's boot, you find pasta with *ceci* (garbanzo beans, or chickpeas) everywhere.

I've included directions for cooking dried chickpeas, but you can always use the canned variety—no one but the pickiest Pugliese grandmother will be able to tell. If you're really rushed, you can even substitute prepared hummus for the blended chickpea mixture, though the result will not be quite as balanced and delicious.

TIMING: About 30 minutes

SERVES 4 TO 6

INGREDIENTS

For the sauce:

1 15-ounce can chickpeas

¼ cup plus 2 tablespoons extra-virgin olive oil

1 pound spicy Italian sausage

3 cups Basic Tomato Sauce (page 285)

½ teaspoon ground fennel seed

For the broccoli rabe and rigatoni:

1 bunch broccoli rabe, cleaned of outer leaves and bottom stems trimmed

1 pound rigatoni

2 tablespoons extra-virgin olive oil

1 clove garlic, sliced Goodfellas thin

¼ teaspoon red pepper flakes

salt and pepper to taste

To finish the dish:

2 tablespoons butter

2 teaspoons extra-virgin olive oil

1 cup grated pecorino cheese

METHOD

TO PREPARE THE SAUCE:

1. Drain the chickpeas well, reserving the liquid. Blend half the chickpeas (about 1 cup) and all their liquid on high until the mixture forms a smooth paste, about 1 minute.

2. Heat the olive oil in a large saucepan over high heat. Squeeze the sausage out of the casing and add the meat to the pan. Brown it, stirring regularly and breaking the meat up into small pieces with a spoon or potato masher.

3. Add the tomato sauce and stir to combine.

4. Add the chickpea purée and the fennel seed and stir to combine. Cook over medium heat until the mixture forms a loose sauce and the flavors are combined, about 15 minutes.

TO PREPARE THE BROCCOLI RABE AND THE RIGATONI:

1. Bring a large pot of salted water to a boil.

2. Blanch the broccoli rabe until the stems are just softened and the color has deepened, about 90 seconds. Remove with a slotted spoon or spider to a bowl of ice water to immediately stop the cooking process.

3. Return the water to a boil, add the rigatoni, and cook until it's al dente. Drain but do not rinse the pasta.

4. Warm the olive oil over medium-high heat in a medium sauté pan. Add the broccoli rabe, garlic, red pepper flakes, and the remaining

>>>

half of the chickpeas. Season with salt and pepper and sauté until the greens are well coated, about 1 minute.

TO FINISH THE DISH:

1. Return the rigatoni to the pot. Add the sauce and cook on medium-high heat, mixing well, until the pasta is well coated, about 1 minute.

2. Remove the pot from the heat and stir in the butter, olive oil, and half the pecorino cheese.

3. Transfer the pasta and sauce to a large serving dish and pour the broccoli rabe and chickpea mixture over the top. Top with the rest of the pecorino cheese and serve immediately.

RIGATONI WITH FAVA BEANS
AND PECORINO

This pasta takes its inspiration from a classic Roman springtime combination: fava beans, pecorino, and black pepper. When the weather warms up, you can find variations on this dish in cafés and restaurants across the city. A lot of restaurants around New York rush to serve fava beans as a hallmark of spring, too—which is kind of funny, since those gorgeous green spring favas are usually flown in from California or Mexico. Around here, local fava beans really are mid- to late-summer vegetables.

If favas grow near you and they sell them at your local grocer or farmers' market, try to get them when they're local and fresh: favas are always delicious, but the flavor and texture of the beans when they come straight to market from the farm is unbeatable. If you can't find fresh fava beans at all, try this dish with peas or sugar snap peas—fresh or frozen. I use basil here, but mint works really well in this dish, too. And don't be afraid to make things really peppery in the end: it makes the dish well balanced and gives it some serious contrast.

One of my discoveries, in my months of cooking at home, was how superior cooking is to dishwashing on the enjoyment meter. This dish calls for two pots because you need to blanch the favas while you're boiling the pasta water—I really didn't want to up the pot-washing lineup to three, so I started reusing the pasta pot to cook the sauce. I give you my technique for this below.

TIMING: Super-super-fast

SERVES 4 TO 6

INGREDIENTS

3 pounds fresh fava beans,
    pods removed (about 2 cups with
    pods removed)

1 pound dried rigatoni

3 tablespoons extra-virgin olive oil

2 tablespoons butter

1 medium onion, sliced thick

2 cloves garlic, sliced Goodfellas thin

¼ cup pine nuts, chopped

¼ teaspoon red pepper flakes

1 teaspoon dried oregano, preferably on
    the branch (Sicilian or Calabrian)

½ teaspoon salt

½ teaspoon coarse-ground black pepper,
    plus some for sprinkling

½ cup grated pecorino cheese, plus
    some for sprinkling

¼ cup fresh basil (about 12 leaves),
    roughly chopped

METHOD

1. Put a large pot of salted water on to boil for the pasta.

2. Put another large pot of salted water on to boil to blanch the fava beans.

3. When the blanching water boils, throw the shelled fava beans into the pot and blanch them for 1½ minutes if small, 2 minutes if large. Remove them with a slotted spoon to a bowl of ice water to stop the cooking process. Then remove the translucent skin from the beans. (The favas don't visibly change color when they're blanched, but when you slip the skins off, the insides should be emerald green.)

4. Meanwhile, when the pasta water boils, cook the pasta until just al dente, about 8 minutes.

5. Drain the pasta (but don't rinse it). Pour 1 tablespoon of the olive oil over the pasta as it rests in the colander and mix it well with your hands, so the pasta won't stick together. (You don't want to do this for every pasta recipe, but here you do because the pasta will sit in the colander for a little while.)

6. Return the pasta-cooking pot to the stove. Turn the heat to medium-high and allow the pot to dry out for about 30 seconds.

7 With the heat still on medium-high, add 1 tablespoon of butter, the onion, and 1 tablespoon of the olive oil and cook until the onion starts to soften, about 2 minutes.

8 Add the garlic and pine nuts and cook until both have begun to toast, about 2 minutes, stirring often to keep the garlic from burning.

9 Add the red pepper flakes, oregano, and ¾ cup of water, and mix to combine.

10 Add the cooked pasta and then the fava beans to the pot and mix well. Cook until the pasta is coated with the onion mixture and the flavors come together, about 1 minute.

11 Remove the pot from the heat. Add the salt and pepper, the rest of the butter, the remaining tablespoon of olive oil, the grated pecorino cheese, and the basil, and mix everything together well. Serve the pasta in individual serving bowls, sprinkled liberally with more pecorino and black pepper.

MY GRANDMOTHER'S RAVIOLI

This is one pasta that makes people happy. I started running "Grandmas" (as we call 'em in the kitchen) as a Sunday-supper dish almost ten years ago; pretty soon, people were coming back during the week and asking for it. Now it's a permanent fixture on my menu. The recipe is not exactly my actual grandmother's actual ravioli—I've done a little chefly tweaking—but it's pretty damned close to her own Sunday-supper specialty.

There's no need to get fancy with sauces here. Basic Tomato Sauce is my favorite with the Grandmas.

TIMING: This one is definitely a project. It's a good idea to make the pasta dough (page 297) and the filling a day or two before you need it—the filling takes some time to cook and cool, but it will hold for up to 2 days in the fridge. That way, you can put the ravioli together and finish the dish without being pressed for time.

MAKES ABOUT 50 RAVIOLI; SERVES 6 TO 8

INGREDIENTS

For the filling:

½ pound veal stew meat, cut into 1½-inch cubes

½ pound beef short ribs, cut into 1½-inch cubes

½ pound pork butt, cut into 1½-inch cubes

1 teaspoon salt

½ teaspoon coarse-ground black pepper

2 tablespoons extra-virgin olive oil

½ cup roughly chopped bacon, in pieces about ½ inch (about 3 ounces)

1 small onion, roughly chopped

1 small carrot, sliced

1 stalk celery, roughly chopped

1 beefsteak tomato, cored and roughly chopped

1 clove garlic, smashed

1 tablespoon tomato paste

1 tablespoon all-purpose flour

1 cup dry red wine

>>>

METHOD

TO MAKE THE FILLING:

1. Place the veal, beef, and pork on a large plate and season the meat all over with the salt and pepper.

2. Heat the olive oil on high heat in a large pot. Add the meat and cook until it's browned, about 2 to 3 minutes.

3. Add the bacon, onion, carrot, and celery and cook together until the vegetables soften and begin to brown—about 5 minutes—stirring occasionally so nothing sticks.

4. Add the tomato, smashed garlic clove, and tomato paste. Stir everything together so that all the ingredients are glazed with the tomato paste, about 1 minute.

5. Add the flour and mix it in well, so that the meat and the vegetables are coated. Cook the starchy flavor of the flour out a bit, about 2 minutes.

6. Add the wine and the bay leaves and mix well. Allow the liquid to reduce by three quarters, about 2 minutes.

7. Add the chicken broth. With a rubber spatula (or a wooden spoon), carefully scrape down the sides of the pot above the mixture, so that any bits that have landed on the sides don't burn and flavor the filling. Lower the heat to medium-low, cover the pot, and simmer until the meat has broken down into little bits, most of the liquid has reduced, and the mixture looks like a thick, delicious, fragrant stew—about 2½ hours. Check the mixture periodically as it cooks to make sure it doesn't come up to a hard boil. (It's important to make

>>>

2 bay leaves

2 cups chicken broth

2 egg yolks

⅓ cup grated Parmigiano-Reggiano

a pinch of nutmeg

1 recipe Pasta Dough for Ravioli (page 297)

For the sauce:

3 cups Basic Tomato Sauce (page 285)

2 tablespoons extra-virgin olive oil

2 tablespoons butter

½ cup grated Parmigiano-Reggiano

½ cup fresh basil, chopped

sure that the mixture is really not wet but just moist when it's done: there should be just a little liquid in the bottom to glaze up the meat.)

8 Remove the pot from the heat and allow the mixture to cool. When the mixture has cooled, you have three options:

A. Use your hands to squeeze the meat bits up and break everything apart (including the vegetables). This is exactly what I do if I'm making these at home and I don't want to dirty up a piece of equipment. It's like working with very messy clay.

B. Use a food processor, pulsing till the mixture is coarsely ground.

C. Put the filling through a meat grinder using a large die.

When you're done, the filling should look as if it's been roughly chopped.

9 Add the egg yolks, Parmigiano-Reggiano, and nutmeg and mix everything thoroughly with your hands, kneading it so that the mixture looks like a rough dough.

10 Form the filling into little balls, about 1 tablespoon's worth (or ½ ounce) for each one.

11 Put the balls of filling in the fridge on a plate covered with plastic wrap, and cool them for at least 1 hour, so the filling gets nice and cold and will retain its shape when you put it in the pasta. The filling will hold in the fridge for up to 2 days.

>>>

TO MAKE THE RAVIOLI:

1. Remove the ravioli dough from the fridge and turn it out onto a well-floured surface. With a wooden rolling pin, roll the dough out into a square or a rectangle, so that it fits inside your pasta machine.

2. Flour the pasta to prevent stickiness and roll it through the pasta machine. Cut the resulting sheet of dough in half (so the final sheet doesn't get too long). Roll the pasta through the machine again, reducing the setting. Repeat until the dough is thin enough to allow you to see the outline and color of your hand through it, but not so thin that it gets fragile: it should feel like a piece of velvet. At this point, run the dough through the machine once more without changing the setting.

3. Make an egg wash by beating the egg together with 1 tablespoon of water.

4. Cut the pasta lengthwise into 3-inch-wide strips and brush the egg wash all over the pasta with a pastry brush so that it's evenly covered.

5. Remove the ravioli-ball filling from the fridge. Place the balls at 1-inch intervals along the middle of the strip of pasta. Fold the dough lengthwise over the tops of the filling balls and pinch it shut at the open edge with your fingers. The dough should be grainy with flour on the outside when you fold it over; if it's not, sprinkle on a little more flour so the top isn't sticky.

6. Using two fingers (one on each side of the filling ball), press the pasta dough down around the filling balls, so that they're sealed in (they look a bit like sand dunes poking up from a desert when you're done).

7. Cut the ravioli using a fluted pastry cutter or a pizza cutter (if you don't have one, you can use a knife, but it won't give you that good-looking ravioli edge). The trick is to press your fingers down next to the ravioli ball and cut on the outside of them, pressing the cutter hard so the edge is clean.

8. If you're not serving the ravioli right away, you can freeze them at this point (they'll keep for up to 2 weeks in an airtight container). But if you're moving on, put them on a plate and proceed directly to cooking.

TO PREPARE THE SAUCE AND FINISH THE DISH:

1. Bring a large pot of salted water to a boil.

2. Drop in the ravioli and cook until they bob to the surface and float, about 2 minutes.

3. Meanwhile, warm the Basic Tomato Sauce in a large pan on the stove over medium heat until it reaches a very slow bubble.

4. Drain the ravioli but do not rinse them; you want all that stickiness so the sauce will adhere.

5. Remove the sauce from the heat and add the ravioli. Toss everything together well, so that all the ravioli are well coated with the sauce. Add the olive oil, butter, Parmigiano-Reggiano, and basil and mix well. Serve immediately, sprinkled with more Parmigiano-Reggiano.

PENNE WITH BACON, RADICCHIO, AND PIAVE CHEESE

Bacon, onion, mushrooms—what is this, France? No, but close enough. The town of Treviso—famous for its radicchio—is closer to Switzerland than to Tuscany, and you feel it in the food. It was in a side-of-the-road trattoria in Treviso, on my first trip to Italy, when I was nineteen, that I discovered there's much more to radicchio than *insalata tricolore*, that '80s bistro staple.

I'm not usually big on cream sauces for pasta, but in the north, especially when you're getting toward Austria and Switzerland, tradition (and the weather) calls for them. Here, the smokiness of the bacon is offset a bit by the sharp flavor and bounce of the radicchio. A bowl of this stuff with a glass of Amarone della Valpolicella (from the same region, naturally) will warm you up, body and soul, on even the coldest night.

Try to find whole slab bacon at your butcher's; it's usually better quality than the sliced stuff in the supermarkets, and you really want to get lots of smoky flavor here. Parmigiano-Reggiano works fine with this pasta dish—but if you can find it, Piave cheese is even better. It's from the same region, named after the river that runs through the Veneto, and it's a great match for the bitterness of the radicchio. There should be just enough sauce here to coat the pasta, not so much that the pasta is swimming in it.

TIMING: Superfast; under ½ hour

SERVES 4 TO 6
INGREDIENTS

For the pasta:

1 pound dried penne

For the sauce:

1 cup bacon, medium diced

1 small onion, diced (about 1 cup)

8 white mushrooms, diced
   (about 1½ cups)

1 clove garlic, minced

1 teaspoon fresh thyme leaves

1 head radicchio, roughly torn

¼ teaspoon salt

½ teaspoon coarse-ground black pepper

2 cups heavy cream

To finish the dish:

¼ cup grated Piave cheese or
   Parmigiano-Reggiano

salt and coarse-ground black pepper
   to taste

METHOD

ORDER OF OPERATIONS: Your aim here is to finish everything at once; I've given you pasta directions not because I think you're an idiot, but to help you out with timing. If something has to get done first, make it the sauce: you don't want the pasta getting clumpy and cold, because it won't combine well with the sauce.

TO MAKE THE PENNE:

1. Put a large pot of salted water on to boil for the pasta.

2. When the water comes to a boil, add the penne and cook until it is just al dente. (Follow the timing on the box, subtracting 1 minute. Be sure to test a couple of pieces in the last 2 minutes of cooking to avoid mushiness.)

3. Drain the pasta but do not rinse it; you want as much stickiness as possible, so the sauce adheres.

TO MAKE THE SAUCE:

1. Cook the bacon in a large, dry pot over high heat until it begins to brown, about 2 minutes.

2. Add the onion and mushrooms and stir to coat everything in the rendered bacon fat. When everything is soft and colored by the bacon

fat, stop stirring and cook so the vegetables caramelize a little—
just until they start to stick to the pot a bit, about 2 to 4 minutes.

3 Add the garlic, thyme, and radicchio and cook until the radicchio is just wilted and has lost its bright color, about 2 minutes,
stirring constantly so the garlic doesn't burn.

4 Add the salt, pepper, and cream. Continue cooking the sauce at
high heat, stirring occasionally, until the cream has reduced by
half, about 3 minutes. When the sauce is done, you should taste
the smoke of the bacon, and the radicchio should have just a little bit of bounce when you bite it.

TO FINISH THE DISH:

1 Add the penne to the bacon-radicchio mixture and toss well, so
the pasta is well coated with the sauce.

2 Cook everything together for about 1 minute on medium heat,
so the flavors come together and really get inside the pasta.

3 Add the grated cheese and mix well.

4 Season with more salt and black pepper, to your taste. Divide
the pasta into individual bowls. If you like, sprinkle each bowl
with a little more cheese before serving.

POLENTA

Polenta is one of those Italian dishes for which everybody thinks they've got the best recipe ever—usually the recipe their mother used. I remember getting yelled at by a customer once about my polenta. It wasn't authentic, she said, wasn't "real" polenta. She wanted the real deal, the way her mom did it—from one of those yellow tubes they sell in supermarkets.

I didn't exactly grow up with yellow-tube polenta. My family comes from the source: southerners call people from Friuli *polano*, or "polenta eaters," and it's not meant as a compliment. After all, this is true peasant food: my dad, who is not the kind of guy who dresses things up in fancy words, calls it "gruel." But the fact is that nothing satisfies the soul like a plate of soft polenta with some grated parmesan on top: it's the ultimate comfort food.

A lot of restaurants serve polenta fried (as we did on *Iron Chef*), but I never do that at home. Soft polenta, the version you most often see in Italy, is just so soul-satisfying, delicious in a childhood warm-cereal-in-the-morning comfort-food kind of way. But that doesn't mean it's not for grown-ups. I love it topped with a fried egg and parmesan cheese; you can turn it into a hearty dinner with a piece of braised meat, or dress it way up by shaving white truffles on top.

There are endless varieties and brands of polenta: premade, quick-cooking, fresh, dried. I like working with dried polenta (my favorite is Moretti, which is easy to find). If you're rushed, the quick-cooking ones are a perfectly good alternative; the only difference is that the polenta is blanched in boiling water before it's dried, so it absorbs liquid faster.

POLENTA

The thing about polenta is that it's only as good as the cook making it. Even if you follow the same ratio every time, with the same brand of polenta, you're always going to end up adding or subtracting a little bit of liquid as it cooks, so you need to sort of use the force here. That's why we call it cooking, folks, and not chemistry.

My dad refers to polenta as "gruel," and he's not wrong—but it can be very elegant, very yummy gruel if you put some love into it. Polenta can be many things: a perfect vehicle for a piece of braised veal or, in the fall, for shaved truffles; a side dish for meats or poultry; a stick-to-the-ribs late-night supper (or breakfast), topped with sautéed mushrooms or fried eggs and parmesan cheese; or, if you're feeling in need of comfort, a big bowl of deliciousness all on its own.

Polenta is incredibly easy to cook, but the ending—the addition of the olive oil, butter, and parmesan—is really important. This is peasant food: it's supposed to be nourishing, not light. If you scrimp on the fat, you might as well skip the carbs too and just have a salad for dinner.

One thing I have definitely learned in cooking polenta at home: if you're the cook *and* pot washer, make sure you start soaking the polenta-encrusted pot before you enter your carb coma. (I usually fill the pot with water and set it to boil on the stove.) Also, don't ever put your polenta-cooking utensils down on a counter or stovetop, and be sure to wipe up all drips and spills with obsessive-compulsive zeal. I've learned the hard way that dried cooked polenta is similar to concrete in its sticking qualities.

TIMING: Supereasy to get started; about 2 hours to cook, depending on which brand of polenta you use

SERVES 12 (OR 6 TO 8 FOR VERY LARGE SERVINGS)

INGREDIENTS

2 cups dried polenta
  (not the quick-cooking stuff)
6 cups whole milk (or water)
2 teaspoons salt
1 teaspoon coarse-ground black pepper
3 tablespoons butter
3 tablespoons extra-virgin olive oil
½ cup grated Parmigiano-Reggiano

Optional:
2 bay leaves
1 whole branch thyme
1 whole branch rosemary

METHOD

1   Take the polenta out of the package and dump it into a pourable mixing cup or similar vessel. (It's important to do this so that the polenta can be added to the mixture evenly.)

2   Pour the milk (or water) into a large pot. Add the salt and pepper. (If you'd like to flavor the polenta, add the bay leaves, thyme, and rosemary, leaving the herbs on the branch.)

3   Bring the milk to a rolling boil on high heat. (If you've added the herbs, reduce the heat and simmer for 2 minutes to infuse the flavors. Remove the herbs with a slotted spoon, then bring the milk back up to a boil.)

4   Pour the polenta into the boiling milk in a steady stream, whisking as you go. There should be a lot of liquid, since the polenta will expand and soak everything up as it cooks; if the mixture is at all thick or sludgy at this point, add some hot water.

5   Scrape down the sides of the pot with a wet spatula, so that any bits that splashed up on the sides don't burn and flavor the polenta.

>>>

6 Reduce the heat to low and cook the mixture at a very low simmer (bubbling like a tar pit—slowly, popping up every once in a while, instead of bubbling all over). Stir it vigorously once in a while with a whisk, and keep wiping the sides down with the wet spatula as you go—but don't worry about it too much if the polenta starts to stick on the bottom. In Venice, the saying goes, *l'é pronta che fae la crosta stulidha dal ran* ("the polenta is ready when it burns in the copper"). But be sure to just leave the burnt bits as they are: don't scrape them up into the polenta so they flavor everything.

7 Let the polenta cook until it's soft but slightly grainy on the tongue and the mixture has achieved your preferred level of thickness, about 2 hours. (I like my polenta to be about the texture of a thick soup, so if it starts to really thicken up, I add water—about 2 cups total over the course of the cooking time, added at intervals as it cooks. If you like it thicker, don't add liquid, or add less. You'll be able to judge it as it cooks.)

8 Remove the pot from the heat and add the butter, olive oil, and Parmigiano-Reggiano. Whisk the mixture well so that the internal heat of the polenta melds everything together.

9 Taste and season with more salt and pepper if you like. Serve immediately.

ABOUT RISOTTO

The trick with risotto is the timing. Everything needs to be added at the right time and at the right temperature, so you'll need to handle a number of operations at once—and there's a whole lot of stirring going on too. Make sure you do all of your prep work before you get started, so you don't end up needing three hands.

The starchiness in the rice is what gives risotto that amazing silkiness. To get it, you need to cook your rice at a good hot temperature, so your stock is always at a boil. There's an old Italian saying: The risotto's ready when you squeeze a grain of rice and the inside shows a "Trinity"—the Father, the Son, and the Holy Ghost, represented in three little white uncooked spots. It sounds crazy, but it's actually a pretty good marker of doneness.

In most risottos, the final step is the addition of butter, olive oil, and cheese after you've removed the pot from the heat: a technique called *mantecare*. (When you see "risotto *mantecato*" on menus, it means risotto finished with butter and cheese.) Don't skip this step or skimp on the fats: they bring everything together. In a three-star Michelin Italian kitchen I worked in, there was one cook responsible only for making risotto—the signature dish of the restaurant. The chef was always yelling at the guy: *"Onde! Onde! Onde!"* he would bellow, at the top of his lungs. *Onde* means "waves," and for the first couple of days, I kept wondering, "Why is he yelling *waves* at him? What is he—a surfer?" Turns out he was talking about the way the finished risotto moves: when you toss it back and forth in the pot, it should act like a wave of water. That's when you know you've hit the perfect coming together of liquid and rice.

ASPARAGUS RISOTTO WITH AN ORGANIC EGG AND LEMON

Some people do asparagus risotto by making a plain risotto and cooking the asparagus in it. That's pretty easy, and it'll give you an okay-nothing-wrong-with-it risotto. But if what you're after is a kick-ass risotto, try it this way. I make a quick purée from the stalk of the asparagus and add it to rice. Presto: intense asparagus flavor. The tips go in at the last minute, as a garnish, so they keep their own flavor and give the dish some contrast and crunch. The lemon—always great with asparagus—cuts through the richness of the dish, opens up the asparagus flavor, and keeps things fresh. The basil and the parsley add a green flavor and even more freshness. The result? Springtime in a bowl.

At the restaurant, I like to add a raw egg to the middle of each dish just before serving. The diner mixes the egg in, and it cooks in the hot risotto. The look is beautiful, and the egg gives everything an added silky richness on the tongue, so I don't need to add any butter. I do the same thing at home. I know people worry about raw eggs, but there's really no danger here if you do things right: I use high-quality organic eggs, and I serve the risotto very hot, straight from the pot, so the pasta cooks the eggs. But if you're skeevy about the whole raw-egg thing, leave out the eggs. (Whatever you do, *don't* put them in the pot while the risotto is cooking—they'll turn into scrambled eggs and wreck the dish.) Add the butter with the cheese and lemon juice at the end to give you some richness instead.

TIMING: Pretty quick; 30 to 45 minutes, depending on broth- and water-boiling time

SERVES 4 TO 6

INGREDIENTS

For the asparagus and the asparagus purée:

5 cups chicken broth or vegetable stock (or water)

1 bunch asparagus (about 1 pound)

½ cup basil

½ cup parsley

For the rice:

3 tablespoons extra-virgin olive oil

1 tablespoon butter

½ large Vidalia or other sweet onion, diced (about 1 cup)

2 cups Arborio rice

1 cup white wine

½ teaspoon each of salt and coarse-ground black pepper

>>>

METHOD

ORDER OF OPERATIONS:

1. Put the broth for the risotto and the water for the asparagus purée on to boil.

2. While the broth and water are heating, prepare the asparagus and add the bottoms to the broth.

3. When the broth is close to a boil, begin the rice, so that the broth is hot but has not boiled down when you need it for the risotto.

4. While the risotto is cooking, prepare the purée, so it's hot when it goes in the risotto—but don't forget to stir the risotto frequently!

TO PREPARE THE ASPARAGUS AND THE BROTH:

1. Put the broth or stock (or water) on to boil.

2. Cut off the bottom inch of the asparagus stalks and reserve. Cut off the asparagus tips about 3 inches from the top and reserve. You should have about 4 inches of stalk remaining; cut these pieces in half.

3   As the broth is coming up to a boil, add the asparagus bottoms to the broth.

4   Bring the broth to a boil and cook the asparagus ends in it for 3 minutes, so that the broth becomes lightly flavored. Remove the asparagus ends with a slotted spoon and discard.

TO PREPARE THE RICE:

1   Heat the olive oil and butter in a large pot over medium-high heat. Add the onion and sweat it until it softens, about 1½ minutes.

2   Add the Arborio rice and stir well, so that all the rice grains are coated in the olive-oil-butter-onion mixture—about 1 minute.

3   When the rice is evenly coated, add the white wine. Mix well and continue cooking, stirring frequently, until the wine has evaporated and the alcohol smell is released, about 1½ minutes or so.

4   Add 3 cups of the broth and continue cooking, stirring well and often, until the rice has absorbed all the liquid, about 7 minutes.

5   Add the remaining 2 cups of broth and the salt and pepper. Mix well, and continue cooking together, stirring well and often, until the rice has absorbed most of the liquid and become a thick, liquidy stew—another 7 to 8 minutes or so.

TO PREPARE THE ASPARAGUS PURÉE:

1   Put a large pot of salted water on to boil.

2   Throw the asparagus tips in the boiling water. Blanch for 1 minute, until they turn dark green and are edible but with some crunch (more crunch than you would want if you were going to serve them right away). Remove the tips from the pot with a slotted spoon or spider to a bowl of ice water to stop the cooking process.

3   Cook the asparagus stalks in the same boiling water until they're softened, about 3 minutes. Remove the stalks with a slotted spoon or spider and put them directly into the blender while they're still hot.

>>>

To finish the dish:

½ cup grated Parmigiano-Reggiano, plus extra for sprinkling

juice of 2 lemons

6 organic eggs; or 2 tablespoons butter

4 Add to the blender the basil, parsley, and ½ cup of the water the asparagus cooked in. Pulse together until the mixture forms a smooth purée, about 30 seconds.

TO FINISH THE DISH:

1 When the rice has just about finished cooking, add 1 cup of the asparagus purée. Cook together for 30 seconds to combine.

2 Turn off the heat and add the asparagus tips to the rice. Add the Parmigiano-Reggiano and the lemon juice and mix together. If you're using butter instead of raw eggs, add the butter here too.

3 Ladle the risotto onto individual plates. Crack an egg (if using) into the center of each serving. Sprinkle generously with cheese and serve as quickly as humanly possible—with or without the egg, risotto must be eaten while it's hot.

RISOTTO MINESTRONE

The base of this dish is *soffrito*, a mixture of carrots, onions, and celery, diced and cooked together quickly. It's the heart of a thousand Italian soups, lending backbone and depth to even the simplest recipes. But I've turned the soup this dish is based on inside-out: instead of adding pasta to soup, I've taken all the flavors of minestrone and put them in risotto.

The stars of this risotto are the vegetables you throw in later in the cooking process. I've used summer vegetables here, and they definitely look beautiful in the risotto, but you can really use any kind of good-looking nonbitter vegetable (it's great in winter with root vegetables, too). Just make sure that everything's chopped up pea-sized, because you want the rice and the vegetables to achieve doneness at the same time.

I've done this dish without meat, and you can easily make it truly vegetarian by using water or vegetable stock instead of chicken stock. On the other hand, if, like my brother-in-law, you strongly believe that a meal without meat will cause you to fall down and die, don't panic. Throw in some diced pancetta or prosciutto and you're good.

TIMING: About 30 minutes

SERVES 4 TO 6

INGREDIENTS

6 cups chicken stock (or vegetable stock or water)

¼ cup extra-virgin olive oil

3 tablespoons butter

1 small onion, chopped (about ½ cup)

½ cup carrots, diced small

½ cup celery, diced small

2 cups Arborio rice

1 cup white wine

1½ teaspoons salt, plus extra for seasoning

2 cups mixed vegetables: English peas, snap peas, haricots vert (green beans), yellow wax beans, zucchini, fava beans, or whatever else appeals to you, all chopped to pea-size

¼ cup grated Parmigiano-Reggiano

⅓ cup Pesto (page 288)

½ teaspoon coarse-ground black pepper, plus extra for seasoning

Optional:

½ cup diced pancetta or prosciutto

METHOD

1. Put the chicken stock (or vegetable stock or water) on to boil.

2. Heat the olive oil and 1 tablespoon of the butter together over high heat in a large stock pot.

3. Add the onion, carrots, and celery to make a soffrito. (If you're adding meat to the recipe, this is where you throw it in.) Sweat the vegetables over high heat until they're really soft (about 3 minutes), stirring as needed, but don't let them brown. (If you're adding meat, it should render, so the fat is released.)

4. Add the Arborio rice and mix well until all the rice grains are coated in the soffrito, about 1 minute.

5. Add the wine and continue cooking—stirring constantly to ensure that none of the rice sticks—until the wine has been completely absorbed and the rice is soft but not sticky, about 1 minute.

6. Add 3 cups of the stock (or water) and the salt, and continue cooking, stirring occasionally, until the rice is al dente, just beginning to cook through, about 6 minutes.

7. Add the mixed vegetables and stir well. Add the remaining 3 cups of stock (or water) and continue to cook, stirring regularly, until the rice is ready and the vegetables are cooked through but retain their snap and flavor, about another 6 or 7 minutes.

>>>

8 Turn off the heat and add the Parmigiano-Reggiano, the remaining 2 tablespoons of butter, the Pesto, and the pepper. Adjust the seasonings with more salt and pepper if necessary. If the risotto is too thick for your taste, add a little leftover stock or water.

Serve in individual bowls, sprinkled with a little more Pesto and Parmigiano-Reggiano on top if you like.

RISOTTO

Risotto's been around for a really long time—it's one of the most basic peasant dishes in Italy. Even before rice came to Italy, the dish existed as a type of gruel, made with farro or barley. These days, you can see the rice paddies when you drive around the Po Valley, stretching through Piedmonte, Lombardia, and the Veneto; like water buffalo (the source of buffalo mozzarella), they're totally out of place and completely Italian at the same time.

You hear all kinds of rules for making "the best" risotto: use only boiling stock, add wine, never add wine, add the liquid one ladleful at a time . . . Everyone's got a perfect method. But in my first cooking stint in Italy, I watched the chef throw everything in a pot and boil the hell out of it—and it was pretty good. So who knows?

I got my recipe down on that first solo trip, and I've made risotto the same way ever since, adding half the liquid first and the rest at the end, stirring constantly. I use Arborio rice for heavier versions, since it's got more starch, and carnaroli or vialone nano for lighter summer risottos.

When I got home from that stint in Italy, I made risotto for my dad. This was kind of a big deal. I'd been hearing about good risotto from him my whole life: it was one of the things his Italian father cooked for him when he was a kid, and he'd never had it the same way since. I'd been cooking in Italy for a year; I'd made about seven thousand risottos; I knew I could finally do one that would blow his mind. I made it with beautiful tomatoes, straight from the garden, and fresh parmigiano from West Side Market in Cleveland. It was as authentic, as perfect, as a risotto made in Ohio could possibly be.

He dipped a spoon, tasted, stopped. He hated it. "It tastes totally different," he complained. "And it's not soft enough. What *is* this?"

My beautiful straight-from-the-source risotto, it turned out, was nothing like the one his father made. Go figure.

RISOTTO ROSSO WITH RED WINE, RADICCHIO, AND SMOKED MOZZARELLA

In the famous radicchio-growing town of Treviso, in the Veneto region of northern Italy, red wine risotto with a little bit of radicchio mixed in is a very traditional wintertime dish. Smoked mozzarella, on the other hand, is not exactly traditional in Treviso.

But in my opinion: mozzarella is good. Smoked mozzarella is *really* good.

So this is my American everything-tastes-better-when-smoked version. The flavors are very deep: the smokiness of the cheese, the bitterness of the radicchio, the astringency of the port. (If you don't happen to have a bottle of port sitting around in your liquor cabinet, you can tart up some red wine with sugar instead.) I finish this dish with Piave cheese, local to the region and delicious, though if you can't find it, Parmigiano-Reggiano will work just fine. Serve it with a good *vino rosso*, of course.

TIMING: About 20 minutes

SERVES 4 TO 6
INGREDIENTS

For the radicchio:

1 large head radicchio

2 tablespoon extra-virgin olive oil

1 clove garlic, crushed

¼ teaspoon salt

¼ teaspoon fresh-ground pepper

½ cup port (or ½ cup red wine mixed
   with 1 tablespoon sugar)

For the rice:

5 cups chicken or vegetable stock
   (or water)

2 tablespoons extra-virgin olive oil

1 small onion, chopped (about ½ cup)

2 cups Arborio rice

1 cup dry red wine

>>>

METHOD
TO COOK THE RADICCHIO:

1. Cut the head of radicchio in half lengthwise. Remove and discard the core. Cut each half into thirds and then cut each of these segments in half.

2. Heat the olive oil in a saucepan or sauté pan over medium-high heat.

3. Add the garlic clove, radicchio, salt, and pepper. Cook, stirring regularly, until the radicchio begins to wilt, about 1 minute.

4. Add the port (or the red wine and sugar), and stir to combine them. Continue to cook the mixture, stirring occasionally, until the port has evaporated and the radicchio pieces are soft but retain a little bit of texture and bounce, about 8 to 10 minutes.

5. Remove the garlic clove. Reserve.

TO COOK THE RISOTTO:

1. Bring the stock (or water) to a boil.

2. Heat the olive oil in a large pot over medium-high heat.

3. Add the onion and sweat until it softens, about 1½ minutes.

4. Add the Arborio rice and stir well, so that all the rice grains are coated in the olive-oil-and-onion mixture. Cook for about 1½ minutes, stirring constantly to avoid sticking, and ensure that every grain is well coated in the fat. (This helps to keep the grains separate while they toast, so there's no sticking and the flavor develops well.)

5 Add 1 cup of the dry red wine. Mix well and continue cooking, stirring frequently, until the wine has evaporated, the risotto has taken on its color, and the alcohol smell is released, about a minute and a half or so.

6 Add 2½ cups of the boiling stock and continue cooking, stirring well and often, until the rice has absorbed all the liquid, about 7 minutes.

7 Add the remaining 2½ cups of stock. Continue cooking, stirring well and often, until the rice has absorbed most of the liquid and become a thick, liquidy stew—another 7 to 8 minutes or so.

TO FINISH THE DISH:

1 Add the radicchio mixture and the thyme leaves to the risotto pot. Cook together, stirring constantly, until everything is well combined, about 1 minute.

2 Remove the pot from the heat and add the salt and pepper, smoked mozzarella, and grated Piave or Parmigiano-Reggiano. Mix well. Spoon each portion of risotto into a shallow bowl. Sprinkle with more cheese and serve immediately.

To finish the dish:

1 tablespoon fresh thyme leaves

¼ teaspoon each of salt and fresh-ground pepper

¾ cup smoked mozzarella, diced (about ¼ pound—you'll need this much for the risotto, plus extra for the snacking-while-cooking-the-risotto, which is definitely going to happen)

¼ cup grated Piave (or Parmigiano-Reggiano), plus extra for sprinkling

RISOTTO TERRAZZO-MAN STYLE

This dish is an ode to my paternal grandma's family. The Bertins were traditional terrazzo artisans; my dad is one of the last of that line. They were hardworking guys from Friuli who could do beautiful things with marble and cement. Every house any member of my dad's family lives in has beautiful terrazzo work somewhere (in my parents' house, that includes a terrazzo table handcrafted by my grandfather and great-grandfather). One of the Bertin men used to make a risotto like this for me. It's kind of a *risi e bisi*: a traditional rice-and-pea *minestre*, a really soupy rice dish from my family's region. When I make it now, it always reminds me of being in the terrazzo workshop with my dad and my uncles.

TIMING: About 30 minutes

SERVES 4 TO 6

INGREDIENTS

5 cups chicken stock or vegetable broth
   (or water)
1 tablespoon extra-virgin olive oil
½ cup diced pancetta
1 small onion, chopped (about ½ cup)
2 cups Arborio rice
1 cup white wine
2 cups green peas (shelled English peas
   or chopped snap peas or a combo)
¼ teaspoon coarse-ground black pepper,
   plus extra for seasoning
½ cup grated Parmigiano-Reggiano or
   Piave cheese, plus extra for sprinkling
1 tablespoon chopped fresh parsley
1 tablespoon butter
salt to taste

METHOD

1. Bring the stock to a boil.

2. Heat the olive oil in a large pot over medium-high heat. Add the pancetta and allow the fat to render, about 3 minutes.

3. Add the onion, stir to coat, and cook until it softens, about 1½ to 2 minutes.

4. Add the Arborio rice and stir well, so that all the rice grains are coated in the mixture. Cook about a minute and a half, stirring constantly to avoid sticking and to ensure that every grain is well coated.

5. Add the wine. Stir well and continue cooking, stirring frequently, until the wine has evaporated and the alcohol smell is released, about a minute and a half.

6. Add 2½ cups of the stock and continue cooking, stirring well and often, until the rice has absorbed all of the liquid, about 7 minutes.

7. Add the rest of the stock and continue cooking for 3 minutes. Add the peas and pepper. Stir continually for 2 minutes, until the rice has absorbed most of the liquid. The peas should be cooked through but still bright green and crunchy.

8. Remove the risotto from the heat. Add the cheese, parsley, and butter. Season with salt and pepper to taste. Serve immediately, sprinkled with more cheese.

SEAFOOD RISOTTO WITH CHORIZO AND LEMON

Most Italian seafood risottos don't include chorizo—but that's because they don't need it. Seafood risottos are an excellent argument for local cooking: they're all about proximity to the sea. Usually, local risottos in Italy are made from stuff that's just come out of the ocean, stuff you can't get anywhere else. (I still dream about the tiny, tiny scampi I bought for a risotto in Viareggio.) That gives the risotto such an amazing, strong seafood flavor that all you need to add is a little parsley and lemon for tempering. But it's pretty hard to get that kind of seafood in ordinary American life, so I add chorizo here to pump up the flavor and give the risotto some texture. (I use Palacios-brand chorizo, which is nice and spicy.) Consider it a meaty, spicy nod to Spanish paella.

In this recipe I remove the clams and mussels from the shells, so you get a little bit of each kind of seafood with every bite, instead of having to plan each bite before you put it in your mouth. For less work and more dramatic effect, you can cover the clams and mussels with plastic wrap to keep them warm while the rice cooks. When the risotto's ready, just pop them on top with their shells.

TIMING: About 30 minutes

SERVES 4 TO 6
INGREDIENTS

For the shellfish:

2 pounds littleneck or Manila clams

2 pounds fresh mussels

¼ cup extra-virgin olive oil

2 cloves garlic, crushed

¼ teaspoon red pepper flakes

2 cups white wine

For the risotto:

2 cups clam juice

2 tablespoons extra-virgin olive oil

⅓ cup chopped chorizo
   (about ½ a sausage)

1 small onion, chopped (about ½ cup)

2 cups Arborio rice

To finish the dish:

½ pound shrimp, peeled, deveined, and
   with heads removed, cut into thirds

juice of 1 lemon

1 tablespoon chopped fresh parsley

METHOD
TO PREPARE THE SHELLFISH:

1 Clean the clams and mussels under cold running water. Scrub with a light brush to remove any sand.

2 Heat the olive oil in a large pot over high heat. Add the garlic and red pepper flakes and sweat, stirring constantly, until the garlic releases its aroma, about 30 seconds.

3 Add the wine.

4 If you're using large clams, add them first, on their own, then cover the pot and cook for 5 minutes to get the clams started before adding the mussels. If you're using small clams, add them and the mussels at the same time. Cover the pot and continue cooking until the clams and the mussels open, 3 to 5 minutes.

5 Drain the shellfish into a colander over a large bowl, saving the juice. Pull the clam meat out of the shells with your fingers. Do the same with the mussels, pulling out and discarding the furry bit. Discard the shells. (If you're not pulling the meat out of the shells, put the shellfish in a bowl and reserve on the counter, covered in plastic wrap to keep the heat inside.)

>>>

1. Pour the liquid from the clams and mussels into a small saucepot, going slowly so that the sediment that will have passed through the colander stays in the bowl.

2. Add the clam juice and 2 cups of water to the pot. Bring to a boil over high heat.

3. In a medium saucepot, heat the olive oil over medium heat. Add the chorizo and the chopped onion and sweat them together until the chorizo renders and the onion is soft.

4. Add the rice. Sweat the mixture together until the rice soaks up the olive oil and is colored by the chorizo, about 30 seconds.

5. Add half the shellfish broth to the rice and continue cooking, stirring well and often, until the rice has absorbed all of the liquid, about 7 minutes.

6. Add the rest of the shellfish broth and continue cooking, stirring well and often, until the rice has absorbed most of the liquid and become a thick, liquidy stew, another 7 to 8 minutes or so. (Keep an eye on your risotto; the liquid amounts are never an exact science, but you want the risotto to be very moist in the end without being liquid.)

TO FINISH THE DISH:

1. Remove the risotto from the heat. Add the shrimp and allow them to cook in the heat of the risotto until they turn white, about 30 seconds.

2. Add the rest of the shellfish and stir to incorporate. Make sure the risotto is smooth and well combined: if necessary, add 1 or 2 tablespoons of liquid and stir well to adjust the consistency.

3. Mix in the lemon juice and parsley. Spoon each portion of risotto into a shallow bowl. Serve immediately.

TOMATO RISOTTO

I've been doing variations on this dish for the past ten years—sometimes getting really crazy, cooking the tomatoes for one dish five different ways. When I won *Food & Wine*'s Best Chef 2000, the magazine featured a very complicated version of this recipe. But complicated isn't always better, and I've finally figured out, in my old age, that the simpler version I was cooking at home is actually more delicious.

This is one recipe that really depends on the season: you definitely want to do this in midsummer, when the tomatoes are at their ripest and most flavorful. Here in New York, we get all different sorts of great tomatoes at the Greenmarkets, including some amazing heirlooms. I like to use both cherry tomatoes and larger sizes: the cherries for garnish on top, the big guys inside the risotto itself.

Two things to keep in mind: I've given a standard measure for the chicken stock (or water), but the amount will vary depending on the juiciness of your tomatoes; if they don't have much liquid, you'll want to up the amount. And if your tomatoes turn out to be not so great (or if you really, really want to make this when tomatoes are not exactly in season), you can always add a teaspoon of tomato paste to your risotto to bump up the flavor.

TIMING: The tomato baking (not exactly labor-intensive) takes about 1 hour, but the rest can be put together in the last 45 minutes of their baking time

SERVES 4 TO 6
INGREDIENTS

For the baked tomatoes:

1 pound tomatoes (about 8 small beefsteaks)

¼ teaspoon each sea salt and coarse-ground black pepper

1 teaspoon fresh thyme leaves

1 teaspoon finely chopped fresh rosemary

1 clove garlic, sliced Goodfellas thin

For the tomato topping:

2 cups halved cherry tomatoes

2 tablespoons extra-virgin olive oil

a pinch of salt

>>>

METHOD
TO PREPARE THE BAKED TOMATOES:

1 Preheat the oven to 400°.

2 Cut the beefsteak tomatoes in half and lay them face-up on a sheet pan. Sprinkle them with the sea salt, pepper, thyme, and rosemary. Lay a slice or two of garlic on top of each tomato half.

3 Bake the tomatoes on the middle rack of the oven, uncovered, until they're a bit grilled-looking and soft and yummy, about 1 hour.

4 Remove the tomatoes from the oven and allow them to cool to room temperature.

5 Chop the tomatoes roughly and reserve them in a bowl, along with as much of their liquid as you can retain.

TO PREPARE THE TOMATO TOPPING:

1 Gently cook the cherry tomatoes, olive oil, and salt together in a small pot over low heat until the oil is bubbly, the tomatoes are soft, and the mixture looks like a chunky sauce, about 20 minutes.

2 Remove the topping from heat and reserve.

>>>

TO PREPARE THE RICE:

1. Put the chicken stock (or vegetable stock or water) on to boil.

2. Melt the butter and the olive oil together over high heat in another large pot. Add the onions and sweat them until they're really soft, about 2 minutes, stirring as needed so they don't color or brown.

3. Add the red pepper flakes to the onion-butter-olive-oil mixture and stir to combine.

4. Add the Arborio rice to the onion-butter-olive-oil mixture and mix well, so all the rice grains are coated, about 1 minute.

5. Add the white wine to the rice mixture and continue cooking, stirring constantly to ensure that none of the rice sticks, until the wine has been completely absorbed and the rice is soft but not sticky, about 1 minute.

6. Add 3 cups of the boiling stock (or water) and the chopped baked tomatoes with their liquid. Continue cooking, stirring occasionally, until the rice is al dente, just beginning to cook through, and the stock (or water) has evaporated, about 7 minutes.

7. Add the remaining 2 cups of stock (or water) and continue to cook, stirring well and often, until the rice has absorbed most of the liquid and become a thick, liquidy stew, another 7 to 8 minutes or so.

TO FINISH THE DISH:

1. Remove the risotto from the heat.

2. Add the mascarpone, Parmigiano-Reggiano, rosemary, salt, and pepper. Mix well, so the risotto becomes rich and well combined. If the risotto is too thick for your taste, add a little leftover stock or water.

3. Serve in individual bowls, topped with the tomato mixture and a little more Parmigiano-Reggiano.

For the rice:

5 cups chicken stock (or vegetable stock or water)

1 tablespoon butter

¼ cup extra-virgin olive oil

1 small onion, chopped (about ½ cup)

¼ teaspoon red pepper flakes

2 cups Arborio rice

½ cup white wine

To finish the dish:

2 tablespoons mascarpone cheese

¼ cup grated Parmigiano-Reggiano, plus more for sprinkling

1 tablespoon chopped rosemary

1½ teaspoons salt

½ teaspoon coarse-ground black pepper

SPAGHETTI PEPE DE VELLIS

My friend Olivier Flosse, sommelier extraordinaire, made this spaghetti for me in his kitchen at home—and as he cooked, he told me the story that goes with it, about his grandfather, Pepe di Vellis. It goes like this:

Pepe was working as a cook on a fishing boat back in the early '40s when his ship happened to dock on Manhattan's West Side piers, right next to an American naval vessel. Pepe was cooking his version of spaghetti *anchoise* that day in port, and the garlicky, anchovy-filled aroma made its way from his galley to the neighboring ship, sparking the interest of the officers on board. They called across to find out what the great smell was. Pepe's captain invited the Navy guys over to taste the pasta. They were so impressed they invited Pepe to cook for a big dinner for invited high-ups in the Navy on their ship the next night. The captain said Pepe could go—as long as the entire crew of the fishing boat could come over for dinner, too. The two captains shook hands, and the next night, the rough-and-ready Napolitano fishermen washed their hands and combed their hair and trooped over to the naval vessel for dinner with the bigwigs. The spaghetti was a huge hit with the brass, and in gratitude, the Navy officers gave Pepe a full U.S. admiral's uniform.

Pepe was born in Naples, but Olivier is from Marseilles, so he added a little Pernod to Frenchify the dish. And to be honest, this pasta tastes like the south of France: strongly aromatic, really herby, but with tang and brininess from the anchovies. Not recommended for dinner dates (unless you really think you've got a keeper).

Your most important tips for cooking Pepe's legendary spaghetti *anchoise*:

I. Cook the garlic very slowly, over medium heat, till it's nicely browned. If you use high heat and the garlic scorches, you're done.

2. Start the spaghetti first. Really. Trust me. The sauce will take about two seconds to cook, and you don't want the pasta sitting around getting clumpy and cold.

TIMING: Superquick

SERVES 4 TO 6

INGREDIENTS

1 pound dried spaghetti

⅓ cup extra-virgin olive oil

5 cloves garlic, sliced Goodfellas thin

10 anchovy fillets in oil

¼ teaspoon red pepper flakes

1 heaping tablespoon fresh thyme leaves

1 heaping tablespoon fresh rosemary
   leaves

2 tablespoons Pernod (or Sambuca or
   other anisette liqueur)

⅓ cup pitted Nicoise olives, whole

4 to 6 tablespoons grated Parmigiano-
   Reggiano

4 to 6 tablespoons Crumbs Yo! (page 291)
   or panko breadcrumbs

METHOD

1 Bring a large pot of salted water to a boil and begin cooking the spaghetti.

2 When the spaghetti has cooked for about 6 minutes, heat the olive oil over medium heat in a large pan.

3 Add the garlic and cook it slowly, until it gets nice and toasted: beige-brown and just a bit crispy, about 2 minutes.

4 Add the anchovy fillets and smash them up in the pan with a fork (you can also do the smashing up beforehand, in another vessel).

5 Add the red pepper flakes, thyme, rosemary, and Pernod, and cook together until the herbs release their aroma, about 30 seconds.

6 Add ½ cup of the pasta-cooking water and then the olives. Allow the sauce to reduce by half, about 30 seconds, then remove the pan from the heat.

7. Drain the pasta (but do not rinse it) and add it to the saucepan, mixing everything together well with tongs so that all the strands of pasta are well coated in the sauce.

8. Distribute the pasta and sauce in individual bowls, topping each portion with 1 tablespoon each of the Parmigiano-Reggiano and the Crumbs Yo! or panko breadcrumbs. Serve immediately.

SPRINGTIME SPAGHETTI CARBONARA WITH RAMPS

The key ingredient in this rich, crisp update on the classic dish is speck: dried, cold-smoked ham from the Südtirol region of northern Italy. The peas give the dish crunch, and the mildly garlicky ramps lend a tiny bit of bite, so the whole thing is balanced and complex. Ramps are one of those vegetables that have suddenly become trendy. I first learned about them when I spent a summer working in western Virginia: I went out foraging for mushrooms with some local guys, and they taught me how to pick ramps too. If they're not growing in your own oak forest, you can usually find them at farmers' markets or in good grocery stores in the spring. And if you can't find them at all, you can substitute the green parts of scallions.

TIMING: Superquick; 20 minutes

SERVES 4 TO 6

INGREDIENTS

2 cups fresh English peas, shelled

2 cups sugar snap peas

1 pound dried spaghetti

2 egg yolks

1 cup heavy cream

2 tablespoon extra-virgin olive oil

1 cup roughly chopped speck
    (or prosciutto or bacon), about
    ½ pound—try to find it in a chunk,
    rather than sliced

1 pound ramps, roots cut off, thoroughly
    washed, and cut in thirds (or green
    parts of scallions)

1 cup chicken stock (or water)

½ cup Parmigiano-Reggiano, plus extra
    for finishing

1½ teaspoons coarse-ground
    black pepper

½ teaspoon salt

METHOD

1 Bring a large pot of salted boiling water to a boil.

2 Blanch the English peas in the boiling water until they turn bright green, about 2 minutes. Remove them using a spider or long-handled strainer and immediately plunge them into a bowl of ice water to stop the cooking process. When they are cold, remove them from the water and reserve.

3 Clean the sugar snap peas by taking off the top corners and the string that runs along the top.

4 Blanch the sugar snaps in the boiling water until they turn bright green, about 2 minutes, and then give them the ice bath, following the same procedure you used for the English peas.

5 Begin cooking the pasta in the pea-blanching water. You're aiming for it to be finished by the end of step 9.

6 When the sugar snaps have cooled, cut them into thirds crosswise and reserve.

7 Beat the egg yolks and cream together in a bowl with a fork or whisk until they are well combined.

8 Heat the olive oil in a large pot over high heat. Add the speck (or prosciutto or bacon) and cook, stirring regularly, until the meat crisps up and releases its fat, about 3 minutes.

9 Add the ramps (or scallions) and the chicken stock.

10 When the pasta is cooked, drain but don't rinse it. Add the English peas and sugar snaps to the speck mixture. Stir well to combine, and then add the pasta and the cream mixture. Cook together, mixing well, so that the pasta becomes well coated with a well-combined sauce, about 1 minute. Your aim here is to have no extraneous sauce, so if it's too liquidy, turn the heat to high and allow the mixture to reduce a bit, stirring constantly, until the sauce sticks to the pasta.

11 Remove the pot from the heat and add the Parmigiano-Reggiano, pepper, and salt, adjusting the seasonings to your taste. Mix well.

12 Divide the pasta into individual bowls, using a big spoon to pull the yummy stuff out of the bottom of the pot and pile it on top of the pasta. Sprinkle generously with Parmigiano-Reggiano and serve immediately.

SQUASH TORTELLONI

In the Po Valley, *zucca*—pumpkin—is everywhere in the fall, and *tortelloni di zucca* appears on restaurant menus all along the via Emilia, the ancient Roman road that runs through the valley from Piacenza to the Adriatic coast. Sometimes it's good not to screw around too much with the classics, and this is definitely one of those times. The sauce I give you here is pretty much the Po Valley classic: brown butter, sage, and *mostarda di frutta* with crushed amaretti cookies (see the sidebar on page 153). I've made one important change: true Italian *zucca* is hard to find in the States, and American pumpkin varieties can be watery, so I use butternut squash instead. It's always great in this dish.

TIMING: This one's a project. As with all stuffed pastas, it's a lot easier to make the dough and filling on Day 1, then put the tortelloni together and finish the dish on Day 2.

SERVES 4 TO 6
INGREDIENTS

For the filling:

1 large or 2 small butternut squash
   (about 3 pounds total)

½ teaspoon salt

½ teaspoon coarse-ground black pepper

1 egg yolk

1 egg

2 tablespoons butter

6 sage leaves

½ cup heavy cream

2 tablespoons grated Parmigiano-
   Reggiano

For the pasta:

1 recipe Pasta Dough for Ravioli
   (page 297)

all-purpose flour for dusting

1 egg

>>>

METHOD
TO PREPARE THE FILLING:

1. Preheat the oven to 375°.

2. Cut the squash in half lengthwise. Scoop out the seeds and stringy bits and discard.

3. Place the squash on a baking rack over a baking tray, cut side up. Sprinkle with ¼ teaspoon each of salt and pepper, and place in the oven on the center rack. Bake the squash until it's very soft and liquid has collected in the seed cups, about 1½ hours, depending on your oven. Rotate the tray halfway through to ensure even baking.

4. Remove the squash from the oven and allow it to cool on the countertop until you can work with it.

5. Scoop the meat out of the squash; you should have about 3 cups. Put the squash meat in a food processor and add the egg and the egg yolk, but don't process it yet.

6. Heat the butter in a large pan on the stove on high heat, allowing it to bubble and turn golden brown, about 1½ minutes.

7. Add the sage and cook until it crackles, about 30 seconds.

8. Add the cream and allow the liquid to reduce by half, about 1 minute.

9. Add the cream mixture to the food processor, along with ¼ teaspoon each of salt and pepper and the Parmigiano-Reggiano. Combine the mixture on medium-high until smooth, about 1 minute.

>>>

To finish the dish:

2 tablespoons butter

2 tablespoons roughly chopped sage
   (about 8 leaves)

¼ teaspoon coarse-ground black pepper

2 tablespoons chopped mostarda
   di frutta (mustard fruit)

½ cup grated Parmigiano-Reggiano

2 amaretti cookies, crushed
   (2 tablespoons)

10 Allow the mixture to cool completely in a bowl in the fridge, covered with plastic wrap, for at least 2 hours. The filling will hold in the fridge for up to 2 days.

TO PREPARE THE TORTELLONI:

1 Remove the ravioli dough from the fridge and turn it out onto a well-floured surface. With a wooden rolling pin, roll the dough out into a square or a rectangle, so that it fits inside your pasta machine.

2 Flour the pasta to remove stickiness and roll it through the machine. Cut the resulting sheet of dough in half (so the final sheet doesn't get too long). Roll the pasta through the machine again, reducing the setting. Repeat until the dough is thin enough to allow you to see the

outline and color of your hand through it, but not so thin that it gets fragile: it should feel like a piece of velvet. At this point, run the dough through once more without changing the setting.

3. Make an egg wash by beating the egg together with 1 tablespoon of water.

4. Using a chef's knife or a dough cutter, cut the pasta lengthwise and then widthwise, so that your sheet of pasta is divided into 2-inch-by-2-inch squares.

5. Place about a teaspoon of tortelloni filling in the center of each pasta square.

6. Using a pastry brush, sweep some of the egg wash lightly over 2 edges of 1 of the squares in an L shape, being careful not to brush the filling.

>>>

7 Here's the fun part: Fold the pasta square into a triangle, so that your egg-washed sides meet your un-egg-washed sides. Squeeze the corners together. Pick up the tortellono and, using your fingers, squeeze the open sides closed to form a pasta pocket. Hold the pocket by one corner of the long side of the triangle, grasping it between your thumb and forefinger. Take the other corner of the long side and roll it around your forefinger, so that the pasta is wrapped around the end of your finger (like a triangle-shaped ring), with the pointy end toward your knuckle and both corners of the long side pinned under your thumb. Squeeze the two corners together to make sure they stick. The resulting tortellono should have the shape of a pope's hat.

8 Repeat steps 6 and 7 for the remainder of the tortelloni.

You can freeze the tortelloni at this point if you're not serving them right away (they'll keep for up to 2 weeks in an airtight container), but if you're moving on, put them on a plate and proceed directly to cooking.

TO FINISH THE DISH:

1 Bring a large pot of salted water to a boil and add the pasta.

2 When the pasta is in the water (but not before), melt the butter in a large pan over high heat until it foams, about 1 minute.

3 Add the sage and continue cooking together until the butter begins to brown, 30 seconds or so.

4 Add the black pepper and the mostarda di frutta and mix together. Stir or shake the pan as the mixture cooks together until the ingredients are well combined, about 2 minutes.

5 When the tortelloni are just cooked (they'll bob up to the top of the water—about 1 to 2 minutes), remove them from the pot with a spider or slotted spoon and add them to the butter-herb mixture, along with 2 to 3 tablespoons of the pasta water. (The starchy water helps provide the sexiness in the mouth-feel department.) Remove the pan from the heat and spoon the sauce over the pasta to coat it thoroughly.

6 Divide the pasta into individual bowls and sprinkle liberally with more Parmigiano-Reggiano. Serve immediately.

AMARETTI

Amaretti are crisp, almondy, bittersweet cookies (hence the name: *amaro* means "bitter"). I love crunch, so I crush 'em up as a topping for gelato and granitas—and believe it or not, we throw 'em in main dishes like squash tortelloni too. No worries about unexpected nut allergies here: the "almond" flavor actually comes from ground apricot kernels. As with everything in Italy, they come with a story, and of course it's romantic, unprovable, and really, really old. It goes like this: amaretti were invented by two young lovers, Giuseppe and Osolina. Seems the Cardinal of Milan was making a surprise visit to Saronno.

Everyone was expected to come up with a welcoming gift, but Giuseppe and Osolina, too busy getting busy with each other, missed the news and were caught empty-handed. In desperation (the Cardinal wasn't known for his Christian charity to those who failed to feed him), they ground up the piths of the apricots they'd been eating with some sugar and egg whites and baked 'em, hoping for the best. The Cardinal was such a fan, he gave the young couple his blessing, and so Giuseppe and Osolina live on in their cookies: amaretti are always wrapped in pairs, together forever, the sweetness tempering the bitter bits—just like true love.

STROZZAPRETI WITH SAUSAGE, GRAPES, AND RED WINE

Grapes and pasta? What, are you outta yer freakin' mind?

Okay, so maybe it's not exactly a combination that leaps to mind when you think "pasta," but you know what? These are, in fact, all the flavors of the Italian grape-harvest time: sage, meaty spicy sausage, and, of course, sweet young grape juice. I've just put it all together. It's totally delicious. Trust me.

I like to use two kinds of sausage for this dish: half sweet, half spicy. But if you're not a fan of spicy food, just tip the balance toward the sweet stuff, or eliminate the spicy sausage entirely.

Strozzapreti pasta looks like little twisted pieces of rope. It's one of two great pastas named for clergymen who have come to unfortunate ends: *strangolapreti* means "strangled priest," and the name of our pasta here, *strozzapreti*, translates to "choked priest." One old Italian chef claimed this had something to do with the land taxes that Italians paid to priests back in the day: the guy who first came up with the name apparently did so as he was serving a bowl of it to his local clergyman. As a Catholic-school boy, I found this explanation hilarious—but strangely enough, every time I cook this pasta, I feel a vague desire to drop everything and go to confession.

TIMING: Superquick—not counting the overnight grape maceration

SERVES 4 TO 6

INGREDIENTS

1 cup seedless red grapes (not the seedless Thompson variety: something small and sweet), cut in half lengthwise

1 cup dry red wine

¼ cup sugar

2 tablespoons red wine vinegar

1 pound dried strozzapreti pasta

3 tablespoons olive oil

1½ pounds Italian sausage (about 4 links, 2 spicy and 2 sweet, or the combination of your choice), casings cut away and meat roughly chopped

1 medium onion, chopped (about 1 cup)

10 sage leaves, roughly chopped

2 tablespoons butter

½ cup grated pecorino cheese, plus extra for sprinkling

½ teaspoon coarse-ground black pepper

1 tablespoon chopped Italian parsley

METHOD

DAY 1:

1   Combine the grapes, wine, sugar, and vinegar in an airtight container, and store in the fridge so that the grapes macerate for at least 8 hours or overnight.

DAY 2:

1   Put a large pot of salted water on to boil for the pasta.

2   Remove the grape mixture from the fridge, place it in a medium saucepot, and bring it up to a boil over high heat. Cook the mixture at a boil until the liquid has reduced by half, about 10 minutes.

3   When the pasta water comes to a boil, add the strozzapreti and cook until the pasta is just al dente (follow the directions on the box, subtracting 1 minute from the cooking time).

4   Heat the olive oil in a large pot over medium heat. Add the meat and begin to brown it for about 3 to 4 minutes, stirring and breaking up the meat as you go.

5   Add the onion and continue cooking, stirring well, until the sausage and onion have cooked through, about 5 to 7 minutes.

6 Add the sage and stir to combine.

7 Add the grape mixture and stir well.

8 When the pasta is cooked, drain it (but do not rinse it). Add the pasta to the pot with the grape-and-sausage mixture and cook together so the flavors combine and the pasta cooks a bit more, about 1½ minutes.

9 Remove the saucepot from the heat and add the butter, cheese, black pepper, and parsley. Sprinkle with more cheese and serve immediately.

TAGLIATELLE WITH HERBS, CAPRINO, AND MARINATED TOMATOES

This sauce may look like a standard-issue alfredo sauce, but there's a whole other thing going on tastewise. This isn't the heavy '80s staple at all: instead, you get a real tang from the goat cheese, the vinegar, and the tomatoes, plus freshness from the herbs.

TIMING: Superquick

SERVES 4 TO 6
INGREDIENTS

For the marinated tomato topping:

2 cups cherry tomatoes (preferably Sungold or Sweet 100 variety), halved

2 shallots, minced fine

1 tablespoon balsamic vinegar

1 tablespoon red wine vinegar

2 tablespoons extra-virgin olive oil

¼ teaspoon each of salt and pepper

2 tablespoons chopped parsley

For the pasta and sauce:

¼ cup milk

¼ cup cream

½ cup chicken stock (or vegetable stock or water)

1 cup caprino or other fresh soft goat cheese

1 teaspoon fresh thyme leaves

1 teaspoon chopped fresh rosemary

1 teaspoon pepper

½ teaspoon salt

1 pound tagliatelle, preferably fresh

To finish the dish:

¼ cup grated Parmigiano-Reggiano

⅓ cup roughly chopped basil

METHOD

TO PREPARE THE MARINATED TOMATO TOPPING:

1. Combine the tomatoes, shallots, both vinegars, olive oil, salt, pepper, and parsley in a bowl and allow the tomatoes to marinate while you prepare the rest of the recipe.

TO PREPARE THE PASTA AND SAUCE:

1. Put a large pot of salted water on to boil for the pasta.

2. Bring the milk, cream, and stock (or water) to a simmer over medium heat in a large saucepan. Whisk in the goat cheese and continue whisking until the mixture thickens into a sauce—just a few seconds.

3. Add the thyme, rosemary, pepper, and salt. Mix to combine, then remove the saucepan from the heat.

4. Cook the pasta. Fresh tagliatelle cooks very quickly—it'll be al dente in no more than 1½ minutes. If you're using the dried stuff, follow the directions on the box, subtracting 1 minute from the cooking time.

5. Transfer the pasta directly from the water to the saucepan with tongs (or if it's easier, drain the pasta and then transfer it). Do not rinse the pasta.

TO FINISH THE DISH:

1. Return the saucepan to the heat. Cook the sauce and pasta together over medium heat until the pasta is well coated with the sauce, about 1 minute.

2. Remove the saucepan from the heat and add the Parmigiano-Reggiano and basil. Mix well to combine.

3. Distribute the dish into individual plates. Spoon the tomato mixture over the top and sprinkle a little of the marinating juice over each plate. Top with more Parmigiano-Reggiano, if you like.

ZITI WITH TUNA, RED ONIONS, AND CANNELLINI BEANS

You might think of tuna-and-cannellini-bean salad as the Italian cousin of that very American invention known as Tuna Casserole—but this was way back before Tuna Casserole started hanging out with that bad influence Canned Cream of Mushroom Soup and went so terribly wrong. The Italians don't use canned soup in their version: they make do with fresh herbs, beautiful canned tuna in oil, and, of course, wine. In this dish, the capers give a real salty, oceany feel, and the lemon keeps the flavors fresh and crisp. I also incorporate a trick I learned at a restaurant I worked at in Italy. The crew would make the salad for lunch for family meal and store the leftovers in the walk-in. After dinner service, they would take the leftover salad, sauté it in olive oil, and mix it up with pasta. *Ecco-la*: a perfect comfort-food meal at the end of a long night.

The key to this pasta salad is the olive oil for finishing: even if you don't bother with good olive oil anywhere else, you want to use it here.

TIMING: Superfast

SERVES 4 TO 6
INGREDIENTS

For the pasta:

1 pound dried penne

1 teaspoon extra-virgin olive oil

For the bean mixture:

2 tablespoons extra-virgin olive oil

1 medium red onion, sliced thin

½ teaspoon salt

¼ teaspoon red pepper flakes

¼ cup white wine

1 15-ounce can cannellini beans, drained

To finish the dish:

1 cup halved fresh cherry tomatoes

1½ cups canned tuna in oil, preferably
    Sicilian or Spanish

½ cup halved pitted Calamata olives

juice and zest of 3 lemons

2 tablespoons roughly chopped
    fresh parsley

¼ cup roughly chopped basil
    (about 12 leaves)

>>>

METHOD
TO PREPARE THE PASTA:

1 Bring a large pot of salted water to a boil.

2 Cook the penne until it's just al dente, stirring occasionally (follow the directions on the box, subtracting 1 minute from the cooking time and tasting frequently toward the end of the cooking to avoid mushiness).

3 Drain the pasta, but do not rinse it.

4 Add the teaspoon of olive oil to the drained pasta in the colander to prevent sticking while you finish the rest of the dish. Mix well.

TO PREPARE THE BEAN MIXTURE:

1 Dry the pasta pot with a towel or by heating it for 30 seconds over the stove.

2 Turn the heat to medium-low and heat the 2 tablespoons olive oil. Add the red onion and salt, and cook until the onion begins to soften, about 3 minutes, stirring to prevent burning or sticking.

3 Add the red pepper flakes and white wine and stir well to combine. Continue cooking until the wine is reduced to a glaze and the onions are shiny, about 2 minutes.

4 Add the cannellini beans and then the pasta, mixing well to combine. Cook for another 1 to 2 minutes.

TO FINISH THE DISH:

1 Remove the pot from the heat and add the cherry tomatoes, tuna, olives, lemon juice and zest, parsley, basil, capers, and oregano. Mix well to combine.

2 Mix in the olive oil, salt, and pepper.

3 Serve immediately, sprinkled with more olive oil and Crumbs Yo! or panko breadcrumbs.

2 tablespoons capers
1 teaspoon dried oregano, preferably on the branch (Sicilian or Calabrian)
¼ cup extra-virgin olive oil, plus extra for sprinkling
¼ teaspoon each of salt and coarse-ground black pepper
2 tablespoons Crumbs Yo! (page 291) or panko breadcrumbs

3

{ SECONDI }

CHICKEN LEG CACCIATORE WITH SWEET PEPPERS, FENNEL, AND GREEN OLIVES

I love chicken cacciatore. When I opened my last place, some very particular food aficionados (who shall remain nameless) busted my chops about it, as did some chefs (who shall also remain nameless). "I can't believe you put something as boring as chicken cacciatore on a serious restaurant menu!" they would holler at me. I would smile politely and walk away. Now, granted, chicken cacciatore is not molecular gastronomy; it's not a French preparation with forty-two ingredients that takes three days and a crew of twelve to assemble; it's not some magical food in which the chicken legs jump up and dance on the table. It's just a friggin' great dish, simple and delicious—and if it's made well, there's nothing boring about it. I like to think that chicken cacciatore AC-style is the opposite of dull. It's one of my favorite home dishes—and people ask for it all the time, so I guess I'm not the only one who thinks so.

Some people make chicken cacciatore with peppers; some incorporate tomatoes; others go with olives. Here I use all three. I roast the chicken separately and then marry the sauce and the roast chicken afterward, so all the flavors and textures get their due. I've also used spicy Italian sausage here. I love sausage in this dish, but if you're not a big fan of pork, you can always leave it out.

TIMING: About 1 hour

SERVES 4
INGREDIENTS

For the chicken:

6 chicken legs

1 teaspoon salt

½ teaspoon coarse-ground black pepper

½ teaspoon dried oregano, preferably on the branch (Sicilian or Calabrian)

1 tablespoon extra-virgin olive oil

Optional:

1 batch of Brine (page 290)

For the cacciatore stew:

2 tablespoons extra-virgin olive oil

2 links fresh hot Italian sausage (about ¼ pound), sliced into ½-inch pieces

1 onion, sliced thin

1 small bulb of fennel, sliced thin

¼ teaspoon salt

1 clove garlic, sliced Goodfellas thin

>>>

METHOD
TO BRINE THE CHICKEN (OPTIONAL):

1. Marinate the chicken legs in the brine in the fridge for 30 minutes.

2. Remove the chicken legs from the brine, rinse, and pat dry.

TO PREPARE THE CHICKEN:

1. Turn the broiler on.

2. Season both sides of the chicken legs with the salt, pepper, oregano, and olive oil.

3. Place the chicken legs on a broiler pan on the middle rack and broil until the chicken skin is slightly rendered, about 2½ minutes.

4. Rotate the pan (to ensure even cooking) and broil until the tops of the legs are crispy, about 2½ minutes.

5. Turn the broiler off, turn the oven on to 375°, and bake the chicken legs until they're cooked through, about 15 minutes (when you cut into a piece, it should be juicy but there should be no red bits).

TO PREPARE THE CACCIATORE STEW:

1. Heat the olive oil over medium heat in a large saucepan. Add the sausage and cook to render the fat, about 2 minutes.

2. Add the onion, fennel, and salt. Cover the pan and let the mixture stew until the vegetables are just slightly soft, about 3 minutes.

3. Add the garlic and stir well to combine all the ingredients. Cook together uncovered until the flavors have combined, about 1 minute.

4. Add the wine and cook until it evaporates, 30 seconds or so.

5. Add the peppers and the tomatoes and cook, uncovered, until the tomatoes are broken down, the vegetables have softened, and the mixture comes together as a sauce, about 20 minutes.

6. Add the green olives, mix well, and continue cooking until the flavors are combined, about 1 minute.

7. Remove the saucepan from the heat and add the basil, parsley, and cooked chicken legs. Mix everything together, being sure to coat the chicken well with the sauce.

8. Serve immediately, with generous helpings of the sauce poured over the chicken.

¼ cup white wine

3 roasted peppers (see How to Roast Peppers the Easy Way, page 294), red and/or yellow, cut into strips—about 1 cup

10 good-quality whole Italian canned tomatoes, preferably San Marzano (about one 28-ounce can)

¾ cup pitted green olives (preferably marinated), halved

¼ cup roughly chopped fresh basil

¼ cup roughly chopped fresh Italian parsley

GRILLED SWORDFISH WITH ORANGE AND OLIVES

Swordfish gets a bum rap because of rumors about overfishing, but don't believe the hype: the swordfish-fishing industry is one of the most highly regulated in the country. (If you're interested, you can check out the National Marine Fisheries Service's "Fishwatch" page at www.nmfs.noaa.gov). Plus, it's delicious and not very difficult to cook, and as you'll see in this recipe, olives and swordfish are like beans and rice: perfect together.

I like to do this dish with spicy Calabrian anchovies, but they can be really hard to find in America if you're not a spoiled New York City chef, so here I use regular anchovies and add a little harissa (if you're lucky enough to find the real Calabrian deal, use those instead). The Crumbs Yo! are key: add them right at the end, so the crunch provides a contrast, bringing out the sweet, sour, salt, and spice.

You want to cook swordfish till it's just opaque in the middle and let it rest for a minute or two off the heat, so the temperature evens out; if you cook it till it's white all the way through, it tastes like sawdust. If swordfish isn't available from your local fishmonger, use tuna or mahi-mahi instead.

TIMING: Superquick; about 30 minutes

SERVES 4

INGREDIENTS

For the olive topping:

4 anchovy fillets, chopped

3 tablespoons chopped olives (preferably oil-cured)

¾ teaspoon harissa

¼ cup extra-virgin olive oil

2 tablespoons pine nuts, toasted and chopped

2 tablespoons chopped fresh parsley

zest of 1 orange

juice of ½ orange

zest of 1 lemon

¼ cup Crumbs Yo! (page 291) or panko breadcrumbs

For the oranges:

2 oranges (preferably navel or Valencia)

14 whole parsley leaves

a pinch of salt

>>>

METHOD

TO PREPARE THE OLIVE TOPPING:

1. Combine the anchovies, olives, harissa, olive oil, pine nuts, parsley, orange juice, orange zest, and lemon zest in a bowl.

2. Stir together until all the ingredients are thoroughly combined. Reserve.

TO PREPARE THE ORANGES:

1. Segment the oranges: With the peel still on, slice the ends off an orange. Set it on one end and, with a small sharp knife, slice off the peel and the white pith together. Holding the peeled orange in your hand, cut along the inside of each white segmenting line. Remove the "supremes" (the meat, the best part) to a bowl, leaving all the membranes attached to the "skeleton." Squeeze all the juice out of this skeleton into the bowl with the supremes, then discard the skeleton. Repeat with the other orange.

2. Add the parsley and salt to the bowl and mix well.

TO PREPARE THE SWORDFISH:

1. Preheat the grill or broiler. If you're using the broiler, set a rack on the middle setting in the oven.

>>>

For the swordfish:

4 swordfish fillets, about 6 ounces each

1 tablespoon extra-virgin olive oil

¼ teaspoon salt

½ teaspoon coarse-ground black pepper

2 Coat the swordfish fillets on both sides with the olive oil and season well with the salt and pepper.

3 Cook the fillets on the grill or on a roasting rack under the broiler until they're grilled on one side, about 3 minutes.

4 Turn the fillets over and continue grilling or broiling until they're white on the outside, just slightly opaque on the inside, and firm to the touch but with a bit of give, about another 3 minutes. Remove the fish from the grill or oven.

TO FINISH THE DISH:

1 Place the swordfish fillets on individual plates. Cover each fillet with 1 to 1½ tablespoons of the olive topping and about 1 teaspoon each of the Crumbs Yo! or panko breadcrumbs.

2 Add a portion of the oranges with some of the juice from the bowl to each plate. Serve immediately.

TAGGIASCA OLIVES

There are a lot of great olive varieties in Italy, but Taggiasca olives are something special. They're grown in Arma di Taggia, on the Ligurian coast between San Remo and Imperia. The olives are named after the town, or after the river, or maybe after the mountain: it's hard to know, since everything seems to be called Taggia. Though they're not exactly natives—all "Italian" olives came over from Asia Minor, way back in the mists of time—they certainly landed in the right place: the rocky Ligurian seaside cliffs are the ideal environment for olive trees, and the mineral-rich soil gives the fruit a rich flavor. Taggiascas are a little like Nicoise olives, only meatier, and with a stronger olive taste, since Taggiascas are stored in olive oil instead of brine. That's the reason I use them so much at the restaurant: the flavor is deep and earthy, but without the tang of salt-cured olives. They're great for olive paste and tapenade, and we also use them in a lot of main-course recipes, like Lamb Shank with Lemon, Oregano, and Olives (page 173). I get my Taggiasca olives from my friend Marco Bonaldo, who sells olives from local growers through his company, Terre Bormane in Arma di Taggia. When I went to visit him, Marco took me up to the olive orchards, and I watched workers collect olives from nets below the trees. Unlike apples and other, more delicate fruit, olives know their own mind. They aren't picked from the branches. They drop when they're good and ready.

When we landed in the Palermo airport—my first time in Sicily—we were starving. It was after nine P.M., we'd been traveling all day with nothing to eat, and the airport had exactly no food in it. (On the other hand, there was plenty of local color: soldiers sweating in their fatigues, fondling their weapons; short, wide dudes with slicked-back hair; women in brightly colored spike heels, plunging tops, and piles of bling.)

We'd heard horror stories about the legendary Palermo traffic, and from the air we'd seen something resembling a long, skinny parking lot leading all the way from the airport to the city. Way too hungry to deal with traffic, we headed the other way, west to Mondello, a seaside hangout for rich Palermitans on the peninsula. It was a warm, clear night, and the narrow sidewalks were crowded with big families, teenage girls in fluorescent miniskirts and chandelier earrings, teenage boys with jeans and crucifixes, old men in caps, vendors selling CDs and jewelry, entrepreneurs offering to "watch" your parked car in exchange for a "watching fee." And there was food everywhere: gelato stands, panini carts, pizza shops, and one seafood restaurant after another. We picked the first promising-looking place. The surly waiter (in Mondello, all waiters are surly) grudgingly allocated us a table on the patio, which was packed with blinged-out families feasting and table-hopping. By now desperately hungry, we scanned our burgundy-colored, laminated menus. The list read like an old-style Little Italy menu: shrimp with cacciacavallo, baked branzino alla parmigiana . . . I felt like I'd been hit in the head with a culinary two-by-four. Could it actually be true? Was all that "American-Italian" food I'd always thought of as tacky and inauthentic actually . . . Sicilian?

When the waiter finally quit flirting with the girls at the table down the way and wandered over to us, I ordered spaghetti with clams and a glass of white wine.

My spaghetti arrived. I wielded my fork. The waiter, faster than I, wielded the cheese grater.

Cheese? With seafood? You've got to be kidding me. Every Italian I had ever met had made it clear that Americans who grate cheese over everything were barbarians. "*Fa schifo!*" they would say, not quietly— "Disgusting!"—as they watched some clueless Yank smother a seafood dish with parmesan. The cheese, they insisted, killed the delicate flavors of the seafood. A Roman friend of mine who ran a restaurant in the East Village actually put a notice on her menu detailing her policies: "No fat-free milk. No salt and pepper on the table. No grated cheese on seafood pastas." These were hanging crimes. I have seen diners walk out of her restaurant in midmeal over the cheese-on-pasta issue, yelling things like, "What do you think this is, *Big Night*?" She never stopped them, never gave an inch—just shrugged, Roman-style, and let them go.

But that night in Sicily, too stunned and weakened by hunger to resist, I allowed the surly waiter to shake a handful of Parmigiano-Reggiano over my spaghetti. I took a deep breath. I raised my fork, opened my mouth, chewed. The subtle brininess of the clams and the quiet warmth of the pasta opened out, punched up by the cheese. I could hear, somewhere, my old friend Pilar screaming, "*Fa schifo!*"—I could picture her violently grabbing the fork right out of my hand—but I ate it anyway. Every bite.

So these days, I serve dishes like Ligurian Bass with Clams (see page 168) with a little bit of cheese in the broth. And when you come to my place, I'll shave cheese on anything you want.

LIGURIAN BASS WITH CLAMS

This dish is a really flavorful way to cook bass—plus it has the added bonus of looking a lot more complicated and sophisticated than it really is. It won't take you very long, but it does involve the walk-and-chew-gum challenge: you need to do a lot of things simultaneously to make it work, and you'll have three pots going on the stove at the same time. Be sure to do all of your prep work first so you don't have to stop to clean the clams or slice the garlic while something else is cooking. If you have some Shrimp Meatballs (page 62) hanging out in your freezer, you can add them to this dish: throw 8 to 12 of 'em in the pan with the fish about 3 minutes before the bass is done.

TIMING: About 1 hour, if you manage to do everything at the same time

SERVES 4

INGREDIENTS

For the croutons:

2 slices day-old sourdough or foccacia
    bread, cut into bite-sized pieces (2
    cups)
1 tablespoon extra-virgin olive oil
a pinch each of salt and coarse-ground
    black pepper

For the vegetables:

¼ pound fingerling potatoes
    (about 6 potatoes)
1 pound green beans or haricots verts
    (about 1½ cups), ends trimmed,
    sliced in half

For the broth:

2 tablespoons extra-virgin olive oil
1 clove garlic, sliced Goodfellas thin
¼ teaspoon red pepper flakes
2 pounds littleneck or Manila clams,
    rinsed well
½ cup white wine

>>>

METHOD

TO PREPARE THE CROUTONS:

1. Preheat the oven to 350°.

2. Spread the bread pieces on a baking sheet or in a small sauté pan. Pour the olive oil overtop and season with the salt and pepper.

3. Bake on the middle oven rack until the croutons are crispy, about 10 minutes. Reserve.

TO PREPARE THE VEGETABLES:

1. Fill a large pot with water, add the potatoes, and bring it up to a boil. Cook the potatoes at a low boil until a fork goes into them easily, about 15 minutes.

2. Meanwhile, bring another large pot of salted water to a boil for the green beans.

3. Blanch the beans until they are dark green and just tender, about 3 minutes. Remove the beans from the pot with a spider or large slotted spoon and place in a bowl of ice water to stop the cooking process. When the beans have cooled, drain them and reserve.

4. When the potatoes have cooked, remove them from the pot and allow them to cool to the touch, then cut them into thirds with the skins on.

TO PREPARE THE BROTH:

1. Heat a large pot on the stove on high heat.

2. Add the olive oil, garlic, red pepper flakes, clams, and wine, in that order. Cover the pot and allow the mixture to cook until the clams steam open, about 2 minutes.

3. Remove the pot from the heat and then remove the clams from the pot to a bowl—but don't discard the liquid! Cover the bowl with plastic wrap and reserve.

TO PREPARE THE BASS:

1. When the croutons are done, turn the oven up to 375°.

2. Add the clam juice to the broth the clams have cooked in.

3. Season the bass fillets on both sides with the salt and pepper and place them in an ovenproof dish with high sides. Pour the clam liquid over the top. Cover the dish with a lid or aluminum foil and place it in the oven on the lower-middle rack.

4. When the fillets have begun turning white on top (about 5 minutes), turn them over and return them to the oven.

5. Continue baking until the fish is white and moist all the way through, about 5 more minutes.

TO FINISH THE DISH:

1. Place each piece of bass in a medium-sized individual bowl. Distribute the clams among the bowls.

2. Add the potatoes, beans, and Pesto (or basil) to the liquid that the fish cooked in and mix well to combine.

3. Pour the mixture over the fish and clams in each bowl. Top with the croutons, and serve immediately.

For the bass:

1½ cups clam juice

4 striped bass or black bass fillets,
    6 to 8 ounces each (2 pounds total)

a pinch each of salt and coarse-ground
    black pepper

To finish the dish:

⅓ cup Pesto (page 288) or
    ½ cup chopped basil

RACK OF LAMB GLAZED
WITH CITRUS AND VINEGAR

Mention rack of lamb to most people and they immediately think of the fancy hotel dish, topped with curly decorative vegetables and carved tableside by a guy in a tux. That's too bad, because great rack of lamb rocks. It ain't cheap, but it's definitely worth the cash if you do it right.

When I make rack of lamb at home, I cook it whole and cut it later, both because it's easier and because you can get the fat really crispy. The marinade and glaze here give the lamb a nice kick, while the sugar in the citrus caramelizes on the outside of the lamb (don't get freaked out by the "burnt" color) and sweetens everything up. When you carve the meat, make sure you leave the fat intact: that's where all the flavor hides out.

TIMING: No big deal; after the 2-hour marinade, it takes about 30 minutes

SERVES 4 TO 6
INGREDIENTS

For the lamb:

2 teaspoons whole fennel seed
    (or 1 teaspoon ground)

juice of 2 lemons

juice of 2 oranges

1 clove garlic, peeled

2 tablespoons extra-virgin olive oil

1 tablespoon harissa or crushed red
    pepper flakes

2 full racks of lamb, about 2 to 2¼
    pounds each (plan on 4 bones per
    person)

1½ tablespoons salt

½ teaspoon coarse-ground black pepper

For the glaze:

½ cup balsamic vinegar

½ cup vin cotto (if you can't find vin cotto,
    up the balsamic vinegar to 1 cup)

¼ teaspoon red pepper flakes

½ tablespoon finely chopped rosemary

sea salt for sprinkling

METHOD

TO PREPARE THE LAMB:

1. Toast the fennel seeds in a small pan over low heat until they become fragrant, about 2 minutes. (If you're using the ground fennel, don't toast it.)

2. Blend the fennel seeds (or ground fennel), lemon juice, orange juice, garlic, olive oil, and harissa or red pepper flakes in the blender on medium until combined, about 30 seconds.

3. Place the racks of lamb in a large container and pour the mixture over the top. Cover with plastic wrap and place in the fridge to marinate for at least 2 hours—the longer the meat rests in the marinade the better, up to 8 hours.

4. Turn the broiler or grill on to high.

5. Remove the lamb from the fridge and allow it to come to room temperature on the counter, at least 30 minutes. Reserve the marinade.

6. Season the lamb on both sides with the salt and pepper, place it on a roasting rack, and put it under the broiler, on the middle rack, or on the grill with the cap of fat facing down.

7. Broil the lamb until the fat cap starts to caramelize, about 3 minutes. Rotate the pan and continue broiling as it browns, about 2½ minutes more. Flip the lamb racks over and continue broiling until the fat on top has started to caramelize and render, about 5 more minutes.

>>>

8 Turn the oven to 400°. Remove the lamb from the oven, brush it with the marinade on both sides, and then return it to the oven. Cook until your desired level of doneness: about 20 to 25 minutes for medium-rare (or 115°F on a meat thermometer). Remove the lamb from the oven and allow it to rest on the roasting rack for 20 minutes, so the meat becomes tender and juicy.

TO PREPARE THE GLAZE:

1 Combine the balsamic vinegar, vin cotto, and red pepper flakes in a small pot over high heat and allow the mixture to reduce by half, about 8 minutes. (Be sure to ventilate the kitchen well while you do this.)

2 Remove the pot from the heat; add the chopped rosemary and mix to combine. The glaze should taste sweet, sour, spicy, and herby all at once.

TO FINISH THE DISH:

1 Cut the chops between the bones.

2 Brush the lamb with the vinegar glaze and sprinkle liberally with sea salt. Serve immediately.

LAMB SHANK WITH LEMON, OREGANO, AND OLIVES

I've braised thousands—no, tens of thousands—of lamb shanks since I turned pro as a teenager. This recipe is one of my favorites. It's a one-pot-cooking version, and though the ingredient section looks longer than your average lamb-shank shopping list, you've probably got just about everything you need in your spice rack.

TIMING: Minor project

SERVES 4
INGREDIENTS

4 lamb shanks (1½ pounds each)

1 tablespoon salt

½ teaspoon pepper

2 tablespoons extra-virgin olive oil

1 medium onion, roughly chopped
(1 cup)

1 carrot, roughly chopped into
2-inch chunks

1 stalk celery, roughly chopped into
2-inch chunks

1 large ripe beefsteak tomato, chopped
into eighths

2 cloves garlic, smashed

1 tablespoon tomato paste

1 tablespoon all-purpose flour

peel of 1 lemon

¼ teaspoon red pepper flakes

¼ teaspoon ground fennel seed

2 dried bay leaves

1 sprig thyme

1 sprig rosemary

1 cup dry red wine

2½ cups chicken broth

½ cup oil-cured black olives, halved

1 tablespoon vin cotto or balsamic
vinegar

1 tablespoon dried oregano, preferably
on the branch (Sicilian or Calabrian)

zest of 1 lemon (fine zested, using a
microplane or box grater)

METHOD

1. Preheat the oven to 375°.

2. Season the lamb shanks on both sides with the salt and pepper.

3. Heat the olive oil over high heat in a large, deep cast-iron pan or oven-safe braising pot. (Make sure your cooking vessel has a tight-fitting lid.)

4. Add the lamb shanks and allow them to brown (about 15 to 20 minutes), turning the shanks a different way every 4 to 5 minutes to ensure even browning. Remove the lamb shanks from the pot and set aside, leaving the pot on the heat.

5. Add the onion, carrot, and celery to the pot. Stir the vegetables around to coat them in the fat in the bottom of the pan, and allow them to cook, stirring occasionally to avoid sticking, until they are soft and browned, about 5 minutes.

6. Add the tomato and garlic. Mix well and continue cooking until the tomato pieces have softened, about 2 minutes.

7. Add the tomato paste. Mix well and cook until the tomato paste caramelizes slightly on the bottom of the pan, about 1 minute. Add the flour, mix well, and cook until the liquid in the pan combines with the flour and forms a paste, about 1 minute.

8. Add the lemon peel, red pepper flakes, fennel seed, bay leaves, thyme, rosemary, and wine. Stir to combine. Turn the heat all the way up and cook the mixture until the wine reduces and glazes the vegetables, about 3 to 5 minutes.

9. Add the broth, return the lamb shanks to the pot, and bring the mixture to a low boil. Cover the pot and put it in the oven on the lower middle rack. Braise the meat until it starts to fall apart and a sharp

>>>

knife slides cleanly into the fleshiest parts (there will be some resistance where there's a lot of fat), about 3 hours total. When the bottom sides of the shanks are dark brown on the edges (about 1 hour into the braising process), turn the shanks over in the pot, so that they cook evenly.

10. When the lamb shanks are done, remove them from the pot using a slotted spoon and place them on a platter.

11. Strain the sauce through a fine strainer into a bowl, preserving the liquid. Be sure to push the sauce through the strainer so all the goodies come through.

12. Return the strained sauce to the pot. Add the olives, turn the heat to medium, and bring the sauce up to a simmer.

13. Add the vin cotto or balsamic vinegar and the oregano. Mix well to blend and cook together to meld the flavors, 1 to 2 minutes.

14. Remove the pot from the heat and add the lemon zest. Season the sauce with salt and pepper if you like. Mix well. Pour the sauce over the lamb shanks on the platter and serve immediately.

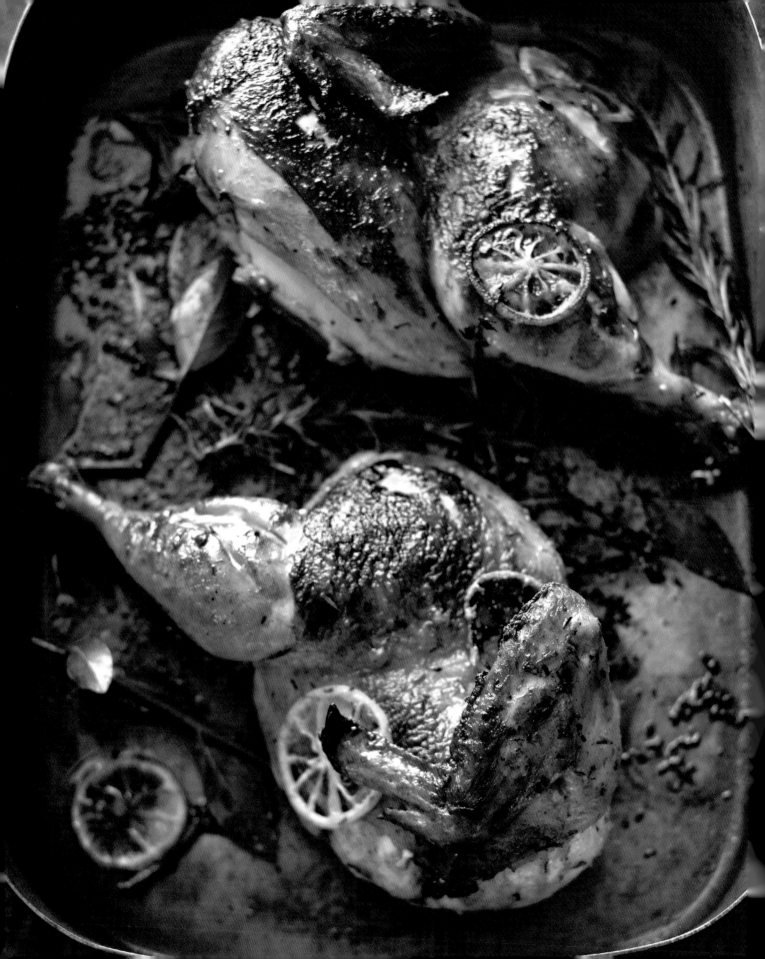

MARINATED CHICKEN ALLA GRIGLIA

This is a simple marinated chicken—I used to make it all the time at home. The first time I tried this baby out, one of my cooks said to me, "Chef! It tastes just like you marinated the chicken in Wishbone salad dressing!" I don't care what anyone says: I think this marinade rocks. Left overnight and grilled the next day, the chicken becomes tender, garlicky, and herbaceous, with a deep, tangy flavor. It pairs well with all sorts of accompaniments. In the summer I like it with Zucchini Bagna Calda (page 237) and a glass of white wine. In the colder months, I pair it with Potatoes Girarrosto-Style (page 226) and Escarole Calabrese (page 216) for a seriously soul-satisfying winter meal.

TIMING: An overnight marinate, plus about ½ hour of cooking time

SERVES 4

INGREDIENTS

For the marinade:

¼ cup roasted garlic purée (use the technique from Garlic Dressing, page 293)

½ cup rice vinegar or white wine vinegar

¼ cup extra-virgin olive oil

¼ cup grapeseed oil or corn oil

2 tablespoons dried oregano, preferably on the branch (Sicilian or Calabrian)

2 tablespoons chopped rosemary

1 lemon, thinly sliced

1 teaspoon red pepper flakes

2 tablespoons salt

1 teaspoon coarse-ground black pepper

1 tablespoon sugar

For the chicken:

2 whole chickens, halved

½ teaspoon each of salt and coarse-ground black pepper

METHOD

1. Combine all the marinade ingredients in a bowl and mix well.

2. Place the chicken halves in a large container and pour the marinade over the top. Cover with plastic wrap and marinate in the fridge for at least 8 hours, or overnight.

3. Fire up the grill or preheat the broiler.

4. Remove the chickens from the marinade (but don't wipe the herbs off; they're delicious charred right on the skin). Season with more salt and pepper.

5. If you're using a grill: Place the chickens skin-side down and grill them on high. After 2 minutes, turn the halves 45°. After another 2 minutes, flip the halves over. After another 2 minutes, turn the halves 45° again. Turn the heat down to medium and cook the chicken until the juice runs clear when you stick a leg with a knife, about 20 minutes, depending on your grill.

OR

If you're using a broiler: Place the chickens on a roasting rack and broil them until the skins are crisp, about 5 minutes. Reduce the heat to 425° and bake the chicken until the juice runs clear when you stick a leg with a knife, about 20 minutes.

6. Serve immediately, with the vegetables and accompaniments of your choice. Leftovers make great chicken salad.

MARINATED LAMB LEG WITH GARLIC, YOGURT, AND FENNEL

Leg of lamb makes a great Sunday dinner—and it's perfect for impressing your date with your meat-cooking artistry. It's delicious, totally serious-chef-looking, and ridiculously easy, since you just marinate the meat for an hour or so, then throw it under the broiler. The broiler sears the outside of the meat, while the acidity of the yogurt in the marinade keeps the meat tender. But if you have an outdoor grill—especially one of the charcoal- or wood-burning variety—use that instead, since it will give the meat even more flavor.

It's really important to slice the meat as thinly as possible, using a diagonal cut and going against the grain, so the meat stays tender. Leg of lamb should be served medium rare to medium. This cooking technique will give you pieces that are more done at the ends and less done in the middle, so you can mix it up when you slice it and give everybody a range.

TIMING: After you marinate the lamb, it's pretty fast and easy; about 20 minutes

SERVES 4, WITH SOME LEFTOVERS FOR THE NEXT DAY. (THE MEAT IS AWESOME IN SANDWICHES, SO IT'S WORTH DOING EVEN IF THERE ARE ONLY TWO OF YOU FOR DINNER.)

INGREDIENTS

For the lamb:

2 pounds boneless leg of lamb, butterflied and laid flat

1 cup plain yogurt (preferably Greek)

2 cloves garlic, roughly chopped

1½ tablespoons whole fennel seed, roughly chopped

1 tablespoon coarse-ground black pepper

¼ teaspoon red pepper flakes

1 teaspoon harissa

2 teaspoons salt

Optional:

¼ cup extra-virgin olive oil

For the sauce:

1 tablespoon balsamic vinegar

1 teaspoon fresh thyme leaves

a sprinkling of sea salt to taste

METHOD

TO MARINATE THE LAMB:

1. Score the top of the leg (where the fat is) in a cross-hatched pattern with a sharp knife, cutting through the skin and fat but not the meat itself. The top should be patterned with diamond shapes, about 1 inch square. (The scoring will stop the fat layer from shrinking and will allow the marinade to penetrate and flavor the meat.)

2. In a large bowl, combine the yogurt, garlic, fennel seed, red pepper flakes, black pepper, and harissa. (If you're using a fairly thin yogurt—like most American-made commercial yogurts—add ¼ cup of olive oil to the marinade for extra yumminess.)

3. Add the lamb to the bowl and, using your hands, massage the yogurt mixture into the meat. Really work the marinade into the lamb, almost kneading it as you would with clay.

4. Cover the bowl with plastic wrap and marinate the lamb in the fridge for at least 1 hour. The longer the meat marinates (up to 24 hours), the better it will be.

TO COOK THE LAMB:

1. Remove the lamb from the fridge and let it come to room temperature, at least 30 minutes.

2. Meanwhile, preheat the oven on broil for about 10 minutes, or fire up the grill.

3   Season the meat very generously with the salt.

4   If you're using the broiler: Place the meat, fat-side up, on a roasting rack set on the second level from the top under the broiler. When the lamb starts to brown on top (about 6 minutes), flip the pieces over. If the lamb seems to be cooking unevenly front-to-back, rotate the rack in the oven to even things out. When the lamb is seared—brown on both sides, pretty loose-feeling but with some bounce when you poke it with tongs, about 12 to 15 minutes—turn the broiler off and turn the oven to 375°. Bake the lamb until the meat is brown all over and has thickened and become bouncy to the touch, about 5 minutes. (If you have a meat thermometer, the internal temperature should be 115° to 120°.)

OR

If you're using a grill: Place the lamb fat-side down on the grill and cook them on high. Turn the meat 45° after 2 minutes; flip the halves over after another 2 minutes; then turn the halves 45° again after another 2 minutes. Turn the heat down to medium and cook the lamb until the juice runs clear when you stick it with a knife, about 15 to 20 minutes, depending on your grill.

5   Remove the lamb from the oven or grill and put it on a plate to rest for 10 minutes, so the juices settle and the meat becomes tender and moist.

6   Remove the lamb to a cutting board, leaving the juices that have collected on the plate. Slice the lamb as thin as possible, cutting on a diagonal to ensure maximum tenderness.

TO PREPARE THE SAUCE AND FINISH THE DISH:

1   Arrange the sliced lamb on a serving platter.

2   Add the balsamic vinegar and thyme to the lamb juices that have collected on the resting plate and mix together with a fork.

3   Pour the juice over the sliced lamb. Sprinkle with sea salt to taste. Serve immediately.

PRAWNS WRAPPED IN PANCETTA AND SAGE

The flavors for this dish come from traditional Roman saltimbocca: veal cutlets with sage and prosciutto. I've just replaced the prosciutto with pancetta and the veal with prawns. The tender prawns balance the meatiness and crispness of the bacon, and the sage, tempered by the lemon, makes it all very fresh-tasting. I've designed this recipe for an indoor broiler, but you can also do it on an outdoor grill if you've got one.

I cook my prawns with their heads on to protect the meat at the top of the prawn and keep it moist. If your dining companions won't appreciate that much nature-red-in-tooth-and-claw, pull the heads off right before serving.

TIMING: Superquick; about 20 minutes

SERVES 4

INGREDIENTS

16 large prawns (about 3 pounds)

¼ teaspoon coarse-ground black pepper

16 fresh sage leaves

1 pound pancetta, sliced by the butcher
    (2 to 3 pieces per prawn)

juice of 1 lemon

METHOD

1. Clean the prawns: remove the shells, then slice the backs open lengthwise and pull out the black vein that runs along the back of the prawn.

2. Turn on the broiler.

3. Lay the prawns flat on a large plate or baking sheet and sprinkle them on both sides with the pepper.

4. Pick up a prawn and put a sage leaf on its back, in the middle, covering the incision you've made. Roll 2 or 3 pieces of pancetta around the prawn and sage leaf, overlapping them slightly so the sage is completely covered as is the meaty part in the center of the prawn. Repeat with each prawn.

5. Lay the prawns on a broiler pan or a slotted pan with a drip sheet below.

6. Put the pan in the oven on the high rack—you want the prawns to get really crispy—and broil them until brown on all sides, about 2 minutes. Remove the pan from the oven and flip the prawns over with tongs. Continue broiling until the bacon is crisp and translucent (so you can see the sage through the bacon) and the prawns are pink, about 2 more minutes.

7. Remove the prawns to a serving platter and squeeze the lemon juice over the top. Serve immediately.

THE BEST VEAL OSSO BUCCO

This is not the first recipe for veal osso bucco in an Italian cookbook—but it is, in my humble opinion, the best one. That's because this sauce is all about building the base through layering—the key to real flavor in a braise.

Thickness is essential to this sauce, so I use a food mill to create a *passito*, or "passed sauce," bringing together the gelatin from the meat and the vegetable purée. If you don't have a food mill, don't despair. The first time I made this dish at home, my food mill was MIA. So instead, I tipped the pot and used a whisk to "pound" the sauce until it was blended and chunky. It's not a bad substitute. Don't put the sauce in the food processor or the blender: the fat will emulsify and the sauce will smooth out instead of staying chunky and meaty.

If you make this in advance, you'll actually enhance the flavor: osso bucco, like all braised meats, tastes better when it's been sitting in the sauce for a while. Cover the meat with the sauce in an ovenproof container and store in the fridge overnight. Heat the next day at 350° until it's warmed through, and you're good to go.

TIMING: About 3 hours total, 2 of them watching the veal cook

SERVES 4

INGREDIENTS

4 pieces veal osso bucco
   (about 3 pounds total)

¾ teaspoon salt

½ teaspoon coarse-ground black pepper

2 tablespoons plus 1 tablespoon
   extra-virgin olive oil

1 small carrot, chopped (½ cup)

1 medium onion, chopped (1 cup)

1 stalk celery, chopped (½ cup)

2 cloves garlic, whole

1 large tomato, chopped (1 cup)

2 tablespoons tomato paste

1½ tablespoons all-purpose flour

½ cup white wine

a pinch of saffron (about 10 threads)

juice of 3 oranges (about 1 cup)

2 dried bay leaves

1 sprig fresh thyme
   (or ½ teaspoon dried)

   >>>

METHOD

1. Preheat the oven to 375°.

2. Season both sides of the osso bucco with the salt and pepper.

3. Heat 2 tablespoons of the olive oil in a large pot over high heat. Add the osso bucco and brown on both sides, about 10 to 15 minutes.

4. Remove the osso bucco from the pot and reserve it on a plate on the countertop. Leave the pot on the stove over high heat.

5. Add the remaining tablespoon of olive oil to the pot, and then add the carrot, onion, and celery. Stir well to coat the vegetables in the oil and then allow the vegetables to soften and caramelize, about 4 minutes. Be sure to scrape the brown bits from the bottom and sides of the pot with a spoon or rubber scraper as you go, so that the stuff doesn't burn and flavor the mixture.

6. Add the garlic, tomato, and tomato paste. Mix to combine and cook until the tomato softens, about 1 minute.

7. Add the flour and stir until the ingredients are well combined, about 1 minute.

8. Add the wine and allow it to evaporate just until the mixture becomes a loose paste, 1 to 2 minutes.

   >>>

1 sprig fresh rosemary
  (or ½ teaspoon dried)
¼ teaspoon red pepper flakes
¼ teaspoon whole fennel seed
2 cups chicken broth
3 to 4 curls lemon peel

9 Stir in the saffron and orange juice. Return the osso bucco to the pot and turn the heat to low. Coat the osso bucco nicely in the sauce mixture.

10 Tie the bay leaves, thyme, and rosemary together with butcher's string (so they'll be easier to remove later) and add this herb packet to the pot; then add the red pepper flakes, fennel seed, chicken broth, and lemon peel.

11 Scrape down the sides of the pot again. Then, to be sure that there's nothing left on the sides of the pot, use a wet cloth or sponge to wipe down the sides. This will stop bits from burning and flavoring the dish when you put it in the oven.

12 Cover the pot and bring the liquid up to a low boil, then put the pot in the oven and cook the osso bucco at a lazy bubble, checking it periodically, until the meat is fork-tender, about 2 hours. Flip the meat over in the pot about halfway through to ensure even cooking.

13 Remove the pot from the oven and return it to the stovetop. Using a slotted spoon, remove the meat from the pot, set it on a serving plate, and cover it with a plate or plastic wrap to keep it warm. Remove the herb packet from the pot and discard it.

14 Turn the heat up to high under the pot and cook the sauce down until it has reduced by half, about 3 minutes.

15 Pass the sauce through a food mill into a saucepot, pushing through as much liquid as possible. Scrape anything that sticks to the underside of the strainer; discard anything bigger that collects in the top without passing through.

16 Put each piece of osso bucco on a plate and pour 2 ladlefuls of the sauce over each piece of meat. Serve immediately.

PORK ARROSTO WITH ITALIAN PLUMS AND GRAPPA

I came across this recipe completely by accident, years ago when I was traveling in Italy with my family. We were cruising along a small road in the Alto Adige, way up in the mountains, when I was struck by an urgent need to visit, as they say, the facilities. We hit a tiny town with a single restaurant, and even though the place wasn't open, I went running in—this is really bad manners in Italy—and begged for permission to use the bathroom, which the old man in charge kindly granted. When I emerged, as I was thanking the man profusely, I was suddenly hit hard by the beautiful aroma in the place: garlic, rosemary, and pork fat. There was a big wood-burning oven going full-blast, and they were roasting a baby pig. "That smells amazing," I said. "How are you doing that?" The old guy cheerfully explained: he made a paste by hand on a cutting board and rubbed the pig with it. Needless to say, I shamelessly stole that generous, bathroom-sharing chef's method. You don't need a baby pig or a wood oven for this home-cooking version (in which I treat the pork like standing rib roast), and I guarantee it will make your kitchen smell amazing.

If you can find fresh Italian prune plums (the season is usually late summer to early fall), they're great for this recipe, but regular plums work really well, too.

TIMING: About 2½ hours if you brine the pork first. The brine will make your pork much more tender, so it's worth doing, but if you don't have time, you can skip this step.

SERVES 4 TO 6

INGREDIENTS

For the pork:

1 rack (or standing rib roast) of pork,
    4 to 5 bones (about 2 to 2½ pounds)

Optional:

1 batch of Brine (page 290)

For the spice paste:

2 cloves garlic, sliced Goodfellas thin

½ tablespoon whole fennel seed

1 tablespoon fresh thyme

1 tablespoon fresh rosemary

10 sage leaves

2 tablespoons sea salt

1 tablespoon coarse-ground
    black pepper

2 tablespoons extra-virgin olive oil

>>>

METHOD

TO BRINE THE PORK (OPTIONAL):

1. Cover the pork with brine in a large container and let it marinate in the fridge for 45 minutes.

2. Remove the pork from the brine and pat it dry with a paper towel.

TO PREPARE THE SPICE PASTE:

1. Place the garlic, fennel seed, thyme, rosemary, sage, salt, and pepper on a cutting board, mixing everything together. With a large chef's knife, roughly chop everything together.

2. Pour the olive oil directly over the mixture, right on the cutting board.

3. Lay a large knife flat over the mixture. Pushing down with your fingers on the top flat side of the knife, rock the blade back and forth over the herbs and spices to grind them up. (You're basically using the flat of the knife as a pestle here.) Be careful not to cut yourself as you do this, since the mixture will be slippery with oil—a wide-bladed knife with lots of room for your fingers is key.

>>>

TO ROAST THE PORK:

1. Preheat the oven to 400°.

2. Rub the pork with the spice paste, being sure to cover all sides.

3. Place the pork on a roasting rack on the middle oven rack and bake it until it's done to medium, about 45 minutes: when you squeeze it, the roast will feel like a perfect summer tomato, with a little bit of resistance and some softness underneath. If you have a meat thermometer, the internal temperature should be 125°.

4. Remove the pork from the oven and allow it to rest for 15 to 20 minutes.

TO PREPARE THE PLUMS AND FINISH THE DISH:

1. About 5 minutes before the roast is going to come out of the oven, start the sauce. In a medium saucepan, combine the plums, sugar, lemon juice, bay leaves, pepper, and 1½ cups water. Cook at a lazy bubble until the plums just start to disintegrate, about 15 minutes.

2. Add the grappa and continue to simmer until the mixture becomes a shiny and well-integrated sauce, 2 to 4 more minutes.

3. Slice the pork across the cylinder of meat, cutting at the bones to make chops with a bone attached to each.

4. Serve each chop topped with a generous helping of the plum sauce.

For the plums:

2 cups plums, pitted and chopped
  (4 to 5 plums)—preferably Italian
  prune plums

½ cup sugar

juice of 2 lemons

2 bay leaves

a pinch of coarse-ground black pepper

¼ cup grappa or other strong
  clear alcohol

SHORT RIBS BRACIOLE

If the name of this dish doesn't ring any bells for you, you're not alone. To be honest, I never knew what *braciole* meant until one of my cooks made it for family meal when I was at Café Boulud. He used his grandmother's recipe: rolled-up flank steak with provolone cheese, prosciutto, and hard-boiled eggs, braised in tomato sauce. I looked for braciole when I traveled through Italy, but it was nowhere—until one day I spotted it in a butcher's window in Puglia, made out of horse. Maybe mine is a little less authentic, but instead of having to compete with the dog-food guys at the racetrack, I've done it with short ribs (and everyone loves short ribs). This dish is great in the depths of winter: real stick-to-your-ribs stuff, if you'll excuse the pun, with deep flavors balanced by the freshness of the topping.

TIMING: About 3 hours

SERVES 4

INGREDIENTS

For the short ribs:

½ cup roughly diced pancetta (about ¼ pound)

4 boneless short ribs (about 2 pounds), cut into thirds

1 heaping tablespoon salt

½ teaspoon pepper

1 small onion, diced (about 1 cup)

1 clove garlic, sliced Goodfellas thin

⅛ teaspoon red pepper flakes

20 canned whole tomatoes (2 28-ounce cans, about 4 cups), preferably San Marzano, plus their juice; or 4 cups crushed tomatoes, plus their juice

>>>

METHOD

FOR THE SHORT RIBS:

1. Preheat the oven to 375°.

2. Cook the pancetta in a large, dry, ovenproof saucepot over medium-high heat until the fat renders, about 2 minutes, stirring occasionally to keep from sticking.

3. Season the short ribs on both sides with salt and pepper, add them to the pan, and brown the meat, about 5 minutes.

4. Add the onion and cook until it softens, about 1 minute. Add the garlic and the red pepper flakes, mix well, and continue cooking.

5. Crush the tomatoes over a bowl with your hands, then add them to the pot along with their juice. Bring the mixture up to a low boil.

6. Remove the pot from the stove and place it in the oven. Check the ribs about every 15 minutes or so to make sure they're not boiling too hard. Cook until the meat is supertender and a fork can pass through it without sticking, about 2½ hours.

FOR THE TOPPING:

1. Toast the pine nuts in a dry sauté pan over low heat, shaking the pan occasionally to avoid burning or sticking, about 8 minutes.

2. Add the olive oil and mix well. Add the Crumbs Yo! or panko breadcrumbs and continue cooking over low heat, mixing occasionally, until everything is toasty brown, about 2 minutes.

>>>

For the topping:

¼ cup pine nuts, chopped roughly

1 tablespoon extra-virgin olive oil

¼ cup Crumbs Yo! (page 291) or panko
   breadcrumbs

2 teaspoons dried oregano, preferably
   on the branch

2 tablespoons chopped parsley

a pinch each of salt and coarse-ground
   black pepper

2 tablespoons grated Parmigiano-
   Reggiano

3 Add the oregano and parsley. Season with the salt and pepper and cook together for a few seconds, so everything is warmed but the parsley does not wilt.

4 Remove from the heat and then add the Parmigiano-Reggiano (not before—otherwise, you'll have a melted-cheese mess).

TO FINISH THE DISH:

1 Remove the pot from the oven and immediately remove the ribs to a plate, using a pair of tongs.

2 Use a ladle to remove some of the fat from the sauce, by pressing the chunky sauce away as you tip the pot so that the ladle fills only with the clear fat. (This is optional, but it definitely makes the sauce prettier—there's about 2 tablespoons' worth of fat there.)

3 Add ½ cup of water to the sauce and stir to bring it together.

4 Place 4 to 5 pieces of meat on each plate. Pour the sauce from the pot directly over the short ribs and sprinkle the topping generously over each dish. Serve immediately.

BAY SCALLOPS WITH DRIED HERBS AND CITRUS

These bay scallops, inspired by the Sicilian seaside, are ridiculously easy to cook: heat a pan and sauté them up really quickly. They're tasty, they look great on the plate, and they'll get you instant chef-cred: everyone will think you spent hours slaving in the kitchen, when really you were watching *Law & Order* reruns all afternoon.

I like to use Nantucket Bay scallops when they're in season, from November to February. If you can't find small bay scallops, buy the larger sea scallops and cut each one into three or four pieces.

TIMING: Very quick

SERVES 4

INGREDIENTS

For the scallops:

1½ pounds bay scallops

1 tablespoon flour

½ teaspoon salt

¼ teaspoon pepper

1 teaspoon Dried Herbs (page 292)

2 tablespoons extra-virgin olive oil

For the sauce:

juice of 4 oranges (about 1½ cups)

1 tablespoon butter

1 tablespoon extra-virgin olive oil, plus extra for drizzling

½ teaspoon dried oregano, preferably on the branch (Sicilian or Calabrian)

2 oranges, cut into supremes (see technique in Grilled Swordfish with Orange and Olives, page 165)

sea salt for finishing

Optional:

juice of 1 lemon

METHOD

1. Pat the scallops very dry with a paper towel.

2. Shake the flour, salt, pepper, and herbs over the scallops and coat them well.

3. Heat a sauté pan over high heat, then add the olive oil and allow it to heat until it starts to smoke.

4. Add the scallops to the hot olive oil (you will probably need to do this in 2 batches to get everything properly brown). Keep turning the scallops with a spoon as they go lightly golden brown on each side and become a bit translucent at the center, so they're just done on the outside, but not opaque—and rubbery—on the inside, about 1½ minutes. Don't remove the pan from the heat to toss the scallops; you want constant contact with that high heat.

5. Remove the scallops to a plate and deglaze the pan with the orange juice. Allow the juice to come to a boil on high heat and keep cooking until it has reduced to a thin glaze, about 5 minutes.

6. Add the butter, olive oil, and oregano. Continue cooking over high heat, stirring to incorporate any bits of scallop and herbs adhering to the bottom, until it starts to become a nice sauce, about 1 minute or so.

7. Add the orange segments and mix everything together. Taste the sauce. If it's a bit too sweet for your taste, add the lemon juice to tarten it up.

8. Pour the sauce over the scallops and sprinkle some sea salt over the top. If you'd like, drizzle the scallops with a bit more olive oil. Serve immediately.

SPICE-GLAZED DUCK

One of the best dishes I ever ate in Italy was duck glazed with spices. A dish like this might not seem very Italian, but in fact rich, cosmopolitan Italians have cooked with lots of spices and vinegar from Roman times on down. Dishes like this one don't turn up much in Italian-American cuisine because the big waves of Italian immigrants were mostly made up of poor country folk, and poor country folk couldn't afford expensive spices. They cooked with herbs and garlic—maybe a leek once in a while to make things fancy. They brought their cooking traditions with them to the States, and so those are the flavors Americans now tend to think of as "Italian." This particular dish is all about indulgence: no poverty food here. It dates all the way back to that great ancient Roman book of epicurian delights, Apicius's *De Re Coquinaria*, in which spices were thrown around like they were going out of style.

Lots of people think of duck as a restaurant dish, but don't be afraid to try this at home: I promise, this method is easy and delicious. You may, however, want to think about cooking in stages. You can cook the duck on the stovetop up to a half hour before you plan on putting it in the oven. This is a very good idea if you're entertaining—and especially if you're entertaining in a poorly ventilated New York City apartment.

Sliced with some of the glaze on top, this duck breast is irresistible: the skin is crispy, the meat ruby red, the glaze rich and complex. At my place, we call this "duck crack."

TIMING: Medium quick; about 45 minutes

SERVES 4

INGREDIENTS

For the duck:

4 duck breasts (preferably Pekin or
    Muscovy), about 2 to 2½ pounds

2 teaspoons salt

½ teaspoon coarse-ground black pepper

For the glaze:

3 tablespoons honey

½ cup red wine vinegar

For the spice mix:

½ teaspoon ground allspice

⅛ teaspoon ground star anise

¼ teaspoon coarse-ground black pepper

¼ teaspoon ground fennel seed

¼ teaspoon ground coriander seed

¼ teaspoon ground cinnamon

METHOD

TO PREPARE THE DUCK:

1 Preheat the oven to 400°.

2 Pat the duck breasts dry with a paper towel, and lay them meat-side down on another piece of paper towel. Using a small, sharp knife, score the skin layer in a cross-hatch pattern, going about three fourths of the way through the skin but being careful not to cut the meat below. (This prevents the skin from shrinking.)

3 Sprinkle both sides of each duck breast with the salt and pepper.

4 Place the duck breasts skin-side down in a large cold sauté pan or saucepan. Put the pan on the stove over high heat and allow the fat to begin to render.

5 Once the fat accumulates in the bottom of the pan to a depth of about ⅛ inch (about 5 minutes), drain off the extra fat: holding the duck breasts down with a large spoon or a pair of tongs, just tip the fat out of the pan into a bowl. (You'll need to remove the fat a couple of times during the cooking process—this ensures that the skin will get nice and crispy.)

6 Turn the heat to medium-low and continue cooking the duck until the skin is really crispy and well browned, about 10 minutes. As the duck fat accumulates in the pan, drain it out periodically. Flip the meat over in the pan and continue cooking until the flesh is just browned, another 1½ minutes or so.

7 Remove the duck breasts to a roasting rack, skin-side up, and place them in the oven on the middle rack. Bake until the flesh is taut and springy to the touch, about 8 minutes. Remove the duck from the oven and allow it to rest for at least 2 minutes.

TO MAKE THE SPICED GLAZE AND FINISH THE DISH:

1 Drain the oil from the duck-searing pan, then return the pan to high heat. Add the honey, bring it up to a boil, and cook, stirring vigorously, until it has a nice smooth caramel color, about 30 seconds.

2 Add the red wine vinegar and reduce, stirring frequently, until there's about ¼ cup left, about 7 minutes.

3 Combine the spices together in a small bowl. Mix the spices into the vinegar-honey mixture.

4 Using a spoon, spread the glaze liberally over the skin side of the duck so the flavors enter the scored side and infuse the meat.

5 Slice the duck into thin slices widthwise and serve it immediately, topped with some sea salt if you like.

CODFISH WITH SHRIMP AND CALAMARI

This is a pretty quick and easy fish-in-broth preparation—kind of like a San Francisco–style cioppino, except easier. You don't have to use the shrimp for this, or the squid either, if you don't want to. Throw in any kind of shellfish you like; add some clams, or even toss in some lobster. The key is to avoid allowing the white wine to evaporate. You're not using it to deglaze here, as we do in other broths; you want that winey flavor.

TIMING: Pretty quick; about 45 minutes

SERVES 4 TO 6
INGREDIENTS

¼ cup extra-virgin olive oil

2 cloves garlic, sliced Goodfellas thin

1 red bell pepper, sliced thin (about
     1 cup)

½ teaspoon red pepper flakes

½ cup white wine

2 cups Basic Tomato Sauce (page 285)

1 cup clam juice

4 6- to 8-ounce deboned codfish fillets
     (2 pounds total)

¼ teaspoon each of salt and coarse-
     ground black pepper

¼ pound rock shrimp, cleaned, shelled,
     and with heads removed

¼ pound squid, cleaned and cut
     into rings

4 basil leaves, chopped (about
     1 tablespoon)

1 tablespoon chopped parsley

METHOD

1. Preheat the oven to 375°.

2. Heat the olive oil over medium heat in a medium-sized saucepot. Add the sliced garlic and toast until it's golden brown, stirring to avoid burning, about 2 minutes.

3. Add the bell pepper and cook, stirring, until the pepper pieces are coated in the olive oil, about 30 seconds.

4. Add the red pepper flakes and the wine, and allow the liquid to come up to a simmering boil.

5. As soon as the liquid comes to a simmer (you don't want the wine to reduce), add the Basic Tomato Sauce and the clam juice. Bring the mixture back to a simmer and continue cooking until the peppers are soft, about 15 minutes.

6. Remove the mixture to a blender and blend on medium until smooth, being careful while working with the hot liquid. (I put a towel over the top of the blender and pulse a few times first to prevent face-scalding catastrophes.)

7. Season the fish fillets on both sides with the salt and pepper, place in an ovenproof dish or saucepan with high sides, and cover with the warm broth from the blender.

8. Cover the dish and bake the fish in the oven until the flesh is white, the inside is just opaque, and the fish is flaky but not falling apart, about 12 minutes. When it's done, use a slotted spoon or spatula to remove the fish from the dish, placing each fillet in an individual serving bowl and leaving the broth behind in the pan.

9 Return the pan to the stove and add the shrimp and squid (or what-ever seafood you're using) to the broth. Cook together slowly, at a very light simmer over medium heat, until the shrimp and squid have cooked through and become opaque, about 1½ to 2½ minutes. Be very careful here: if you cook the seafood too fast or let the broth come to a boil, you'll end up serving some expensive pieces of rubber.

10 Turn off the heat and add the basil and parsley, mixing well to com-bine.

11 Spoon a generous helping of the seafood broth over each individual piece of fish. Serve accompanied by a spoon, so your guests can get at the yummy broth.

BLACK BASS WITH SICILIAN-STYLE PESTO

For years, I thought Sicilian pesto was some weird, made-up American sun-dried-tomato abomination. It wasn't until my first trip to Sicily that I discovered that *pesto alla Siciliano* was actually Italian—and more to the point, that there was a reason to eat it. I did some research, diving into old Sicilian cookbooks, and I found a handful of recipes, all using the tender leaves at the heart of celery as a key ingredient.

Black bass is my favorite fish for steaming, because it's so delicate and flakes perfectly, but if you can't find it, you can always substitute another flaky white fish—cod or halibut, for example.

TIMING: Superquick; about 15 minutes

SERVES 4

INGREDIENTS

For the bass:

2 tablespoons extra-virgin olive oil

4 boneless black bass fillets (about 2 pounds total)

¼ teaspoon each of salt and pepper

½ teaspoon dried oregano

1 teaspoon each of lemon zest and orange zest (3 passes of the microplane)

2 scallions, whites only, chopped very fine

¼ cup white vermouth or white wine

1 tablespoon butter

For the pesto:

¾ cup oil-packed sun-dried tomatoes

¼ cup extra-virgin olive oil, plus more for drizzling

1 clove garlic, peeled

½ cup sliced blanched almonds

½ cup fresh basil (about 15 leaves), chopped

½ cup parsley, chopped

½ cup celery leaf, chopped

METHOD

TO PREPARE THE BASS:

1. Preheat the oven to 375°.

2. Pour the olive oil into a baking dish.

3. Using a sharp knife, make 4 shallow diagonal incisions in the skin side of each fillet. (This keeps the fish from curling up and getting tough.) Season the fillets with salt, pepper, oregano, and the lemon and orange zest and shake the scallions over the top. Lay them in the baking dish skin-side up.

4. Pour the vermouth or wine over the fish.

5. Break up the butter with your fingers and place little bits across the fish.

6. Bake the fish, uncovered, until the flesh turns just white and is semi-firm to the touch, about 5 to 8 minutes. When you cut into the fish, the center should be just opaque.

TO PREPARE THE PESTO:

1. Drain the sun-dried tomatoes and put them in the blender with the olive oil, garlic, almonds, and 1 cup of hot tap water. Blend on high until the ingredients have combined into a chunky sauce, about 1 minute.

1. Remove the fish from the baking dish to a plate but do not discard the juices in the bottom of the pan.

2. Add half the pesto to the juices in the baking dish and mix together over low heat until everything is combined. Add the chopped basil, parsley, and celery leaf, and mix to combine all the ingredients. If the pesto seems too thick for your taste, adjust the consistency by adding a little more hot tap water.

3. Spoon a portion of the pesto onto the bottom of each serving plate and place a fish fillet on top. Drizzle more extra-virgin olive oil over the top. Serve immediately.

STEAK PICANTE WITH SALSA VERDE

Beef and salsa verde is a classic Italian combination, and spicy steaks are a classic American favorite. This ridiculously simple preparation will wean you off A1 sauce for good.

Proper steak doneness is crucial, of course. At my first job, working the grill at a crappy Italian-American restaurant, this beat-up, drugged-out, greasy grill cook showed me his personal secret method for testing the doneness of a steak. It works like this:

A. Put your thumb right next to your forefinger and press on the fleshy pad below the thumb on the palm of your hand with your opposite forefinger. Feel that? That's what a rare steak feels like when you poke it.

B. Move your thumb an inch away from your forefinger and do it again. Medium rare.

C. Halfway along the thumb arc: that's a medium steak. (That's the preparation I'm giving you times for here, but feel free to adjust to your personal favorite level of doneness.)

D. And your thumb extended as far as it'll go away from your forefinger? That, my friends, is well done.

TIMING: Very fast; about 30 minutes—even less if you made the Salsa Verde the day before

SERVES 4

INGREDIENTS

4 8- to 10-ounce New York strip steaks, preferably dry aged

½ teaspoon salt

1 tablespoon red pepper flakes (or harissa) blended in ¼ cup extra-virgin olive oil

4 tablespoons Salsa Verde (page 301), plus extra for plating

OR

Last-minute Salsa Verde substitute:

1 tablespoon chopped capers

4 anchovies, chopped fine

2 tablespoons chopped parsley

METHOD

1. Preheat the broiler or the grill. If you're using the broiler, set a rack on the middle setting.

2. Place the steaks in a large container. Shake the salt over them on both sides.

3. Coat both sides of the steak well with the mixture of red pepper flakes (or harissa) and olive oil; reserve whatever you don't use. Allow the steaks to marinate in this mixture on the countertop for at least 15 minutes.

4. Put the steaks in the oven on a broiler pan, or right on the grill, if you're using one. Broil or grill until the marinade has caramelized and the steak looks crispy at the edges (or marked from the grill), about 5 minutes. Turn the steaks and return them to the heat and continue broiling or grilling until the second side looks like the first, about 5 more minutes.

5. Take the steaks off the heat and allow them to rest on a plate or in a low bowl for 5 minutes, so that they firm up but remain juicy.

6. Remove the steaks from the plate to a cutting board and slice them as thin or thick as you like.

7 Combine the resting juices that have gathered at the bottom of the plate with the leftover marinade. If you didn't have time to throw the Salsa Verde together, combine only half of the resting juices with the marinade; add the other half to the capers, anchovies, and parsley to form an instant salsa.

8 Arrange the steak on individual plates and distribute the marinade mixture over the meat with a spoon. Top each serving with about 1 tablespoon of Salsa Verde (or your instant salsa), and pile more on the side for dipping. Serve immediately.

TRIPE ALLA PARMIGIANA

Chances are, if you're going to make this recipe at home, you truly love to eat. Lots of people are afraid of tripe, but I love it. Tripe is serious comfort food, warm and rich and filling and delicious, the opposite of fancy cooking, and not in any way gross. (The tripe you buy from the butcher these days is treated, extremely clean, and very easy to work with.) Tripe, sweetbreads, head—these are common foods in city markets and butcher shops in Italian cities.

Traditionally, these foods belonged to the poor, who couldn't afford to waste any part of an animal. When I was a kid, I used to see tripe for sale in the ethnic meat stalls at the West Side Market in downtown Cleveland. But nobody I knew cooked it, so I didn't taste tripe until I went to Italy. When I started cooking in New York, French restaurants had tripe on the menu, but only Europeans ordered it. That's all changed as Americans have become much more adventurous eaters. In the last ten years, offal has become high cuisine everywhere. In my kitchen, we go through upward of sixty pounds of the stuff every week.

Tripe is great for dinner on a cold winter's eve—but it also makes great middle-of-the-night food. Extremely late one extremely cold winter's night—or early morning, to be exact—I found myself in the kitchen with one of my sous-chefs, Rich Torrisi, a little worse for wear after a night of celebrating something or other (the details are a little murky) with the kitchen crew. We fried up some eggs and put them on top of this tripe recipe. It was one of the most satisfying post-drinking early breakfasts ever.

TIMING: This is a good Sunday-afternoon project. It takes about 5 hours.

SERVES 4 TO 6
INGREDIENTS

For the tripe:

2½ pounds honeycomb beef (or veal) tripe (2 large or 3 medium-sized pieces)

¼ cup extra-virgin olive oil

2 medium onions, sliced thin (about 2 cups)

¼ teaspoon red pepper flakes

1 tablespoon butter

1 cup white wine

2 cups chopped canned tomatoes (preferably San Marzano) with their juice (1 28-ounce can)

3 cups chicken broth

1½ teaspoons salt

>>>

METHOD
TO PREPARE THE TRIPE:

1. Preheat the oven to 375°.

2. Bring a large pot of salted water to a boil. Place the tripe in the boiling water and push it under using a spoon or tongs. (It will bob up a little bit but should be mostly submerged.) Cook the tripe for about 15 minutes.

3. Using tongs, remove the tripe to a bowl. Allow it to cool on the countertop until it can be handled (or speed things up by putting the bowl in the freezer for a few minutes).

4. Once the tripe has cooled, pour off any excess water. Cut the tripe pieces roughly into thirds—long 3- to 4-inch-wide strips. Cut off any fibrous edges that stick up (they will get tough when cooked). You'll probably end up cutting off about 15 percent of the tripe this way, which is fine. Then cut the strips into smaller pieces, about 1 inch wide by 3 to 4 inches long.

5 Heat the olive oil on medium heat in an ovenproof casserole. Add the onions and cook slowly, without allowing them to color, until they're soft, about 5 minutes.

6 Add the red pepper flakes and the butter. Mix well and continue cooking until the butter has melted, about a minute.

7 Add the tripe and stir well to coat every piece in the butter mixture. Turn the heat to high, then add the white wine and cook until the alcohol smell disperses, about 3 minutes.

8 Add the tomatoes and their juice, the chicken broth, and the salt and pepper and stir to combine.

9 Cover the casserole and allow the mixture to come up to a simmer.

10 Transfer the covered casserole to the oven and continue simmering about 3 hours, stirring occasionally.

11 Remove the casserole from the oven and place it on the stove. Add the celery and carrots to the casserole and continue cooking on the heat, uncovered and at a low simmer, until the liquid has reduced by half, the vegetables have cooked, and the liquid has formed a nice sauce (sort of a medium-thick stew), about 1 more hour.

TO FRY THE EGGS (OPTIONAL):

1 When the tripe is nearly done, heat the olive oil in a nonstick pan.

2 Add the eggs, salt, and pepper and fry the eggs up to your liking.

TO FINISH THE DISH:

1 Add the vinegar. Season with more salt and pepper if needed.

2 Transfer the tripe to individual serving dishes and sprinkle with the Parmigiano-Reggiano and Crumbs Yo! or panko breadcrumbs. Drizzle the olive oil over the top.

3 Serve with a fried egg on top of each dish, if you like.

¼ teaspoon coarse-ground black pepper

6 stalks celery, roughly cut (about 2 cups)

2 medium carrots, sliced (about 1 cup)

For the fried eggs (optional):

2 tablespoons extra-virgin olive oil

4 to 6 eggs

a pinch each of salt and coarse-ground black pepper

To finish the dish:

2 tablespoons sherry vinegar or red wine vinegar

¼ cup grated Parmigiano-Reggiano

2 tablespoons Crumbs Yo! (page 291) or panko breadcrumbs

2 tablespoons extra-virgin olive oil

VEAL TENDERLOIN WITH PANCETTA AND MUSHROOM MARSALA SAUCE

When I was a kid, working at my local Italian eatery, I made so many veal Marsalas that by the end of each night I would have what we call, in the business, "sauté arm." Later on, when I started working at fancy New York City restaurants, I blew off Marsala sauce as old-fashioned. But lately I've come back around to it. There's a reason so many people order veal Marsala: it's really good. These old classics can get pretty heavy, though (think Tony Soprano–heavy), so I've lightened this one up a little for modern living. I use veal tenderloin instead of scallopini, so that the meat stays super-super-tender; instead of pouring on the veal stock, I caramelize the onions really well to make the sauce taste rich; and I add tomatoes to give it all a tempering acidity. (But this ain't diet food, kids: it's still veal with pancetta and cream. That's why it tastes good.) This is pretty easy cooking, but it looks—and tastes—like hours slaving over a hot stove. Perfect for those with champagne tastes, Rat Pack–style.

TIMING: About 1 hour

SERVES 4

INGREDIENTS

For the veal:

2 veal tenderloins (about 1½ pounds total), silver skin removed by the butcher (or see method)

¾ pound pancetta, sliced as thin as the counterperson will slice it

½ teaspoon fresh thyme leaves

½ tablespoon coarse-ground black pepper

2 tablespoons extra-virgin olive oil

For the sauce:

1 medium onion (about 1 cup), sliced thin

¼ pound mixed mushrooms (white, cremini, portobello, wild—whatever appeals to your palate and won't endanger your net worth), about 2 cups, cleaned and cut into large chunks

1 tablespoon extra-virgin olive oil

>>>

METHOD

TO PREPARE THE VEAL:

1 Heat the oven to 375°.

2 If the butcher hasn't cleaned the silver skin off the veal, do it yourself: slide the blade of a long sharp knife (like a fish knife) underneath the silvery membrane on the top of each tenderloin and cut it away, with the blade facing away from you and angled up so that you don't nick the meat beneath.

3 Place a tenderloin on the cutting board. Lay a row of pancetta rounds, overlapping, on the cutting board along the length of the tenderloin. Put another row behind that, and another behind that, so that there's a layer big enough to wrap the loin. (You'll probably need about 9 rounds; remember to use only half the pancetta.) Sprinkle the pancetta with half the thyme and the black pepper. Place the tenderloin on top of the pancetta slices. Roll the loin in the pancetta, using your fingers to press the pancetta against the veal so that it's wrapped well. You should have enough pancetta to wrap the loin all the way around; the pancetta pieces will stick to one another as they wrap around. If this isn't happening for you, tie the whole thing around with butcher's string.

4 Repeat for the second veal tenderloin with the remaining pancetta.

5 Heat the olive oil in a large sauté pan over high heat until it's smoking. Add the pancetta-wrapped tenderloins and cook, rotating and turning periodically, until the meat is browned on all sides, about 5 minutes.

6 Remove the meat to a roasting rack and place it in the oven on the middle rack. Dump about half the veal juices out of the sauté pan, but leave the rest. Roast the tenderloins 12 to 14 minutes for medium rare (115° to 120° on a meat thermometer), longer if you prefer your meat more cooked. Remove the meat from the oven and place on a rack or a plate. Allow the tenderloins to rest for 10 minutes, so the meat is firm but tender and juicy.

TO MAKE THE SAUCE:

1 Return the sauté pan, with the reserved veal cooking juices, to the stove over medium heat. Add the onions and stir to coat them in the fat. Allow the onions to caramelize a bit, about 2½ minutes.

2 Add the mushrooms and turn the heat to high. Add the olive oil. The pan will still be fairly dry (mushrooms always soak up whatever's in the pan), and there will be caramelized bits on the bottom; those will help flavor the sauce, but you want the mushrooms to sauté, not burn. Allow the mushrooms and onions to caramelize a bit, about 2½ minutes.

3 Add the Marsala wine and mix well. The wine may flame a bit if you're cooking on a gas stove, so watch out—if it does catch fire, just mix everything around and the flame will subside. (If you're a pyro or a show-off, you can do like I do and just tip the pan a bit so the wine catches a flame. The fans, they love the fire.) Continue cooking until the alcohol has almost evaporated and everything looks all glazy, about 30 seconds or so.

4 Add ¼ cup of water, the heavy cream, tomatoes, thyme leaves, salt, and pepper, and continue cooking until everything has combined and the sauce has reduced to a thick consistency, about 10 minutes more.

5 Remove the pan from the heat and add the parsley, mixing to combine.

TO FINISH THE DISH:

1 Slice the veal into ½-inch-thick rounds and remove to a serving platter.

2 Pour the sauce over the top. Sprinkle with sea salt and serve immediately.

¼ cup Marsala wine

¼ cup heavy cream

¼ cup canned peeled cherry tomatoes or good-quality Italian canned plum tomatoes (about 10 tomatoes)

1 tablespoon fresh thyme leaves

¼ teaspoon each of salt and coarse-ground black pepper

1 tablespoon chopped parsley

4

{ CONTORNI }

ARTICHOKES ALLA CONTADINO

Contadino means "farmer" or "peasant," and this dish can definitely be a really rustic, lazy-Sunday-afternoon kind of thing. But it also cleans up pretty good: it makes a great addition to a more elegant meal, because artichokes are just inherently fancy. Either way, it's supereasy one-pot cooking.

TIMING: About 30 minutes

SERVES 4 TO 6

INGREDIENTS

¼ cup extra-virgin olive oil

½ cup pancetta, cut into large chunks

1 small onion, chopped (about ½ cup)

6 artichokes, cleaned, halved, and
    with chokes removed

¼ teaspoon each of salt and pepper

1 clove garlic, peeled and crushed

2 whole tomatoes, chopped

¼ cup white wine

¼ cup pitted Taggiasca olives

¼ cup basil, chopped

1 tablespoon fresh rosemary

1 tablespoon fresh thyme

¼ cup parsley, chopped

¼ cup Crumbs Yo! (page 291) or
    panko breadcrumbs

METHOD

1. Heat the olive oil in a large saucepot over medium-high heat. Add the pancetta and onion and cook together 2 minutes, until some of the pancetta fat is rendered and the onion starts to soften.

2. Add the artichokes and season the mixture with the salt and pepper. Cook for 2 minutes, until the artichokes are lightly sautéed.

3. Add the garlic, tomatoes, and wine and cook for 2 minutes, until the alcohol evaporates.

4. Add ½ cup water, lower the heat to medium, and cover. Cook for 15 minutes at a medium simmer. When you can insert a sharp knife into an artichoke and pull it away cleanly, turn off the heat. (You can make this part in advance and keep it in the fridge for up to 2 days; the dish will actually be better, because the sauce really gets into the artichokes. You'll want to bring the dish back up to heat gently on the stove, adding up to ¼ cup water as needed.)

5. Add the olives, basil, rosemary, thyme, and parsley, and mix everything together well.

6. Remove the mixture to a serving dish and top with Crumbs Yo! or panko breadcrumbs. Serve immediately.

ASPARAGUS WITH CITRUS AND OREGANO

Asparagus in the microwave is awesome.

Yup. You read that right.

I'm sure some food snob somewhere is recoiling in horror and throwing this book across the room, but I don't care. The microwave can be a good cooking tool, if you don't abuse it. I learned how to do asparagus in the microwave like this from my mom—and *nobody* is going to insult my mom's cooking: everything she makes is gold. This technique is no exception; when I cook asparagus at home now, I don't put a big pot of water on. But don't get carried away, my friends: the microwave technique is great for asparagus, but it doesn't work so well with other green vegetables. (And I definitely wouldn't roast a chicken in there.)

TIMING: Super-super-fast; 10 minutes or less, depending on your knife skills

SERVES 4 TO 6
INGREDIENTS

For the asparagus:

1 bunch of the largest green asparagus
    you can find (jumbo is best)
2 tablespoons extra-virgin olive oil
zest of 1 orange

For the dressing:

2 oranges
4 tablespoons extra-virgin olive oil
2 scallions, finely chopped
1 teaspoon dried oregano, preferably on
    the branch (Sicilian or Calabrian)
juice of 1 lemon
salt and coarse-ground black pepper
    to taste
sea salt for sprinkling

METHOD

TO PREPARE THE ASPARAGUS:

1. Cut off an inch or two from the bottom of the asparagus and discard.

2. Place the asparagus in a microwave-safe dish with high sides. Add the olive oil and ¼ cup water. Using a microplane or box grater, grate the orange zest over the top.

3. Cover the dish with plastic wrap and put it in the microwave for 2 minutes on high. Rotate the dish and cook for 2 more minutes, until the asparagus stalks are bright green and crunchy-tender. (The exact time will depend on the size of your asparagus.)

TO PREPARE THE DRESSING:

1. Segment the oranges: with the peel still on, slice the ends off an orange. Set it on one end and, with a small, sharp knife, slice off the peel and the white pith together. Holding the peeled orange in your hand, cut along the inside of each white segmenting line. Remove the "supremes" (the meat, the best part) to a bowl, leaving all the membranes attached to the "skeleton." Squeeze all the juice out of this skeleton into the bowl with the supremes, then discard the skeleton. Repeat with the other orange.

2. Add the olive oil, scallion, oregano, and lemon juice. Combine with a spoon. Season with salt and pepper to taste.

1 When the asparagus has finished cooking, remove the plastic wrap. There shouldn't be a lot of water on the bottom, but if there is, drain that from the dish.

2 Spoon the dressing over the asparagus and sprinkle with sea salt.

CALABRIAN OREGANO

The best oregano you can buy is the Calabrian or Sicilian stuff that comes dried on the branch. The plant grows wild, and it's picked, dried, and sold whole, in one-ounce bags—it looks, to me at least, like the bushel of twigs that stooped old man is carrying on his back on the cover of *Led Zeppelin IV*. At the restaurant, we like to use the TuttoCalabria brand, which is fairly easy to find in Italian specialty stores. It stays really green when cooked, and the flavor is very intense. You can smell the oregano from across the room when you open the package: very fragrant, rich, herbal—almost more like something you'd find at a Zeppelin reunion concert than in a kitchen.

ONIONS

When asked about their favorite ingredients, some fancy chefs say, "Oh, truffles," or "Caviar, of course." Now, I'm just a simple dude from Ohio, so maybe I'm just not refined enough—but when it comes down to it, I think onions are really my favorite ingredient. There are so many different varieties (red, Vidalia, green, Spanish . . .), and they add such a range of surprising flavors and textures: sweetness, body, crunch, you name it. Not that I want to sit around eating raw onions, you understand. But for good cooking—especially good Italian cooking—they're key. A lot of traditional Italian (and Italian-American) cooking is basically peasant fare. And in the poverty-stricken Italian countryside, spices were just too expensive. For flavoring, Italians had only the onions and garlic they grew in their gardens and on their farms. They learned how to cook onions to make them sweet, mellow, rich, to take on all the flavors and textures that they couldn't afford to get from more expensive ingredients. So don't be ashamed of loving onions—but pay attention to how you cook 'em.

BROCCOLI RABE WITH GOAT CHEESE, ONIONS, AND PINE NUTS

Broccoli rabe, or *cima di rapa*, is a bitter green from southern Italy that's ubiquitous as a restaurant side dish across the U.S. You usually find it sautéed with browned garlic and olive oil; in the south, they roll it into bread dough and bake it. In New York, Royal Crown Pastry Shop in Brooklyn is the king of broccoli rabe bread. The bread is studded with sautéed sweet onions, and the rabe is totally overcooked, supersoft—and absolutely delicious.

My take on broccoli rabe plays with sweet onions too—plus goat cheese and sun-dried tomatoes to balance the bitterness of the greens. I blanch the broccoli rabe so that it retains a little crunch, but if you want that smooth Brooklyn feel, just keep it in the water a little longer.

TIMING: Superquick; under 30 minutes

SERVES 4

INGREDIENTS

3 tablespoons pine nuts

1 bunch broccoli rabe

2 tablespoons extra-virgin olive oil

1 Vidalia onion, thinly sliced

1 clove garlic, finely chopped

½ teaspoon red pepper flakes

6 sun-dried tomatoes in oil, julienned

a generous pinch each of salt and
    coarse-ground black pepper

2 tablespoons fresh goat cheese

METHOD

1. Bring a large pot of salted water to boil to blanch the broccoli rabe.

2. While the water is boiling, slow-roast the pine nuts over very low heat in a dry pan until golden brown, about 5 minutes (longer on an electric stove). Shake the pan regularly to avoid burning the nuts. Remove from the heat and reserve.

3. Cut off the bottoms of the broccoli rabe stems and remove any large, bruised leaves.

4. Blanch the broccoli rabe for 1 minute, until the leaves have softened but the stems are still straight and hold a nice, firm texture. Remove to a bowl of ice water to stop the cooking process. (Blanching helps the rabe to hold its color: if you just sauté it without blanching, it gets brown and crispy.)

5. Heat the olive oil in a large sauté pan. Add the onion and sauté, stirring steadily, until it's nice and soft and translucent.

6. Add the chopped garlic and red pepper flakes and stir to combine. Add the broccoli rabe, sun-dried tomatoes, and salt and pepper and stir to combine. Cook the mixture over high heat until the flavors come together, about 2 minutes.

7. Remove the mixture to a large serving bowl. Crumble the goat cheese over the top. It's important to add the cheese just before the dish is served, so it doesn't get runny or melt completely from the heat of the broccoli rabe—but do let it sit for just a moment, so that it softens and melts a tiny bit, for a sexy mouth-feel. Sprinkle the pine nuts over everything and serve immediately.

CAULIFLOWER WITH PEARS, SAGE, AND HAZELNUTS

There are a lot of anti-cauliflower types out there in the world—mostly people who were traumatized by boiled rubber-vegetable cauliflower as children. But don't hate on the big white guy: cauliflower, believe it or not, can be really sexy. There are two ways to make that happen, in my opinion: either you make it super-super-smooth in a purée, or you sauté it in brown butter till it's crispy and unvegetable-like. Here we're going with option B, dialed up a notch with a combination of pears and hazelnuts that's very Piedmontese. If Italians celebrated Thanksgiving, this would be one of their side dishes.

TIMING: Super-super-fast; about 15 minutes

SERVES 4 TO 6

INGREDIENTS

½ medium head cauliflower, thoroughly washed and cut into florets (about 4 cups)

3 tablespoons butter

¼ cup peeled hazelnuts, chopped

4 sage leaves, chopped

½ teaspoon salt

¼ teaspoon coarse-ground black pepper

1 ripe pear, sliced thin

1 tablespoon roughly chopped parsley

METHOD

1. Cut each floret into slices no more than ½ inch thick.

2. Melt the butter in a large sauté pan over medium-high heat until it bubbles white. Add the hazelnuts, sage, and sliced cauliflower and cook together, stirring or shaking the pan every 30 seconds or so to keep them from sticking, until the cauliflower begins to soften, about 2 minutes.

3. Add the salt and pepper and cook for another 4 to 5 minutes, until the cauliflower browns a bit (just as a sautéed onion browns).

4. Turn off the heat and add the pear slices and parsley. Remove from the stove and mix all the ingredients together. Serve immediately.

ESCAROLE CALABRESE

The inspiration for this dish is Calabrian: spicy sopressata, lots of garlic, cherry tomatoes. The canned cherry tomatoes I use here can be a little tough to find, but they're worth searching out because they're supersweet—much sweeter than regular canned tomatoes—and that sets off the slightly bitter escarole really beautifully. Texture is important here too: the escarole should be just wilted, not cooked to death, so you get a little bounce between your teeth.

TIMING: Superquick and easy; 20 minutes plus prep time

SERVES 4

INGREDIENTS

1 head escarole

⅓ cup extra-virgin olive oil, plus more
   to drizzle

3 garlic cloves, sliced Goodfellas thin

1 cup spicy sopressata or other dried
   Italian sausage, roughly chopped

1 small onion, roughly chopped
   (about ½ cup)

¼ teaspoon red pepper flakes (you may
   use more or less, depending on the
   spiciness of your sopressata, but don't
   be afraid of the spice on this one)

2 cups canned cherry tomatoes or
   good-quality Italian canned plum
   tomatoes, drained

¼ teaspoon salt

¼ teaspoon coarse-ground black pepper

2 tablespoons grated Parmigiano-
   Reggiano

1 tablespoon Crumbs Yo! (page 291) or
   panko breadcrumbs

METHOD

1. Wash the escarole and remove any brown outer leaves. Cut off the stem 2 inches from the bottom and then cut the head of escarole in thirds widthwise.

2. Heat the olive oil over medium-high heat in a large pot. Add the garlic and toast it, but do not allow it to color.

3. Add the sopressata and the chopped onions. Cook everything together so the oil from the sopressata mixes in with the onions. Add the red pepper flakes and the tomatoes. Allow everything to cook together for about 5 minutes, crushing the tomatoes lightly with a wooden spoon, until the flavors come together and the tomatoes begin to break apart.

4. Add the escarole (it will take up a lot of space—this is why you need a big pot) and stir the ingredients together. Let the escarole cook down a bit, and as it shrinks, mix it in with the tomato mixture. The volume will decrease a great deal as the escarole cooks.

5. When the escarole leaves wilt to softness and turn a darker green (about 2 minutes), remove the mixture from the heat and season with salt and pepper.

6. Serve in a large bowl, topped with the Parmigiano-Reggiano and breadcrumbs and drizzled with a little olive oil.

FENNEL WITH ORANGE AND SAMBUCA

I love this side dish: a classic combination gone wild, playing spicy, sweet, sour, and savory notes all at once. This version is full of surprises: the Sambuca intensifies the licorice flavor of the fennel, while the raisins riff on its sweet side. This one-pot dish tastes even better the next day, when the sauce has melted into the center of the bulbs.

TIMING: Superquick; about 20 minutes plus raisin-soaking time

SERVES 4 TO 6

INGREDIENTS

3 fennel bulbs

2 tablespoons extra-virgin olive oil

2 tablespoons butter

1 onion, peeled, halved, and sliced

1 garlic clove, peeled and crushed

1 teaspoon fennel seeds, crushed with
   the flat of a knife

¼ teaspoon red pepper flakes

¼ teaspoon salt

coarse-ground black pepper to taste

¼ cup Sambuca, plus 1 tablespoon for
   finishing

¼ cup golden raisins, soaked to
   rehydrate for 20 minutes and soaking
   water reserved

1 cup orange juice (freshly squeezed or
   store-bought)

1 cup low-sodium chicken broth (or
   water)

zest of one orange

2 tablespoons Crumbs Yo! (page 291) or
   panko breadcrumbs

METHOD

1 Cut the tops off the fennel where the green stalks meet the white bulb. Trim the ends off the bulbs and cut the bulbs in half lengthwise. Remove the outer layers and anything that's browned, and trim away any excess stem. Cut each half into eighths. Chop the fronds and reserve.

2 In a large saucepan, heat the olive oil and butter over medium heat. Add the onion slices and sweat them, stirring, until they start to soften—but don't let them brown.

3 Add the fennel, garlic, fennel seeds, and red pepper flakes, and season the mixture with salt and pepper. Deglaze the pan with the Sambuca, and cook until the liquid in the pan has evaporated, about 1 to 2 minutes.

4 Add the raisins and the raisin-soaking water, orange juice, and chicken broth (or water). Cook, periodically turning the fennel and glazing it with liquid from the pan, until the liquid is reduced by three quarters (it should be a thin layer on the bottom of the pan). The liquid will thicken and the fennel will be well glazed, shiny, fattened, and softened.

5 Remove the pan from the heat, pick out the garlic clove, and mix in the chopped fronds and 1 tablespoon of the Sambuca. Transfer the fennel to a serving platter and sprinkle the breadcrumbs and orange zest over the top.

GRILLED RADICCHIO WITH THYME AND PECORINO

Radicchio is one of the great winter vegetables, but because it's got such a strong flavor (there's that Italian bitterness again), you either have to pair it with something sweet, like vin cotto or balsamic vinegar, or throw it on the grill to get that charred smoky flavor to balance things out. This recipe—my favorite way to eat radicchio— does both. Because more is better, right?

The best way to do this recipe is on the grill, but if you don't have one, don't worry: I do this under the broiler in my apartment, and while the color isn't as pretty, the flavor and texture are still pretty damn good.

TIMING: Superfast; about 20 minutes

SERVES 4

INGREDIENTS

2 heads radicchio, preferably Trevisano variety

¼ cup extra-virgin olive oil

¼ teaspoon salt

¼ teaspoon coarse-ground black pepper

2 teaspoons fresh thyme leaves

3 tablespoons grated pecorino cheese

1 tablespoon vin cotto or balsamic vinegar

METHOD

1. Heat the grill, if you have one, and heat the oven to 400° at the same time. If you don't have a grill, just heat the broiler in your oven.

2. Remove any dark or bruised leaves on the outside of the radicchio, remove the core, and cut each head in quarters lengthwise.

3. Place the radicchio on a baking tray and drizzle the olive oil on top. Sprinkle with the salt and pepper.

4. Place the radicchio directly on the grill or under the broiler on the baking tray, cut-side down. Grill or broil until the radicchio is slightly crispy: about 3 minutes on the grill, 5 minutes under the broiler.

5. If you're using the broiler, turn the oven to 400° and move the tray to the middle rack. If you're using the grill, lay the radicchio back on the baking tray and place it in the oven on the middle rack. Bake until the radicchio is fragrant and shriveled, about 10 minutes.

6. Remove the radicchio from the oven, sprinkle on the thyme, and then top with the grated pecorino. Drizzle the vin cotto or balsamic vinegar over the top. Serve immediately.

VIN COTTO

I like to call vin cotto "the poor man's balsamic," but don't mistake this stuff for vinegar. The Italians call it a *condimento*, like *mostarda*. In Apulia and Emilia-Romagna, they make vin cotto—literally "cooked wine"—by drying Black Malvasia or Negromaro grapes on trestles, then boiling the juice down to a thick syrup. Then they mix it with some vinegar mother to balance out the sweetness. You can find it now in an assortment of flavors, from fig to chili pepper, but I just like to use the regular stuff. It's great in sauces, dressings, marinades, and glazes—anywhere I'm looking for that sweet-and-sour taste. (The Italians also give this stuff to kids when they're down with a cold—sort of like an internal menthol rub.) Vin cotto is a lot like reduced balsamic vinegar, so I suggest it as a substitute in lots of places in this book: it's much cheaper than the good stuff, and you avoid the danger of poisoning your neighbors if you're cooking in a poorly ventilated apartment like mine.

LUKE'S WILD MUSHROOM ORZO

Luke Ostrom is a great cook. We've worked together for a long time; we've spent long nights drinking and talking food; we even traveled through Italy together. He knows his stuff, no doubt. So when he tells me we should try something, I usually listen. But when he started going on about orzo in our opening-menu-planning sessions, I was less than enthusiastic. He loved it when he was a kid, he said. It was so soul-satisfying and delicious, he said. It would make a great side dish on our menu, he said. But I wasn't buying it. I thought orzo was the kind of comfort food you fed to children and invalids: too bland, too soft, too … boring.

Boy, was I wrong.

Luke's take on orzo can definitely qualify as comfort food: it's hearty, warm, and delicious, the kind of thing you can't stop eating. But it's also grown-up and complex: the wild mushrooms give it a rich earthiness, and the orzo has a great mouth-feel. It's sort of like the mushroom risotto of your dreams—only it's way easier. It's a great match with poultry or meat; but as far as I'm concerned, ain't nothing wrong with sitting down to a big heaping bowlful of this stuff all on its own, topped with a handful of Parmigiano-Reggiano.

TIMING: 1 hour or so

SERVES 6 TO 8
INGREDIENTS

For the mushroom stock:

½ cup dried porcini mushrooms (about 1 ounce)

1 sprig fresh thyme

For the orzo:

2 tablespoons extra-virgin olive oil

1 small onion, chopped (about ½ cup)

1½ cups mixed wild mushrooms (about 4 ounces), washed, dried, and chopped into 2-inch pieces

1½ teaspoons salt

¼ teaspoon coarse-ground black pepper

2 tablespoons dry vermouth

1½ cups orzo

>>>

METHOD
TO PREPARE THE MUSHROOM STOCK:

1 In a small pot, immerse the dried porcinis in 4½ cups of water. Add the sprig of thyme whole.

2 Bring the mushroom mixture to a boil over high heat, then remove immediately from the stove and set aside for 5 minutes.

TO PREPARE THE ORZO:

1 Heat the olive oil in a medium saucepot. Add the onion and cook over medium heat until it takes on a light golden color, about 3 minutes, stirring regularly to prevent burning.

2 Add the mixed wild mushrooms and stir well to combine. Sauté on medium-high heat for 1 to 2 minutes, until the mushrooms are just starting to color. At this point, but not before, add the salt and pepper (if you do it earlier, before the mushrooms have opened up, the salt will pull out all the moisture). Mix well to combine and continue cooking for another 30 seconds, until the mushrooms have started to reduce and color.

3 Move the pan well away from the heat (so you don't catch fire) and add the vermouth. Stir to combine and then return to the heat for just a few seconds, until the vermouth and mushroom juices form a syrupy mixture in the bottom of the pan.

4 Remove the pan from the heat, add the orzo, and mix well, so the grains are all coated with the pan juices.

5 Remove the thyme sprig from the porcini mixture and discard. Pour the porcinis and liquid over the orzo.

6 Return the pan to medium-high heat and bring up to a low boil, stirring well to combine. Turn the heat down to low, and keep the mixture at a very lazy bubble for about 15 minutes, stirring occasionally. The orzo is done when it's swelled up and become tender, but still has a bit of a bounce between the teeth. There should be just a little bit of syrupy liquid on the bottom, but the orzo mixture should be a bit wet. (If you cook it till the liquid is completely absorbed, you'll have a sticky mess.)

TO FINISH THE DISH:

1 Remove the pot from the heat. Add the butter and mix in well; then add the Parmigiano-Reggiano and continue stirring. Add the parsley and thyme leaves and mix well, until the texture of the dish is softer and richer from the butter and cheese and all the ingredients are well combined. If you're using the truffle oil, add it and mix well so the oil is absorbed.

2 Serve as quickly as possible, topped with a little more of the grated Parmigiano-Reggiano.

To finish the dish:

2 tablespoons butter

¼ cup grated Parmigiano-Reggiano

1 tablespoon roughly chopped fresh parsley

1 teaspoon fresh thyme leaves

Optional:

1 teaspoon white-truffle oil

POTATOES ANTICO MODO

These potatoes are rich, man—no question about it. That's because the cooking process takes all the starch out, so while the outsides crisp up, the insides get really creamy. The spark for these came from a trip up into the Dolomite mountains in northern Italy: in a dark, low-ceilinged little restaurant, I had roast goat in a wood-fired oven with these crazy, crispy, buttery potato pies with tons of herbs and garlic.

TIMING: About an hour and a quarter

SERVES 4

INGREDIENTS

3 Idaho potatoes

1 cup butter (2 sticks)

1 tablespoon fresh thyme leaves

1 tablespoon rosemary leaves

½ teaspoon sea salt plus more for sprinkling

¼ teaspoon coarse-ground black pepper

1 garlic clove, thinly sliced

METHOD

1. Preheat the oven to 450°.

2. Peel the potatoes and slice them as thin as possible; if you happen to have a mandolin slicer sitting around your kitchen, this would be a good time to use it.

3. Half-fill the bottom of a double boiler with water and put the butter in the open top half. Set it on the stovetop on high heat. (If, like me, you don't have a double boiler in your kitchen, you can make a DIY one: fill a medium saucepan halfway with water and put a metal bowl large enough to fill the mouth of the pot on top.)

4. When the water has come to a low boil and the butter has melted, add the potatoes to the top of the double boiler. Use a wooden spoon to coat the potatoes in the butter, being careful not to break them.

5. Add the thyme, rosemary, sea salt, pepper, and garlic. Continue cooking on high heat—flipping and shaking the potatoes occasionally to avoid sticking and to help them cook evenly—until the potatoes have gone a bit translucent, about 20 minutes.

6. Spoon the potatoes onto a baking sheet. Using a fork, layer the potatoes into either one large ovenproof baking dish or four small ones, filling each dish to the top and being careful not to break the potatoes.

7. Place the potatoes in the oven and bake until they're crispy on the outside and creamy and delicious on the inside, about 30 minutes, give or take. Serve plated or right in the baking dish, sprinkled with sea salt if you like.

GIRARROSTO FRANCIA

To most young American cooks, there's nothing more romantic than the idea of spending a year working in European restaurants—and I was definitely one of those cooks. I used to daydream of roasting huge cuts of game meat on spits in stucco-lined kitchens; of rolling pasta with the chef's nonna; of baking bread with artisanal bakers in hundred-year-old brick-lined bakeries; of sipping wine in low-ceilinged cellars with ruby-cheeked masters. I would be the hot young American cook, the one the chef took under his wing. On my days off, I would take off in search of adventure on my Vespa, the wind in my hair, a beautiful Italian girl on the seat behind me with her arms wrapped around my waist.

That's not exactly how things turned out for me.

In my first Italian kitchen gig, this hot young American cook was challenged by such exciting and atmospheric tasks as washing the floors, taking out the trash, and dicing mountains of vegetables for twelve hours at a time. Since I was basically working for free, I had no money for Vespa rentals or anything else, so on my days off (during the limited window of time when I was actually awake), I hung around Torino, which, being a northern industrial town, didn't feature the ancient stony streets, sun-kissed hills, and sweeping fields of flowers I had planned on Vespa-ing through with my fantasy girl. And I was way too poor to do any culinary adventuring. Instead, I found a café where they kept a supply of tiny panini piled on a platter on the counter, the way an American bar might put out popcorn or nuts. I would order a coffee, sip as slowly as possible (no bottomless cups in Italy), and try to be subtle about stuffing myself with free panini. Presto: authentic Italian dinner, 1,000 lire! (That's about 35 cents.) The waitstaff called me "riccone"—big spender— and went out of their way to avoid taking my order.

But my favorite Sunday dinner for cheap was from Girarrosto Francia, a little rotisseria around the corner from my place. It was a hole-in-the-wall take-out joint with two items on the menu: rotisserie chicken and potatoes. The birds turned on gas spits on a high scaffold; the potatoes cooked in the drippings below, with some sea salt and herbs thrown on top. The chicken was always just fine (I mean, how wrong can you go with a locally grown chicken cooked on a spit?), but I was really there for the potatoes. Crispy on the outside, soft and flaky on the inside, buttery-rich from the chicken juice, fragrant, herby, salty—every week, when I had a few lire to scrape together, those potatoes saved my soul.

The place had no tables, not even a counter, so I would hand over my hard-earned lire and carry my feast back to my room, where I would dine like a king on the end of my bed. As a midwesterner, I was more or less born a potato expert—and I'm pretty sure I've tried potatoes every way they can be cooked since then—but those potatoes at Girarrosto Francia were the best I've ever had. They were the perfect cure for my chilly, unromantic winter—no Vespa, no girl, no glory—in that gritty northern Italian town.

POTATOES GIRARROSTO-STYLE

These were inspired by the potatoes I ate during my long, cold, wet, dark winter in Torino—the ones that sat underneath the rotisserie chickens in the rotisserie-chicken joint all night long, basting in fat drippings and crisping up in the heat (page 225). This version doesn't call for chickens—but it's still all about the crispiness.

The big chef's secret here? The stovetop stage. The potatoes and onions caramelize on the stove before they go back in the oven, so you end up with really crisp, really flavorful hash browns, Urban Italian–style.

TIMING: About 90 minutes, including 1 hour of potato-baking time

SERVES 4 TO 6

INGREDIENTS

4 Idaho potatoes

½ cup extra-virgin olive oil

2 medium onions, cut in half and sliced

3 cloves garlic, finely chopped

2 tablespoons butter

¼ teaspoon red pepper flakes

1 tablespoon fresh rosemary leaves, chopped

1 heaping tablespoon fresh thyme leaves

¼ teaspoon coarse-ground black pepper

½ teaspoon sea salt

¼ cup chopped fresh parsley

METHOD

1 Preheat the oven to 425°. (Use a convection oven if you've got one; it'll cook the potatoes faster and crispier.)

2 Prick the potatoes with a fork (so they don't blow up), place them on a baking tray, and bake them on the middle rack until a fork goes in easily, about 1 hour. Remove the potatoes from the oven and let them rest on the countertop until they're cool enough to work with.

3 When the potatoes are cool, roughly cut them into large chunks with a small knife.

4 Bring the oven back up to 425°. Pour the olive oil into the bottom of a large roasting pan. (Pick one that's safe to use on the stovetop too.) Scatter the onions in the pan and layer the potato chunks on top. Bake uncovered on the middle rack for about 15 minutes, turning the contents every 5 minutes, until the onions begin to soften and caramelize.

5 Remove the pan from the oven (leaving the oven on) and cook over high heat on the stovetop for 2 minutes to caramelize the potatoes and onions, being sure to shake the pan or stir the contents every 30 seconds or so to avoid burning.

6 Return the pan to the oven and continue baking for another 5 to 10 minutes, pulling the pan out periodically to shake the potatoes around with a spoon. Bits of potato on the bottom of the pan will brown up so they look almost like hash browns. Scrape these little flavor-and-crispiness bombs off the bottom and mix them in with the rest of the potatoes. When the potatoes are finished baking, they will be golden and crispy, with lots of brown bits.

7 Remove the pan from the oven and return it to the stove over medium-high heat. Add the garlic, butter, red pepper flakes, rosemary, and thyme. Stir, and season very liberally with salt and pepper. The potatoes should be crispy and crunchy on the outside, soft on the inside—think Italian hash browns. Cook for a few more minutes so the flavors meld. Remove the pan from the heat and add the chopped parsley. Serve immediately.

SPAGHETTI SQUASH WITH SAGE AND WALNUTS

Spaghetti squash is fun to eat: it's like kid food for grown-ups. The taste isn't kid stuff, though. This dish is aromatic and full of fall flavors, so it makes a great textural complement to meaty dishes—it's great with Pork Arrosto with Italian Plums and Grappa (page 185), for example. Plus it's stupid-easy to make.

TIMING: Stupid-easy, yes—but I didn't say it was fast. Give yourself 2 hours, because every oven and every squash is different.

SERVES 6 OR SO, DEPENDING ON THE SIZE OF YOUR SQUASH

INGREDIENTS

1 spaghetti squash (about 3 pounds)

¾ teaspoon salt

½ teaspoon coarse-ground black pepper

5 tablespoons butter

15 fresh sage leaves

½ cup shelled walnuts, roughly chopped

1 tablespoon grated Parmigiano-Reggiano or pecorino cheese

METHOD

1. Preheat the oven to 400°.

2. Place the squash on a cutting board. Using a large, very sharp knife, cut the squash in half lengthwise. Scoop out the seeds with a spoon and discard them.

3. Place the squash halves on a roasting rack and season with ¼ teaspoon each of the salt and pepper. Place 1 tablespoon of butter and 2 sage leaves in the hollowed-out core of each half.

4. Bake the squash on a tray on the oven's middle rack until the flesh is just soft—about 1 hour (or longer—it all depends on your oven). Remove the squash and let it cool until you can work with the flesh comfortably, about 15 minutes.

5. Using a fork, scrape the meat of the squash away from the skin, so that you get fluffy spaghetti-like strands. Reserve these and discard the skins, unless you're saving them for the presentation (see below). The squash will hold at this point up to a day ahead of time, in an airtight container in the fridge.

6. Heat the remaining 3 tablespoons of butter in a large saucepan over medium heat. When the butter has melted, add the walnuts. Toast the nuts and allow the butter to bubble, about 1 minute.

7. Add the sage leaves. When the leaves release their aroma and begin to crackle in the pan (about 1 minute), add the squash and stir to coat it with the flavored butter. Cook for 2 minutes over medium heat until the squash is warm, stirring frequently so the flavors get inside the squash. Season with the rest of the salt and pepper.

8. Serve on a large plate or platter, topped with the cheese. Or if you're going for that fancy '70s-hostess-style thing, serve the squash inside its own skin.

PEPERONCINI

Americans tend to think that there's no real spice in Italian cooking, but actually these tiny hot chili peppers play a major part in cooking traditions from all over the country: it's just that the heat is really subtle. Grown mostly in the south of Italy, peperoncini are the raw material for the chili flakes you find in glass shakers on the table at your local pizzeria. I use peperoncini in just about everything I make. For restaurant cooking, I like the pickled whole peppers, which have the perfect amount of sweet and spicy heat, but at home we just keep a shaker of the flakes beside the stove. The spice kicks up the flavor of soups, marinades, sauces, pastas, fish, salad dressing— even chocolate gets better with a shake of this stuff.

SPICY CORN WITH HOT BANANA PEPPER AND PINE NUTS

I'm from Ohio, so naturally I'm a big believer in corn on the grill—but these days, I'm a barbecue-deprived city kid. I came up with this stovetop recipe in desperation: it was killing me to see all that beautiful Greenmarket corn boiled, boiled, boiled. Corn in the pan has a totally different texture, and it's delicious, even sweeter than corn on the grill.

This dish is definitely Urban Italian: American corn (prized on this side of the ocean; fed to livestock on the other) and New World spicy peppers, plus the unmistakably Italian flavor of pine nuts. The dish is spicy—you know that thing about eating hot things on a hot day to cool yourself down?—but the pine nuts temper the spice with some sweetness and meatiness. It makes a kick-ass side dish with steak or grilled fish—so good I'd be tempted to do it this way even if I had a barbecue.

TIMING: Superfast; under ½ hour, including chopping and corn-cleaning time

SERVES 4 TO 6

INGREDIENTS

- 1 tablespoon extra-virgin olive oil
- 1 tablespoon butter
- 1 small onion, diced (about ¾ cup)
- 1 large hot banana pepper, sliced (about ¼ cup)
- 6 ears of corn, cleaned and kernels sliced off the cob (about 5 cups of kernels)
- ½ teaspoon salt
- ½ cup pine nuts, roughly chopped
- ¼ cup chopped basil
- ¼ cup chopped parsley

METHOD

1. Heat the olive oil and the butter together in a medium-to-large sauté pan. Add the onion and cook until it's soft, 1 to 2 minutes. Add the banana pepper and cook for 1 minute.

2. Add the fresh corn to the pan and stir. After 2 to 3 minutes, add the salt. (Don't put the salt in any earlier: you want the corn to retain its moisture.) Continue cooking until the corn is cooked through and takes on some spice from the peppers, about 5 minutes total. (You don't want to cook the corn into mushiness.)

3. Remove the pan from the heat and sprinkle with the pine nuts, basil, and parsley. Serve immediately.

SPINACH WITH CRISPY CHICKPEAS AND RICOTTA SALATA

Chickpeas have been all over southern Italian cooking ever since the Saracens; and spinach with garlic, of course, is very Italian. But this recipe was pure NYC in inspiration: I came up with it strolling through the Union Square Greenmarket while eating a falafel from my local joint. I fry the chickpeas up crispy to jack up the flavor and texture, using a really simple, apartment-friendly frying technique. In the restaurant world, you would probably achieve that crispiness in a fryer, but I think this low-stress home technique works even better.

TIMING: Super-super-quick; maybe 20 minutes, including prep time

SERVES 4

INGREDIENTS

For the chickpeas:

1 15-ounce can chickpeas (about
   1½ cups)
1 tablespoon all-purpose flour
3 tablespoons extra-virgin olive oil
¼ teaspoon each of salt and coarse-
   ground black pepper

For the spinach:

1 tablespoon extra-virgin olive oil
2 cloves garlic, sliced Goodfellas thin
¼ teaspoon red pepper flakes
1 pound fresh spinach, leaves picked and
   thoroughly washed
¼ teaspoon each of salt and coarse-
   ground black pepper
⅓ cup grated ricotta salata

METHOD

FOR THE CHICKPEAS:

1. Drain the chickpeas thoroughly in a strainer and let them dry, then place them on a paper-towel-lined plate so that any excess liquid is absorbed.

2. Place the flour in a deep bowl. Add the chickpeas and shake them around until they're all coated with the flour.

3. Heat the olive oil in a large, high-sided pot over high heat. When the oil begins to smoke, add the chickpeas and shake the pot around to coat them with the olive oil. The chickpeas will begin to snap-crackle-pop: that's the sound of crispiness happening. Keep shaking or stirring periodically so the chickpeas turn golden brown on all sides, about 4 minutes. Season with the salt and pepper, stir to coat, and then remove the chickpeas to a bowl and reserve.

FOR THE SPINACH:

1. Return the chickpea pot to the stove. Heat the olive oil over medium-high heat, then add the garlic and sweat 30 seconds, stirring constantly to avoid burning.

2. Add the red pepper flakes and then the spinach. When the spinach has begun to wilt—about 1 minute—add the salt and pepper. Cook for another 30 seconds, until the spinach has wilted thoroughly.

TO FINISH THE DISH:

1. Pile the spinach on a serving plate and load the chickpeas on top. Sprinkle the ricotta salata over everything. Serve immediately.

SPRING PEAS WITH ONIONS AND SAUSAGE

The French (and the English) have peas and bacon; the Italians have peas and sausage. It's a basic, slammin' peasant dish, best made in late spring and early summer and designed for people who do hard work all day long: it puts meat on your bones while giving you a nice taste of spring. The key is to cook the meat and onions together till the meat is brown and the mixture is rich and flavorful; then add the peas at the last minute, so they give the dish freshness, sweetness, and crunch.

When I brought this recipe to the restaurant, it was early summer, and the Union Square Greenmarket was full of pea tendrils, the young tops of the pea plant. So I added 'em in. They're a nice finishing touch; if you happen to find tendrils at your local farmers' market, throw a handful in at the end.

TIMING: Superquick; under ½ hour

SERVES 4 TO 6

INGREDIENTS

1 pound sugar snap peas (about 3 cups)

1 cup English or sweet peas

½ pound sweet Italian sausage (about 2 large links); you can use spicy sausage if you prefer

2 tablespoons extra-virgin olive oil

1 Vidalia or large sweet onion, sliced thin

¼ teaspoon coarse-ground black pepper

¼ teaspoon salt

Optional:

a handful of pea tendrils

METHOD

1. Bring a large pot of salted water to a boil.

2. Clean the sugar snap peas by snapping the ends off and pulling off the top string, but leave them whole.

3. Blanch the English peas, cooking them for about 1 minute, so that the color intensifies and the crunch is preserved. Remove them from the boiling water with a spider or long-handled strainer and immediately place them in a bowl of ice water to stop the cooking. Do the same with the whole sugar snap peas.

4. Remove the sausage meat from the casing and break it up into small pieces using your hands.

5. In a large sauté pan, warm the olive oil over high heat and sauté the meat until it browns, about 4 to 6 minutes. Add the onion and continue to sauté until the onion is soft and slightly caramelized.

6. Add the sugar snap peas and the English peas and season with the salt and pepper. Remove the pan from the heat as soon as the peas are hot—about 1 minute or so. If you're using the pea tendrils, throw them in as soon as you remove the pan from the heat and stir-fry them for a few seconds so they wilt. Serve immediately.

YELLOW WAX BEANS WITH PINE NUTS, MINT, AND LEMON

This is a side dish—it goes well with any summer chicken, pork, or fish dish—but I've been known to eat an entire bowlful on its own. It's full of surprises: savoriness with a buttery mouth-feel, deep flavors from pine nuts and fresh mint, and a sweetness that makes it almost dessert-like. I throw the nuts in the blender to intensify the flavor, but the lemon zest is really the key to this dish, the top note that makes it all come together.

TIMING: Superfast; under ½ hour

SERVES 4

INGREDIENTS

For the beans:

1 pound yellow wax beans

For the pine-nut butter:

½ cup pine nuts

3 tablespoons butter

1 tablespoon extra-virgin olive oil

To finish the dish:

2 tablespoons extra-virgin olive oil

1 onion (Vidalia if possible), quartered and sliced

1 cup chicken stock, vegetable broth, or water

zest of 1 lemon

2 tablespoons mint leaves, chopped (roughly 20 leaves)

¼ teaspoon salt

¼ teaspoon coarse-ground black pepper

METHOD

TO PREPARE THE BEANS:

1 Bring a large pot of salted water to a boil.

2 Cut the ends off the beans and blanch them in the boiling water till the beans are soft but still have a little bit of snap, about 5 minutes. Remove to a bowl of ice water to stop the cooking process. Reserve.

TO PREPARE THE PINE-NUT BUTTER:

1 Roast the pine nuts over very low heat in a dry pan on the stove until they're golden brown, about 5 minutes (longer on an electric stove). Shake the pan regularly to avoid burning the nuts.

2 Combine the pine nuts, butter, and 1 tablespoon of olive oil in a blender. Blend on medium speed until you have a chunky pine-nut butter (much like chunky peanut butter).

TO FINISH THE DISH:

1 Heat 2 tablespoons of olive oil in a pan over medium-high heat. Add the onion and sweat until it softens, about 2 minutes. When the onion has softened but has not yet turned color (about 2 minutes), add ½ cup of the stock. (This is a good trick to get onions to keep cooking but quit browning—adding water or stock lets them steam.)

2 When the liquid has reduced by half (about 2 minutes), add the beans, the pine-nut butter, and the remaining stock. Cook over medium heat, tossing constantly, quickly, and thoroughly, until the pine-nut butter and liquid thicken into a sauce and the beans are coated and shiny.

3 Remove the pan from the heat and stir in the lemon zest and mint. Season generously with salt and pepper—at least 2 twists of pepper and the equivalent in salt. Serve on a large platter.

ZUCCHINI BAGNA CALDA

Bagna calda—"hot bath"—usually refers to a Piedmontese hot-oil-anchovy-garlic dressing for vegetables. But here we're talking about the hot, spicy bath we're going to give some just-barely-cooked zucchini. It's a great way to jazz up what tends to be a sort of plain vegetable. Be careful with the cooking time: mushy, overcooked zucchini will kill this dish. The vegetables should be crunchy, and the sauce zesty, tangy, and spicy. It's best served at room temperature, and it's great with grilled fish.

TIMING: Superquick; 20 minutes or so

SERVES 4 TO 6

INGREDIENTS

For the sauce:

2 cloves garlic, sliced Goodfellas thin

½ cup chorizo (1 small link), finely chopped

½ teaspoon tomato paste

¼ cup sun-dried tomatoes (about 8), cut into strips

¼ teaspoon red pepper flakes

2 tablespoons extra-virgin olive oil

juice of 1 lemon

For the zucchini:

1 pound mixed zucchini, heirloom varieties if you can find them: yellow squash, gold bar squash

1 tablespoon extra-virgin olive oil

a pinch each of salt and coarse-ground black pepper

To finish the dish:

1 cup celery (3 stalks), sliced thin on the diagonal

½ medium red onion, chopped (½ cup)

1 tablespoon chopped parsley

salt and pepper to taste

METHOD

TO PREPARE THE SAUCE:

1. Combine the garlic, chorizo, tomato paste, sun-dried tomatoes, and red pepper flakes in a small pot off the heat.

2. Add the olive oil and heat the mixture over medium-low heat. Cook slowly until the oils from the chorizo come out, about 3 minutes. Remove the pot from the heat and stir in the lemon juice. Reserve.

TO PREPARE THE ZUCCHINI:

1. Cut the zucchini into pieces about 2 inches long and 1 inch wide. (It's okay to vary the size if your zucchini are smaller; just be consistent so that all the pieces cook at the same rate.)

2. Heat a sauté pan over medium heat and then add the olive oil. Sauté the zucchini in batches, tossing to coat with the oil. After each batch of zucchini has been coated with the oil, season it in the pan with the salt and pepper. Cook, tossing occasionally, until the zucchini pieces are soft along the seed side but still quite firm elsewhere, about 2 minutes per batch (though cooking time will vary with the size of your zucchini pieces).

TO FINISH THE DISH:

1. Place the zucchini in a large bowl. Add the uncooked celery and red onion. Pour the sauce over the vegetables and combine well, coating all the vegetables with the sauce.

2. Add the parsley and mix well. Season with more salt and pepper to taste. Serve at room temperature.

5

{ DOLCI }

ALMOND GRANITA

Granita is a big seller in Sicily: every seaside town has a big chrome-and-glass dessert café on the busiest public square, serving up granitas in every flavor you can think of. In the summer, couples, gangs of teenagers, old ladies, whole families sit around till the early hours of the morning at outdoor tables, eating these seasonal desserts (and drinking and smoking, of course) as they flirt, fight, gossip, and watch the crazy summer scene.

In this recipe, the key is the almond milk. Pastry cooks have been using this stuff—a rich, subtly flavored replacement for dairy—since the Middle Ages; it's very Sicilian, bringing out the flavors of the medieval trade routes up from Africa and the Middle East into Europe.

TIMING: Prep time: superquick. Freezing time: 2 hours.

SERVES 6 TO 8
INGREDIENTS

3 cups sliced almonds
½ cup sugar
¼ cup amaretto
½ teaspoon almond extract

METHOD

1. Preheat the oven to 325°.

2. Place the sliced almonds on a baking sheet and bake in the oven until they turn golden brown, about 8 minutes. When the almond slices begin to brown, about halfway through the baking process, pull out the tray and shake the almonds around so that everything browns evenly.

3. Remove the almonds from the oven and allow them to cool thoroughly. (If you're in a rush, remove the almonds to a cool sheet tray with a wider surface area.)

4. When the almonds are cool, put them in a food processor. Add 1½ cups of water and blend on high until the mixture becomes a chunky paste (like a rough-ground peanut butter). Be sure to scrape down the sides with a rubber spatula partway through to make sure everything is mixed in. Add another 1½ cups of water and continue blending until the mixture has a milky froth on top.

5. Strain the almond milk through a fine sieve into a bowl, pressing on the mixture with the back of a ladle to squeeze out as much milk as possible. Discard the remaining almond solids.

6. Add 1 cup of water and the sugar, amaretto, and almond extract to the liquid. Mix with a spatula or whisk until the sugar has dissolved and everything has blended into a very nutty, sweet mixture.

7 Pour the liquid into a shallow pan and put it in the freezer to harden until it achieves a frozen, granular consistency, about 2 hours.

8 Remove the pan from the freezer and scrape a fork back and forth over the top of it, the way the guy on the corner would scrape shaved ice, so that pencil-shaving-like curls result.

9 Serve the granita in small bowls or rocks glasses, over fruit or sorbet, or on its own, with biscotti on the side.

CAPPUCCINO GRANITA

Coffee runs deep in my family: the Carmellinis had a coffee-roasting plant in Livorno, on the Tuscan coast, up until World War I. (The coffee cup on page 239 is a family heirloom from the old days.) So we take our caffeination seriously, and I love coffee-flavored desserts. Most granitas are served with a little bit of fruit and a biscuit. Coffee granita comes with a big dollop of whipped cream on top instead. It looks a lot like a cappuccino, until you dig into it and it becomes a big mush of frozen, creamy, caffeinated goodness. In this version, I use cream flavored with vanilla to make things even more cappuccino-like. And I give the whole thing a Carmellini-family-style twist: my dad taught me that all desserts taste better with some booze inside, so I spike the coffee with Kahlúa. You can also use Sambuca, grappa, Frangelico, or amaretto.

TIMING: The actual dessert-making is superquick, but this dessert needs at least 2 hours to freeze

SERVES 5 TO 6
INGREDIENTS

For the granita:

2 cups fresh-brewed coffee

⅔ cup Kahlúa

½ cup whole milk

1 tablespoon sugar

½ teaspoon coffee extract

For the vanilla cream:

½ vanilla bean (or 1 teaspoon vanilla extract)

2 cups heavy cream

2 tablespoons sugar

Optional:

1 recipe Mom's Biscotti (page 262)

METHOD

TO MAKE THE GRANITA:

1. Combine all the granita ingredients in a medium bowl and whisk together until everything is well blended.

2. Pour the mixture into a shallow pan and place it in the freezer until it's frozen through, about 2 hours. The granita will hold in the freezer for up to 2 weeks.

3. Remove the pan from the freezer and scrape a fork back and forth over the surface of the frozen mixture, so that it curls up into shavings.

TO MAKE THE VANILLA CREAM:

1. Cut the end off the vanilla bean half, split it open, and scrape the meat out into the mixing bowl of a KitchenAid or blender. Add the heavy cream and sugar and combine.

2. Whisk on medium-high (speed 8 on a KitchenAid) until the cream is fluffy, being careful not to overmix (which would make the cream stiff on the spoon)—about 2 minutes. If you're not ready to serve the granita immediately, hold the cream in the fridge until you're good to go—but don't let it sit for more than a few hours.

TO FINISH THE DISH:

1. Spoon the granita into individual small bowls or rocks glasses, about ½ cup per serving. (To really dress this dessert up, frost the glasses for about 30 minutes before you dole out the granita.) Place a generous scoop of cream on top of each glass. Serve immediately, with biscotti on the side if you like.

BAKED FIGS WITH RED WINE AND ALMOND CROSTATA

Italians love fresh figs as an antipasti, especially with prosciutto (I play with that idea in the Fig Salad with Arugula, Parmigiano-Reggiano, and Prosciutto, page 73), but they also eat this grown-up fruit for dessert, baked in red wine. This version puts that sophisticated, but not terribly sweet, Italian classic together with a great American midwestern classic: cobbler. And just like peach or apple cobbler, this dessert is even better when you eat it fresh out of the oven, topped with vanilla or butter-pecan ice cream.

Figs are in season in the U.S. in the summertime, but this dessert is really best when the cold weather begins to set in, as the closer to a hearty meal. So plan ahead: buy some great figs in midsummer, and throw them in the freezer in a ziplock bag. They'll stay beautiful for six months at least.

TIMING: About 1 hour

SERVES 4 TO 6
INGREDIENTS

For the almond crumble:
¼ cup light brown sugar
1 tablespoon butter, cold
⅓ cup all-purpose flour
⅓ cup almond flour
2 tablespoons sliced almonds

For the wine mixture:
4½ cups red wine
2 cinnamon sticks
5 whole cardamom pods
1 teaspoon whole allspice

For the figs:
20 fresh figs (preferably Black Mission
    or Brown Turkey)

METHOD

TO PREPARE THE ALMOND CRUMBLE:

1. Combine the sugar, butter, flours, and sliced almonds in the bowl of a food processor at low speed, using the paddle attachment. As the mixture begins to come together, slowly increase the speed to medium and continue mixing until the butter has been thoroughly incorporated and the mixture has the texture of wet sand.

2. Remove the bowl from the food processor and break up any remaining pieces of butter with your fingers.

3. Cover the bowl with plastic wrap and allow the mixture to rest in the fridge for at least 30 minutes. The crumble will keep in the fridge for up to 2 days.

TO PREPARE THE WINE MIXTURE:

1. In a medium-sized pot, bring the red wine to a boil over high heat.

2. Add the cinnamon sticks, cardamom pods, and allspice and continue boiling until the flavor comes together and the wine reduces slightly, about 5 minutes. Remove the pot from the heat and allow the mixture to rest on the countertop so that the flavors infuse the wine, about 5 minutes.

3. Strain the wine mixture through a fine sieve into a bowl and reserve the liquid.

>>>

TO PREPARE THE FIGS AND FINISH THE DISH:

1. Preheat the oven to 350°.

2. Remove the stems from the figs with a sharp knife. Slice the tops and bottoms off, removing the undesirable bits but leaving as much of the fig intact as possible, and then slice each fig in half.

3. Place the fig halves upright, standing on end, in a shallow, ovenproof serving dish. Be sure to use a dish that allows you to pack the figs in one tight layer, so that little of the bottom is visible.

4. Pour the wine mixture over the figs, so that the wine covers the figs to a little more than halfway up. Place the serving dish on top of a sheet tray (to catch any wine that may bubble up and spill over once things heat up) and bake on the middle oven rack until a sharp knife slides right through the figs, about 15 minutes.

5. Remove the figs from the oven and turn the oven up to 400°.

6. When the oven comes up to temperature (but not before), remove the crumble from the fridge and scatter it on top of the figs. (It's important to bake the crumble straight from the fridge, so that the figs can bake completely before the crumble burns.) Return the figs to the oven and continue baking until the crumble turns golden brown, about 8 minutes or so.

7. Serve immediately, topped with ice cream if you like.

RICOTTA CHEESECAKE WITH BISCOTTI CRUST AND CANDIED LEMON

When I was cooking at San Domenico way back in the day, I used to go to one of the great midtown Jewish delis for a big hunk of cheesecake after a long night. It was sweet and savory and soft and crunchy, huge and filling, completely delicious and over-the-top. Totally NYC.

This cheesecake is a lot like the version I used to wolf down in the middle of the night, with some Italian tweaking. We use ricotta here instead of cream cheese, for a slightly more textured cake. We throw in lemon zest and candied lemon slices, to provide some contrast in flavor and texture. And the crust is biscotti, not graham crackers, so it's Italian-coffee-friendly.

This recipe isn't very difficult, but there are a number of steps involving refrigeration, so be careful with the order of operations; since the candied lemon slices need to chill in the fridge overnight, you need at least two days to put this together. The lemon slices must be as thin as possible—otherwise, they'll be chewy and distracting. There are lots of other options for topping the cheesecake: fresh berries, sautéed cherries, preserves. Consult your local market and your inner chef.

TIMING: Once the lemons are made, you'll need about 1½ hours

SERVES 6 TO 8

INGREDIENTS

For the candied lemon slices (optional):

3 lemons

7 cups sugar

For the biscotti crust:

18 Mom's Biscotti (page 262) or
    store-bought biscotti

¼ cup sugar

1 stick butter, melted

For the cheesecake:

2½ cups ricotta cheese

¾ cup sugar

3 eggs

4 tablespoons heavy cream

zest of 2 lemons

To finish the dish:

1 cup shelled pistachios, crushed

METHOD

TO PREPARE THE CANDIED LEMON SLICES (OPTIONAL):

1. Put the whole lemons in the freezer for 30 minutes. This will allow you to slice them extra-thin, a crucial move for this dish.

2. Meanwhile, add 3 cups of the sugar to 4 cups of water in a small pot over high heat. Stir well so the sugar dissolves, and then allow the mixture to come to a boil.

3. While the sugar water boils, use a serrated knife to slice the lemons widthwise into the thinnest slices possible: ⅛ inch or less.

4. Add the lemon slices to the pot and reduce the heat to keep the liquid at a low simmer. Cook the lemons until they are softened but not falling apart, about 15 minutes. This removes much of the bitterness from the lemons and begins the candying process.

5. Remove the pot from the heat and allow the mixture to cool at room temperature for 15 minutes, so that it can be handled.

6. Carefully strain the mixture, discarding the liquid and reserving the lemon slices.

7. Add the remaining 4 cups of sugar to 4 cups of water in a small pot over high heat. Stir well so the sugar dissolves, and then allow the mixture to come to a boil.

>>>

8 Add the lemon slices, reduce the heat to a low simmer, and continue cooking until the lemons are shiny and the syrup thickens, about 35 minutes.

9 Remove the pot from heat and let the mixture cool completely at room temperature. Place the sliced lemons and the syrup in an air-tight container and refrigerate for at least 8 hours. The lemon slices will hold in the fridge for up to 1 week.

TO PREPARE THE BISCOTTI CRUST:

1 Preheat the oven to 325°.

2 In the food processor, grind the biscotti into fine crumbs. (You should have about 2 cups.)

3 In a medium mixing bowl, combine the biscotti crumbs, sugar, and melted butter. Mix the ingredients together with your hands until everything is thoroughly incorporated and the mixture holds its shape when pressed together.

4 Line a tart pan with the crust mixture, spreading it with your fingers and pressing down so that the mixture forms a thin layer around the entire pan.

5 Bake the crust mixture until it turns golden brown and dry, about 10 minutes. Remove it from the oven and set it aside to cool at room temperature.

TO PREPARE THE CHEESECAKE AND FINISH THE DISH:

1 Return the oven to 325°.

2 Combine the ricotta cheese, sugar, eggs, heavy cream, and lemon zest in a food processor with the blade attachment, and mix on medium until everything is thoroughly combined, about 2 minutes.

3 Fill the crust completely with the cheesecake mixture. Return the tin to the oven and bake until a knife inserted in the cake comes out clean, about 20 to 25 minutes. Turn the cheesecake out onto a plate

or a cookie rack and allow it to cool completely on the countertop. When the cheesecake is completely cool, refrigerate it for 2 hours. It will hold in the fridge up to 2 days.

4. When you're ready to serve the cheesecake, remove the candied lemons from the fridge, if you're using them, and drain off any excess syrup. Garnish the top of the cheesecake with the candied slices, starting from the outside and working to the center. You'll probably have extra lemons left over, so pick out the nicest slices to use. (If you're using a different topping, add it now.)

5. Sprinkle the crushed pistachios over the top before serving.

TUSCAN DOUGHNUTS

I love Italian road food. Even at three in the morning, in any rest stop on the autostrada, you walk into a neon-lit rest stop and find people standing at the counter feasting on fresh-squeezed orange juice, made-to-order panini, and the most amazing espresso you've ever tasted. There are doughnuts, too: doughnuts stuffed with cream and rolled in sugar. But whereas in the U.S., doughnuts on the road are the best, in Italy you're better off dipping something else in your coffee: the doughnuts tend to sit around all day, getting stale and turning tasteless. When you taste them straight out of the kitchen, on the other hand, it's a whole different story. Then they're light, airy, melt-in-your-mouth yummy and rich with just enough of a bounce to keep things interesting.

It's no surprise that these doughnuts are the kind of dessert you can't take off the menu, ever: everybody loves them. What could be more fun, at the end of a long, boozy meal, than fluffy doughnuts filled with pastry cream and dipped in chocolate? The secret ingredient here is orange-blossom water, a Mediterranean ingredient (you can find it in specialty stores) which gives these Tuscan babies an airy fragrance way more grown-up and delicate than your average doughnut.

This dessert is definitely a challenge: it's the lengthiest and most involved recipe in *Urban Italian*. The individual steps aren't that hard, but there are lots of 'em, so be prepared. You'll also need many tools, so check out the recipe carefully before you go shopping. You don't want to get all the way through to the end and then realize at the last minute that you don't have a pastry bag, for example. That would suck.

TIMING: Major project

SERVES 6 TO 8
INGREDIENTS

For the dough:

1 cup whole milk

2 tablespoons plus 2 teaspoons active
   dry yeast

1 vanilla bean

4¾ cups bread flour

½ cup plus 3 tablespoons sugar

1 teaspoon salt

9 egg yolks

juice of 1 lemon, strained through a sieve
   to remove all the pulp

⅓ cup brandy or rum

1 tablespoon orange-blossom water (or
   zest of 2 oranges mixed with 1
   tablespoon brandy)

1 stick butter (¼ pound), cubed and
   kept cold

>>>

METHOD

TO PREPARE THE DOUGH:

1. Bring ½ cup of the milk to room temperature in a medium-sized bowl. Add all the yeast to the milk and stir until it dissolves. Allow it to activate until the yeast begins to foam, about 5 minutes.

2. Cut the ends off the vanilla bean, split it lengthwise, and scrape out the meat. Combine the vanilla-bean meat, flour, sugar, and salt in the large bowl of a mixer or KitchenAid.

3. Add the activated yeast (in its milk), the remaining ½ cup of milk, and the egg yolks, lemon juice, brandy or rum, orange-blossom water, and butter to the bowl.

4. Mix all the ingredients at low speed (speed 1 on a KitchenAid) with the hook attachment. When everything begins to combine (just a few seconds), increase the speed to medium-low (speed 2 on a KitchenAid) and continue mixing until all the ingredients are well combined and there are no chunks of butter. The dough should have some play to it: it will be a little bit sticky and stretchy, and will not tear easily.

>>>

For the pastry cream:

2 cups milk

meat of ½ vanilla bean, scraped (or
    1 teaspoon of vanilla extract)

¼ cup sugar

1 tablespoon all-purpose flour

1 tablespoon cornstarch

3 egg yolks

For the chocolate sauce:

½ cup corn syrup

1 cup sugar

¾ cup cocoa powder

2 tablespoons butter (1 ounce)

½ cup heavy cream

⅓ cup roughly chopped 64 percent dark
    chocolate (1½ ounces)

**For frying the doughnuts and finishing
the dish:**

½ gallon canola oil (look for high-heat
    oil or special canola oil for frying)

3 cups granulated sugar

5 Remove the dough to a large bowl or container (at least twice as large as the dough), coated with an unflavored nonstick spray or a thin coating of canola oil (or some other neutral oil that won't flavor the dough—do not use butter). If the container is square or rectangular, be sure to spread the dough out a bit to fit. Cover the container with plastic wrap, being sure to keep the wrap from touching the dough, place it in a warm area (about 70°), and allow the dough to proof until it has doubled in size and become very soft and almost silky to the touch, about 2 to 3 hours.

6 Turn the dough out on a lightly floured work surface. Beat some of the air out with flat palms, pushing down on all areas of the dough with the heel of your hand. Then form the dough into a large, tight ball, folding and rolling it to make it smooth.

7 Reflour the work surface and lightly flour the dough. Roll out the dough with a rolling pin, rolling in every direction, until the dough is a more or less circular shape, 1½ feet or so across and about ½ inch thick. There will be air bubbles in the dough; they're important for the consistency of the doughnuts. Continue to flour the dough and the surface as you work to prevent sticking.

8 Place a piece of parchment paper over a baking sheet and transfer the dough to the sheet by placing the rolling pin over one end and rolling the dough around the rolling pin (like rolling a skein of wool). Cover the sheet with plastic wrap and place it in the freezer until the dough has cooled and firmed, about 30 minutes. (If you have a really small, Manhattan-apartment-style freezer, and a sheet tray won't fit, cut the dough in half and place it in the freezer on 2 smaller trays.)

9 Flour the dough on both sides and place it on a lightly floured work surface. Roll the rolling pin across the dough to make sure that it's even in thickness (sometimes the dough continues proofing in the freezer). Then, using a round 2-inch cutter, cut out rounds: place the cutter over the dough, press down evenly with the heels of both hands, and then twist the cutter back and forth quickly to release the edges. Remove each round as it is cut. (The rounds will look exactly like dough-colored macaroons.) Save a little bit of the cutout leftover dough for testing the oil later—and remember you'll need to proof these leftover bits along with the rounds.

10 Place a sheet of parchment paper on a baking sheet and lightly spray with an unflavored nonstick spray or brush with canola or another neutral oil. Place the rounds (and your bits of leftover dough) on the baking sheet, leaving enough room between each one (about ½ inch all round) to allow them to proof without touching one another. Spray or brush the tops very lightly with more oil, so that the rounds glisten; this will stop them from drying out, and from sticking if they touch. Place the baking sheet in a warm area and allow the rounds to proof until they have doubled in size, about 1½ hours. When you poke the top of a proofed doughnut, the dough will indent and then spring back; the rounds will be light but firm. Be sure the doughnuts are fully proofed: otherwise, they'll stay raw on the inside when you finish them.

>>>

TO MAKE THE PASTRY CREAM:

1. Combine the milk and the vanilla-bean meat (or vanilla extract) in a medium-sized saucepan, and bring to a boil over medium-high heat.

2. Combine the sugar, flour, and cornstarch in a small bowl.

3. Place the egg yolks in a medium-sized bowl and slowly whisk the dry ingredients into the yolks, so that you have a thick mixture.

4. Pour about ⅓ of the hot milk into the egg-yolk mixture and whisk until all the ingredients are combined. Whisk in the rest of the hot milk and pour the combined liquid back into the saucepan.

5. Cook the liquid over medium heat until the mixture starts to thicken and coats the back of a spoon, about 3 minutes. Remove the cream mixture from the heat and strain it through a chinois or fine strainer into another bowl, so that any lumps are removed.

6. Immediately cover the cream with plastic wrap, placing the plastic directly on the surface of the cream so that a skin does not form. Refrigerate the pastry cream for at least 2 hours, until it's completely cold. The cream will hold in the fridge for up to 1 day.

TO MAKE THE CHOCOLATE SAUCE:

1. Combine ¾ cup of water and the corn syrup in a small pot and bring the mixture to a boil over high heat.

2. Combine the sugar with the cocoa powder in a small bowl.

3. Add the sugar-cocoa mixture to the corn-syrup-and-water mixture and bring it back up to a boil, then reduce the heat to low.

4. Add the butter, heavy cream, and dark chocolate, whisking well until everything dissolves. Increase the heat to medium-high and bring the mixture back up to a simmer, whisking continuously until the mixture becomes a shiny sauce, about 2 to 3 minutes.

5. Strain the sauce through a chinois or fine strainer and reserve. The sauce will hold in the fridge for up to 5 days.

TO FRY THE DOUGHNUTS AND FINISH THE DISH:

1   If the chocolate sauce is in the fridge, set it out so that it comes to room temperature by the time you're ready to serve the doughnuts.

2   Pour the canola oil into a large stockpot (about 1 foot deep) and heat over medium heat until the temperature reaches 350°. (If you don't have a thermometer, you can test the oil by throwing a little bit of the leftover dough into the pot. If the oil bubbles when the dough hits it and the dough fries up, you're good to go.)

3   Remove the chilled pastry cream from the refrigerator and place it in a pastry bag with a pastry tip, being sure to tie the end of the bag.

4   Fry 4 or 5 of the doughnuts at a time, turning them when they are brown on the bottoms (about 30 seconds), and pressing them down to submerge them in the oil. Lift the doughnuts out with a slotted spoon or spider and transfer them to a paper towel. The finished doughnuts will be very light and yeasty inside and well browned outside, and should pull apart easily.

5   While they're still warm, fill each doughnut with pastry cream until it starts to feel a little heavy (about 2 tablespoons' worth).

6   Pour the sugar into a large bowl. Roll each doughnut in the sugar so it's lightly coated.

7   Serve the doughnuts immediately, piled on a serving platter with a bowl of the chocolate sauce on the side for dipping.

CITRUS TIRAMISU

Classic tiramisu is great, but I wanted to try something fresh and a little bit different, so in this take, we've combined the old-school Italian flavors of tiramisu—the ladyfingers, the creaminess—with an equally old-school Italian lemon flavor, more often found in granitas and sorbetti. The combination, with the fruit, is fresh and bright, with an unexpected bounce to the texture. This dessert is best made in wintertime, when Texas Ruby Red grapefruits and Florida Valencia oranges are really good. It's great for parties: it looks really fancy (when you do it in rocks glasses, as I suggest here, it looks like a dressed-up trifle), plus you can make it ahead of time and hold the individual servings in the fridge for a couple of hours while you eat dinner. When it's time for dessert, just pull the rocks glasses out of the fridge and drop 'em on the table. Boom: dessert is served.

One very important warning, though: this dish may be sweet and fresh and a bit delicate, but to make it, you'll need a very strong whisking arm.

TIMING: Under 2 hours, including resting time

MAKES 6 TO 8 TIRAMISUS IN ROCKS GLASSES

INGREDIENTS

For the mascarpone mixture and the zabaglione:

1½ cups mascarpone cheese

1 egg yolk

zest of 1 lemon

⅓ cup plus 3 tablespoons sugar

2 whole eggs

⅓ cup limoncello

For the lemon cream:

1¼ cups fresh lemon juice (about 5 to 6 lemons)

zest of 1 lemon

1 cup sugar

3 whole eggs

7 egg yolks

For the ladyfingers syrup:

1 cup sugar

⅓ cup limoncello

>>>

METHOD

TO PREPARE THE MASCARPONE MIXTURE AND THE ZABAGLIONE:

1. Combine the mascarpone, egg yolk, and lemon zest in a large bowl. Mix together very gently with a rubber spatula until everything is smooth and combined. (If you mix too hard, the mascarpone will separate and become grainy.) Reserve.

2. Heat 3 cups of water in the bottom of a double boiler over medium heat until it steams, but do not allow the water to boil.

3. Make the zabaglione: Combine the sugar, eggs, and limoncello and whisk together thoroughly. Place the mixture in the top half of the double boiler (or in a stainless-steel bowl over the pot of boiling water, if you don't have a double boiler). Whisk the mixture constantly over the heat until it has become an airy, vanilla-colored foam, about 8 to 10 minutes. Make sure the water continues to steam, not boil; otherwise, you'll curdle the eggs. If the eggs do begin to coagulate in the bottom of the bowl as you whisk, take the top bowl off the heat and continue whisking on the countertop until they cool down, and then return the bowl to the heat.

4. When the mixture is thickened and can hold streaks (when you drip it from a whisk into the bowl, the drips are thick enough to hold their shape on the top of the mixture), remove the bowl from the heat and continue whisking until it reaches room temperature. (If you add the

>>>

To finish the dish:

about ½ of a 7-ounce package
    ladyfingers (depending on
    serving size)

3 oranges

2 grapefruits

zabaglione to the mascarpone when it's too hot, it will cause the mascarpone to melt and separate.)

5   Fold the zabaglione into the mascarpone mixture, a third at a time. After the first addition, mix vigorously with a spatula to break up the mixture; once the mascarpone mixture is nice and smooth, with no lumps, it will be able to absorb more of the zabaglione. Add another third of the zabaglione and fold it in gently. Once that's completely mixed in, fold in the remaining third. The mixture should be light and lemony to the taste, not too sweet.

6   Remove the mixture to a container and allow it to set in the fridge for about 1 hour. This mixture will hold in the fridge for up to 6 hours.

TO PREPARE THE LEMON CREAM:

1   Combine the lemon juice, lemon zest, and ⅓ cup of the sugar in a medium-sized pot and whisk them together. Bring the lemon mixture to a boil over high heat. Boil until the sugar has dissolved, about 30 seconds, then remove the pot from the heat.

2   In a large bowl, combine the remaining ⅔ cup of sugar, the whole eggs, and the egg yolks and whisk vigorously for 20 seconds, until everything is combined. (Sugar will partially cook raw eggs, so it's important to whisk well to avoid curdling.)

3   Pour a third of the lemon mixture into the egg mixture to raise the temperature, whisking briefly; then pour in the rest of the lemon mixture and whisk to combine for 10 seconds.

4   Return the combined mixture to the pot and return it to the stove over medium heat, stirring with the whisk to prevent the eggs from curdling, until the mixture begins to thicken up significantly. Turn the heat to low and whisk vigorously until the mixture foams up.

5   Remove the pot from the heat and whisk for a few seconds more. The mixture should be thick but light and airy and should hold a streak. It will be lemon-yellow and very smooth and sweet-tart-tasting.

6   Immediately strain the lemon cream through a fine sieve, pushing it through with the whisk, in order to catch any bits of egg that might have curdled during the cooking process.

7   Pour the cream into a flat tray with a wide surface area (to help the cooling process) and spread it evenly with a rubber spatula. Cover the tray with plastic wrap, being sure that the whole surface is covered and patting the wrap down to ensure that it touches the cream everywhere—this will prevent a skin from forming on top. Cool the cream in the fridge for at least 15 minutes. This mixture will keep in the fridge for up to 24 hours.

TO PREPARE THE LADYFINGERS SYRUP:

1   Combine the sugar with 2 cups water in a small pot and heat it on the stove at high heat, whisking regularly, until the sugar dissolves, about 2 minutes. Remove the pot from the heat and add the limoncello. Whisk the mixture together. Reserve.

TO FINISH THE DISH:

1   Segment the oranges and grapefruits: With the peel still on, slice the ends off each orange and grapefruit. Set it on one end and, with a small sharp knife, slice off the peel and the white pith together. Holding the peeled fruit in your hand, cut along the inside of each white segmenting line. Remove the "supremes" (the meat, the best part) to a bowl, leaving all the membranes attached to the "skeleton." Discard the skeleton. Place orange and grapefruit slices on the bottom of each rocks glass (about 2 segments of each in each glass, alternating for color).

2   Remove the lemon cream from the fridge. Scoop out a large dollop with a soup spoon and place it over the fruit slices.

3   Break the ladyfingers in half. Set aside a few ladyfingers for crumbling on top at the end. Dip the rest very quickly and completely into the syrup (as quickly as putting your ATM card in a slot and pulling it out again).

4   Lay 3 ladyfinger halves on top of the lemon cream, so that the pieces overlap and the cream is covered. Lay 1 more slice each of orange and grapefruit on top of the ladyfingers.

5   Cover the top of the fruit and cookies with generous servings of the mascarpone mixture; the idea is to top it as you would an ice-cream sundae, so the mixture drips down the sides inside the glass, over the fruit, cookies, and lemon cream.

6   Just before serving, crumble the undipped ladyfingers with your fingers and sprinkle them on top.

HAZELNUT AND
WHITE CHOCOLATE COOKIES

Italian cookies are not exactly famous for their moistness: they're usually superdry almond-flour sawdust discs, because they're meant mainly for dipping in coffee. So when I started working on Italian desserts my way, I wanted to try to bring a little American decadence to the cookie-making process. Here, I've used hazelnuts for the Italian flavor—and white chocolate not for the taste (the white chocolate is really just part of the dough, and you don't get a lot of flavor from it) but for the texture. White chocolate in cookies is decadent-tasting and really sweet. In this recipe, it just keeps things moist, so if you wanted to, you could actually eat these subtly flavored cookies without any coffee at all.

TIMING: Superquick; about 20 minutes, not counting resting time

MAKES ABOUT 45 COOKIES

INGREDIENTS

½ cup hazelnuts, whole

½ cup (3 ounces) chopped white
 chocolate

6 egg yolks

1 cup sugar

zest of 1 orange

14 tablespoons (7 ounces; just under
 2 sticks) butter, softened

1 tablespoon plus 1 teaspoon baking
 powder

2 cups all-purpose flour

¼ teaspoon salt

METHOD

1. Grind the hazelnuts and white chocolate in the food processor until the mixture has a mealy, pebbly texture: about 30 seconds.

2. Using the whisk attachment on a KitchenAid, whip the egg yolks, sugar, and orange zest together at medium speed (speed 6) until the mixture is foamy and pale, about 5 minutes.

3. Add the soft butter and continue to whisk until the butter is thoroughly incorporated.

4. Change the attachment from the whisk to the paddle. Add the baking powder, flour, and salt, and mix until everything is incorporated and smooth.

5. Add the hazelnut-and-white-chocolate mixture and combine on low speed until you have a cookie dough, about 20 seconds.

6. Place the dough in an airtight container and refrigerate for at least 30 minutes, so that the dough can be easily worked with. The dough will hold in the fridge for up to 3 days.

7. Preheat the oven to 325°.

8. Line a baking sheet with parchment paper. Using a soup spoon, scoop the cookie dough into tablespoon-size dollops and place them in rows on the lined baking sheet with ample space between each dollop. (You'll get about 25 on a baking sheet.)

9. Bake the cookies until they turn golden brown, about 10 to 15 minutes. These cookies are best straight out of the oven: serve them immediately if possible.

MOM'S BISCOTTI

Biscotti are the most basic and most important of Italian desserts: Italians eat them with ice cream and granita, they layer them in tiramisu, they serve them with after-dinner drinks, and, of course, they dip them in coffee. Some people, in fact, think of biscotti as nothing more than a vehicle for espresso, and so they miss the vital importance of a good biscotti recipe. The perfect biscotto should offer lots of flavor and punch all on its own, while also actually enhancing the coffee-drinking experience. My mom uses two key ingredients to give her biscotti that well-balanced kick: anise seed and booze. The anise gives it that Italian flavor and a little bit of complexity. Anise seeds (small spice seeds with fuzzy tails) can be hard to find, so if they're not at your local, use crushed fennel seeds instead. And booze, as I've mentioned before, is crucial to the Carmellini family dessert experience: we strongly believe it makes everything better.

TIMING: About 2 hours

MAKES ABOUT 40 BISCOTTI
INGREDIENTS

3 whole eggs

1 cup sugar

4 tablespoons butter, melted

2 cups all-purpose flour

1 teaspoon baking powder

zest of 2 lemons

¾ cup whole shelled pistachios

1 tablespoon anise seed (or crushed
   fennel seeds)

1 tablespoon Sambuca

METHOD

1 Using the whisk attachment on a KitchenAid, whip 2 of the eggs and the sugar together at medium speed (speed 4) until the mixture becomes foamy and pale and doubles in volume, about 15 minutes. In the last 2 minutes of the egg-whipping process, pour in the melted butter and allow it to incorporate.

2 Remove the whisk attachment and replace it with the paddle attachment. Add the flour, baking powder, and lemon zest to the bowl and mix at a low speed (speed 2) until everything is combined.

3 Add the pistachios and mix for 30 seconds, so the nuts are combined into the sticky dough.

4 Refrigerate the dough in the mixing bowl for 20 minutes, covered in plastic wrap, so that the dough cools and becomes workable.

5 Preheat the oven to 350°.

6 Line a baking sheet with parchment paper. Remove the dough from the fridge; take half the dough out of the bowl and shape it into a log about 9 inches long by 1½ inches wide. Repeat with the remaining dough. Lay these logs out on the cookie sheet, leaving 3 inches between them to allow for expansion during the baking process.

7 Whisk the remaining egg briskly in a small bowl. Lightly brush the dough with this egg wash.

8 Bake the dough until the loaves start to brown, about 15 minutes. Rotate the tray in the oven, and continue baking until the loaves are golden brown, about 10 to 15 minutes more.

9. Remove the loaves from the oven and let them cool until the logs are warm, but not hot, to the touch, about 10 to 15 minutes.

10. Lower the oven temperature to 325°.

11. Place the loaves on a cutting board. Using a serrated knife, cut them on a slight diagonal into ¼-inch biscotti-sized pieces, discarding the end pieces.

12. Place the cookies back onto the lined baking sheet, one by one, and return the sheet to the oven. Bake until the biscotti are crunchy, another 15 minutes or so.

13. Allow the biscotti to cool before serving. They will keep in an airtight container for up to 1 week.

NERO COOKIES

When I was a kid, I used to invent cookies. I even had a notebook where I kept careful records of some of my inventions. I baked with my mom, whose cookies are still the gold standard for me. But I never came up with anything as tasty and beautiful as her Russian teacakes.

I wanted to do a great Italian version of those teacakes: something delicate and yummy and dippable in coffee. I came up with these—and while nothing is as good as Mom's baking, of course, these are pretty damn fine. The cookies crack as they bake, and the sugar makes the cracks and fissures stand out. To me, they looked like an old city wall, broken with age, like the ones you see all over Rome. I guess I could have called them "Caesar cookies" or something, but I went with the rich, decadent emperor with the crazy appetites—the one who's said to have fiddled while his great city burned.

These cookies are rich and decadent too. If you don't have mint extract on hand, you can use crème de menthe; the flavor will be less intense, but the cookies will still be delicious.

TIMING: About 2 hours, including 1 hour of dough-resting time

MAKES ABOUT 30 COOKIES

INGREDIENTS

1 cup sliced almonds

2 eggs

⅓ cup sugar

8 ounces (2 cups) roughly chopped
  70 percent dark chocolate

2 tablespoons butter

¼ teaspoon mint extract (or
  crème de menthe)

½ cup all-purpose flour

1 teaspoon baking powder

2 cups granulated sugar for coating

2 cups confectioners' sugar for coating

METHOD

ORDER OF OPERATIONS: It's a little tricky but imperative that you roast and cool the almonds, whip the eggs and sugar, and melt the chocolate over the double boiler all at the same time, so that you can add the cooled melted chocolate to the still-whipping eggs and then add the almonds a minute or two later.

1. Preheat the oven to 325°.

2. Toast the almonds in the oven on a baking sheet until they're golden brown, about 10 minutes.

3. Allow the almonds to cool until you can work with them (about 5 minutes), and then grind them into small flakes in the food processor.

4. While the almonds are toasting and cooling, using the whisk attachment on a KitchenAid, combine the eggs and sugar at medium speed (speed 4) until the mixture is foamy and pale and has increased in volume, about 15 minutes.

5. Meanwhile, bring 3 cups of water to a gentle steam in a small pot over medium heat, but do not let the water boil.

6. Place the chocolate, butter, and mint extract (or crème de menthe) in a stainless-steel bowl. Melt the chocolate by placing the bowl on top of the small pot of water, creating a double boiler. When the chocolate has melted (about 3 minutes), remove the bowl from the heat and allow the chocolate mixture to cool slightly.

>>>

7.   Pour the chocolate mixture into the egg-and-sugar mix as it reaches the very end of the whipping process. Once all the chocolate is incorporated (about 25 seconds), stop whisking and change the attachment from the whisk to the paddle.

8.   Add the flour, baking powder, and crushed almonds to the bowl and mix for 30 seconds, until everything is combined into a dough.

9.   Refrigerate the dough in an airtight container for at least 1 hour, so that it's well chilled. The dough will hold in the fridge for up to 3 days.

10.   Return the oven to 325°.

11.   Remove the dough from the fridge. Scoop the dough into tablespoon-sized dollops and roll each one between your palms to form a small ball. Place the dough balls on an ungreased baking sheet or a plate and refrigerate them for 5 minutes so they become very cold.

12.   Pour the granulated sugar and the confectioners' sugar into 2 separate bowls. Roll each ball first in the granulated sugar and then in the confectioners' sugar, so that it's coated, then place it on a baking sheet lined with a piece of parchment paper.

13.   Bake the cookies on the middle rack until they expand and start to crack, about 15 minutes. They'll look awesome, like an old Roman wall.

These cookies are best eaten not hot from the oven but warm, the day they're baked.

We drove down into Modica in the dark-gold light of late afternoon. Modica is a fifteenth-century baroque city; because it's in a deep valley, protected by a ring of citadel towns, it's been almost entirely preserved. It's a calm, prosperous place: tree-lined streets, dense traffic moving at a reasonable pace, business types, ladies who lunch, schoolkids fooling around on the way home from class. Everyone in town seemed to be thin, attractive, well behaved, and totally without bling or D&G or enormous fake boobs. There were no rust-ridden trucks screeching through the streets at 100 clicks, no burnt-out buildings, no chunks of falling terra-cotta, no graffiti, no crack vials. It felt as though we'd suddenly been airlifted out of the craziness that is Sicily and dropped into one of those ads for international corporate shipping, in which shiny young executive types walk through some unnamed European city, swinging their briefcases and talking on cell phones.

But Modica hides a strange and delicious secret behind its north-European façade. Turn down a little alley or follow a path around one of the chic little stores in the city center to a back courtyard, and you'll more likely than not find yourself in front of one of the dozens of dolcerias where chocolate is made in exactly the same way the Aztecs did it. That's thanks to the Spanish, who ruled Sicily in the fifteenth and sixteenth centuries and brought the technique from their colonies in the New World, turning Modica into an unlikely Baroque-era center of Aztec-style chocolate-making. Artisans have been carrying on that tradition here ever since.

Once we'd finally found a legal parking spot more than six inches wide, we followed one of those narrow pathways behind a boutique on the main street. There, in a converted Baroque carriage house, was L'Antica Dolceria Bonajuto. From the outside, it's nothing special (a kid played in the yard; outside stairs went up to the second floor); but inside, the place is a hushed minimalist temple to chocolate (or *xocolatl*: the Aztec word is still in use here). This is Willy Wonka's chocolate factory for grown-ups. The walls of the two-story space are lined with chocolate-colored drawers with brass pulls, and every one of them is filled with a different kind of chocolate. There are explanatory panels and other museum-quality aids to learning. Once we'd done the tour, studied the list of choices, and made a selection, the very well-dressed twentysomething woman in charge (think young, severe Parisian antiques dealer) began opening the unmarked drawers and making precise withdrawals. *Xocolatl* has no cream (which is fortunate, since there isn't a cow within a hundred miles of Modica), but it does feature cinnamon, chili, and vanilla flakes. It made us think of Mexico, and it made us very happy. Scientists say that chocolate is a natural mood-enhancer. I can tell you for sure that, loaded up with bars and heading down the road in a mild chocolate coma, we found the toxic semis and roadside shantytowns of Sicily to be absolutely no problem. If you're looking for your own happy place, you'll be pleased to know that Dolceria Bonajuto sells its rich, darker-than-dark chocolate on the Internet.

THE PERFECT PANNA COTTA

Panna cotta means "cooked cream," but that's not totally accurate: here, we warm the cream but never actually bring it to a boil and cook it through, so it retains its flavor and texture. The raspberry compote is an American addition; I love this with fresh, beautiful local raspberries at the height of the season. The lemon zest at the end brightens everything up a bit, giving a tiny spark to this bowlful of sweet, creamy, rich summer deliciousness. The texture should be much looser than Jell-O, closer to custard or soft ice cream than it is to that green stuff that jiggles on kindergarten tables.

TIMING: Pretty quick; about 15 minutes for assembly, 1 hour to set

MAKES 6 TO 8 INDIVIDUAL PANNA COTTAS

INGREDIENTS

For the panna cotta:

3 gelatin sheets or 4 teaspoons powdered gelatin

1¼ cups whole milk

1 cup heavy cream

¾ cup sugar

1 vanilla bean, split lengthwise (or 1½ teaspoons vanilla extract)

1¾ cups buttermilk

For the raspberry compote:

2 tablespoons sugar

1 tablespoon lemon juice

3 cups fresh raspberries (or any other fresh delicious summer berries)

To finish the dish:

zest of 1 lemon

METHOD

TO PREPARE THE PANNA COTTA:

1. Bloom the dry gelatin in cold water until the gelatin sets, about 2 minutes. (It should feel, of course, like Jell-O).

2. Combine the whole milk and heavy cream in a saucepot. Add the sugar and both the meat (the scraped-out innards) and the pod of the vanilla bean (or the vanilla extract).

3. Heat the mixture over medium heat, whisking constantly and without allowing the mixture to bubble or boil, until the sugar has completely dissolved and the mixture is just starting to steam, about 3 minutes; the vanilla bits will start to rise to the surface and fleck the mixture. Remove the pot from the heat.

4. Remove the gelatin from the water (squeeze out the excess water if you're using gelatin sheets). Add it to the pot with the cream mixture, mixing until it dissolves completely.

5. Strain the mixture through a fine sieve into a bowl. It will be sweet and rich (avoid the temptation to just drink the stuff warm). Set the bowl in a larger bowl of ice, stirring the mixture occasionally, until it cools to room temperature.

6. When the mixture has cooled, add the buttermilk and stir until it is thoroughly incorporated.

7. Pour the mixture into a large bowl or, to be fancier, a number of small dessert bowls. (The larger the bowl, the longer the panna cotta will take to set.) Cover lightly with plastic wrap, being sure to avoid contact between the panna cotta mixture and the plastic. Refrigerate the panna cotta until it's set, about 2 hours. The top should be set in a

>>>

thin, fragile layer, and the panna cotta should be soft inside, with a little bit of the wobble of gelatin.

TO PREPARE THE RASPBERRY COMPOTE:

1. Put the sugar, lemon juice, and 1 cup of the raspberries in a food processor and purée until the mixture is smooth, about 30 seconds.

2. Place the remaining raspberries in a medium-sized bowl. Pour the purée over the fresh raspberries and gently coat them with a spoon.

3. Place the compote in an airtight container and chill in the refrigerator until you're ready to serve the panna cotta (at least 10 minutes).

TO FINISH THE DISH:

1. Remove the panna cotta from the fridge immediately before serving.

2. At the last possible second, spoon a dollop of the compote over each serving of panna cotta and very finely grate the lemon zest over the top.

CHOCOLATE PANNA COTTA

Panna cotta is the quintessential finish to a decadent Italian meal. Here I've added a bit of Middle America, Bill Cosby–style, by hitting this classic creamy dessert with a hint of chocolate puddin'.

There are many possible toppings for this dessert. I think amarena cherries are perfect here, though they can be a bit tough to find. You can throw in some fresh berries; if you want to add some crunch, crush up some chocolate wafers or biscotti to sprinkle on top. It's up to you.

TIMING: Pretty quick; 10 minutes for assembly, 1 hour to set

SERVES 6 TO 8

INGREDIENTS

4 sheets gelatin or 4 teaspoons
   powdered gelatin

½ cup sugar

¼ cup cocoa powder

1 cup milk

1½ cups heavy cream

2½ cups roughly chopped bittersweet
   chocolate (11 ounces)

2 cups crème fraîche or plain yogurt

toppings of your choice

METHOD

1. Submerge the gelatin in cold water and allow it to bloom, so that the gelatin has the bouncy consistency of Jell-O and the appearance of plastic, about 2 minutes.

2. Combine the sugar and cocoa powder in a small bowl and mix together well.

3. Combine the milk and cream in a small pot and heat it gently over medium-low heat. When the mixture is warm to the touch, whisk in the sugar and cocoa powder and combine thoroughly. Be sure to scrape down the sides of the pot as you go, so that bits of cocoa don't burn and flavor the mixture.

4. Bring the mixture to a boil and cook for 30 seconds to activate the starch in the cocoa powder, so that there's no floury taste. Remove the pot from the heat.

5. Place the chopped chocolate in a large bowl. Strain the cream mixture through a fine sieve into the bowl, and mix everything together with a whisk until the chocolate melts and the mixture becomes smooth and liquid.

6. Remove the gelatin from the water (squeeze out the excess water if you're using gelatin sheets). Add the gelatin to the bowl and continue stirring. (It's important to do this while the mixture is hot, so that the gelatin dissolves thoroughly—otherwise you'll have huge chunks in your panna cotta.)

7. Place the crème fraîche or yogurt in another large bowl and pour the cream-chocolate mixture over the top. Whisk the mixture together

>>>

until it's smooth, then scrape a rubber spatula along the sides and bottom of the bowl to make sure that there's no crème fraîche or yogurt sitting around unblended.

8. Pour the mixture into a large bowl (or, to be fancy, divide it into 6 to 8 small dessert bowls), being sure to leave some space at the top of the bowl. Cover the mixture with plastic wrap, stretching the wrap taut so it doesn't touch the panna cotta, and refrigerate for at least 2 hours. The panna cotta will hold in the fridge for up to 2 days.

TO FINISH THE DISH:

1. Remove the panna cotta from the fridge and top with the topping of your choice. Serve immediately.

PINE NUT CAKE

Pignolata cookies are a staple in every Italian-American bakery from New York to San Francisco. This is a teacake version, and it's great for dunking in coffee or tea, but you can definitely eat this one without sticking it in liquid: it's very moist, but not too rich or sweet. The meringue lightens up the batter, so it won't be like one of those stone-weight cakes. And, as I discovered by accident, this stuff is perfect for ice-cream sandwiches. Two slices of pine nut cake with a layer of chocolate ice cream in between? Awesome.

TIMING: About 1 hour including baking time

MAKES 3 CAKES

INGREDIENTS

For the cake batter:

2 cups pine nuts

1¼ cups sugar

1 pound (4 sticks) butter, cut into
    ½-inch cubes, at room temperature

zest and juice of 2 lemons

4 cups all-purpose flour

2 tablespoons baking powder

4 whole eggs

¾ cup yogurt

For the meringue:

4 large egg whites

½ cup sugar

METHOD

TO PREPARE THE CAKE BATTER:

1   Preheat the oven to 350°.

2   Toast the pine nuts over very low heat in a dry sauté pan until they have just begun to take on a golden color, about 8 minutes. Remove from the stove and reserve.

3   Meanwhile, cream the sugar, butter, and lemon zest together in a KitchenAid with the paddle attachment, beginning on low and then increasing the speed to medium as the mixture combines. Be sure to scrape down the sides as you go to make sure everything mixes evenly.

4   When the mixture is quite smooth, add the flour and baking powder. Mix until the dry ingredients are just incorporated, and then begin adding the eggs, one by one, waiting until each egg is thoroughly mixed in before adding the next. Turn the KitchenAid up to high for about 5 seconds to combine everything thoroughly, then scrape down the sides and the bottom with a spatula and mix in any bits that have failed to incorporate.

5   Add the yogurt, and mix in with the paddle attachment until it's thoroughly incorporated.

6   As you continue mixing, add the lemon juice and incorporate. The batter should be stiff and airy, a homogenous mix. Scrape down the sides and bottom and mix well with a spatula to make sure that there are no lumps of butter and that the flour is all incorporated. Then transfer the mixture to a large bowl.

>>>

TO PREPARE THE MERINGUE:

1. Beat the egg whites in the mixer with the whisk attachment at medium speed until they've formed a froth.

2. While the egg whites are still whisking, add the sugar in a slow stream. Mix at medium for 20 seconds to combine.

3. Turn the mixer up to high and continue beating until the meringue forms stiff peaks, about 4 minutes; when you lift the whisk, the meringue should form a bird's-beak shape off the end.

TO FINISH THE CAKE:

1. Fold a third of the meringue into the batter, using a rubber spatula to combine well.

2. Add the rest of the meringue and fold in well until the mixture is combined.

3. Fold in the pine nuts.

4. Spray 3 2-pound loaf pans evenly and on all sides with a nonstick coating.

5. Fill each loaf pan two-thirds full with the batter. Smooth and flatten the tops with the spatula or the back of a wooden spoon, then bake the loaves on the middle rack until you can put a knife into each loaf and bring it out clean, about 45 minutes.

6. Remove the cakes from the oven, turn them out on a cake rack, and let them rest for 30 minutes before serving.

RASPBERRY INVOLTINI

Involtini refers to anything rolled, and that's what these cookies are: halfway between Jewish rugelach and a fruit roll-up. You can put any kind of jam you like inside, but raspberry is my favorite.

TIMING: About 3 hours, most of it chilling time

SERVES 6 TO 8
INGREDIENTS

For the almond crema:

2 sticks butter, cubed

¾ cup sugar

½ cup almond paste

1½ cup almond flour

½ cup plus 2 tablespoons all-purpose flour

4 eggs

For the involtini dough:

1 stick cold butter, cubed

1⅓ cups flour

2 teaspoons salt

½ teaspoon sugar

½ cup raspberry jam

For finishing:

1 cup turbinado sugar

1 egg

METHOD
TO MAKE THE ALMOND CREMA:

1. Combine the butter, sugar, and almond paste in the bowl of a KitchenAid. Using the paddle attachment, cream the ingredients at medium speed (speed 3) until the mixture is smooth and no lumps remain, about 2 minutes.

2. Add the almond flour and all-purpose flour and continue mixing for 30 seconds at a low speed until everything is incorporated.

3. With the mixer still running, add the eggs one at a time, making sure each egg is thoroughly blended into the mixture before adding the next one.

4. When all the eggs have been added and the mixture is well combined, scrape the sides of the bowl with a rubber spatula and mix in anything that has stuck to the sides. Then refrigerate the crema in an airtight container until it sets, about 20 minutes. It will keep in the fridge for up to 1 day.

TO MAKE THE INVOLTINI DOUGH:

1. Mix the butter, flour, salt, and sugar in a clean bowl in the Kitchen-Aid at medium speed (speed 3) until the butter is broken up into pebble-sized pieces. Add 3 teaspoons of water and continue mixing until the dough is smooth, about 1 minute. Then remove the dough from the mixer bowl, wrap it in plastic wrap, and let it rest in the fridge for 2 hours. It will keep in the fridge for up to 2 days.

2. Roll the dough out on a floured surface with a rolling pin until it is ⅛ inch thick. Once the dough is rolled out, place it on a cookie tray and chill it in the fridge for 30 minutes. Then cut the dough into 2 rectangles about 7 inches by 9 inches and put it back in the fridge, so that the butter in the dough stays cold.

>>>

3. Take the almond crema out of the fridge and let it sit at room temperature until it becomes soft. Then remove the dough from the fridge and immediately spread a thin layer of the crema on top of it. Chill the dough in the fridge for another 15 minutes. Remove the dough from the refrigerator and spread a thin layer of jam across the crema. If the dough is very soft, place it back in the refrigerator until it becomes pliable.

4. Roll the dough into a tube: with the long side of the rectangle facing you, fold ¼ inch of the dough over itself. Once that initial fold is complete, place both hands on that fold and gently begin to push the dough, rolling it until it resembles a squeezed-out tube of toothpaste. Repeat with the other rectangle of dough.

5. Wrap the logs loosely in plastic wrap and cool them in the freezer for 1 hour, so the dough is easy to cut.

TO FINISH THE INVOLTINI:

1. When the dough has almost finished chilling, preheat the oven to 350°. Sprinkle the turbinado sugar on a baking sheet, and beat the egg in a small bowl using a fork. Remove the dough from the freezer, remove the plastic wrap, and brush each log on all sides with the egg. Then roll the log in the sugar, coating it evenly on all sides.

2. Cut the logs widthwise into ¼-inch rounds, and place the rounds on a baking sheet lined with parchment paper. Bake for 15 to 20 minutes, until the involtini are golden brown.

SEMOLINA COOKIES

Sesame seeds are a really common Sicilian ingredient (see, for instance, the semolina bread with sesame seeds on the outside, referred to by Italian-Americans as "Sicilian loaf"). Sicilian cuisine is full of Arabic influences like these: all the flavors of North Africa have blown over the island at one point or another, which is why Sicilian-Italian food is totally different from any other Italian cooking. These sesame-coated cookies are great, and pretty easy to make. If you can't find black sesame seeds, don't stress: the white ones work just fine by themselves. The combo of black and white seeds just looks really cool.

TIMING: About 2 hours including chilling, freezing, and baking time

MAKES ABOUT 45 COOKIES

INGREDIENTS

½ pound (2 sticks) butter

1½ cups confectioners' sugar

2 tablespoons brown sugar

1 teaspoon salt

½ teaspoon baking powder

1 cup all-purpose flour

1½ cups semolina flour

2 eggs

½ teaspoon vanilla extract

½ cup black sesame seeds

½ cup white sesame seeds

METHOD

1. Place the butter, confectioners' sugar, and brown sugar in the bowl of a KitchenAid. Using the paddle, cream all of the ingredients together at medium speed (speed 4) until the mixture is smooth and no lumps remain, about 2 minutes.

2. Add the salt, baking powder, flour, and semolina flour. Mix at low speed (speed 2) until all the dry ingredients are incorporated, about 30 seconds.

3. Add the eggs and vanilla extract and mix until everything is well combined into a dough, about 30 seconds.

4. Remove the bowl from the KitchenAid and refrigerate the cookie dough until it is quite cold, at least 20 minutes.

5. Remove the dough from the refrigerator and place it in a piping bag fitted with a ¼-inch tip.

6. Line a baking sheet with parchment paper. Pipe a straight tube of dough running all the way from one side of the sheet to the other. Repeat this procedure with the remaining dough, making sure that the tubes are close to each other but not touching.

7. Place the baking sheet in the freezer and let it set until it's frozen through, at least 1 hour.

8. Preheat the oven to 325°.

9. Using a chef's knife, slice the dough into 2½-inch tubes.

10. Line another baking sheet with parchment paper.

>>>

11 Mix the black and white sesame seeds together in a medium-sized bowl. Roll each tube in the bowl to coat it in the sesame seeds. Place the tubes on the new baking sheet, leaving about 2 inches between cookies for expansion during baking. (If the tubes start to soften at any point in this operation, return them to the freezer until they are firm and manageable.)

12 Bake the cookies until they're golden brown, about 10 to 15 minutes.

These cookies are best if they sit for half an hour or so after they come out of the oven. They'll keep well for a couple of days in an airtight container.

{ B A S E S }

BASIC TOMATO SAUCE

This is the most important recipe in the book. If you make only one recipe from *Urban Italian*, I hope it's this one. Tomato sauce is, of course, the most-used base in Italian cooking—and also the most abused. In Italian-American cooking, the Sauce is near-sacred. But the lore confuses meat-based sauces with the fresh tomato variety. People add all kinds of things to fresh sauce: onions, garlic, piles of herbs ... and then they cook it for hours and hours, until it's the color of dried blood and tastes like winey paste. Call me crazy, but I like my tomato sauce to taste like...tomatoes. The best way to achieve that is to cook the sauce as quickly as possible, to preserve the freshness, and to add any other flavors only at the end, so that they deepen the tomato-y-ness and make it more complex, instead of obscuring it.

Making tomato sauce is a messy operation—you need to get your hands into it, like finger painting, or changing the oil in your car—and you will most likely end up with tomatoes all over you and your kitchen. It's definitely not the kind of thing you want to start an hour before guests start knocking at your door in their nice clothes. But this is a great make-ahead sauce. It keeps beautifully in the fridge for three days or so, and it freezes really well, so you can make big batches ahead of time and keep them on hand. If you're cooking a lot from this book, that's not a bad idea, since there are a number of recipes that work best when made with Basic Tomato Sauce.

I've given you a method for peeling the tomatoes here, but peeling is not mandatory. If it's six o'clock Sunday evening and I want to make some fresh sauce for dinner, I'm not going to get all fancy with the tomatoes—I'll just core 'em and chop 'em. If you can't find great tomatoes (or you're really short on time), you can use a good Italian variety of canned whole tomatoes.

TIMING: About 40 minutes if you're using canned tomatoes; 1 hour to 1½ hours if you're using fresh tomatoes

MAKES 4 CUPS
INGREDIENTS

For the base:

12 beautifully ripe beefsteak tomatoes (about 5 pounds), washed, cored, and scored; or 10 cups (about 2½ 35-ounce cans) good-quality Italian canned tomatoes—I like San Marzano

1 heaping teaspoon sea salt or kosher salt

For the flavored oil:

1 head garlic

1¼ cups extra-virgin olive oil

1 packed cup basil leaves, washed, with stems on

1 teaspoon red pepper flakes

METHOD
TO PEEL THE TOMATOES:

1. Bring a large pot of water to a boil.

2. Wash and core the tomatoes, then cut an X in the bottom of each so the skins loosen as they cook.

3. Plunge the tomatoes into the boiling water for about 30 seconds. They're ready to come out when the skins start to shrink, split, and wrinkle; don't leave them in too long, or the tomatoes will start to cook. You'll probably have to do these in batches to avoid overcooking. Remove the tomatoes with a spider or strainer and immediately plunge them into a large bowl of ice water to stop the cooking process.

4. Once the tomatoes have cooled down, pull the skins off with your fingers.

>>>

TO PREPARE THE SAUCE:

1. Cut the tomatoes in half widthwise. Squeeze out the seeds and juice and discard. (This step is crucial. The key is to bring the sauce to the right consistency as quickly as possible, to preserve the fresh, bright tomato flavor. The more liquid there is, the longer you have to cook the sauce, and the less fresh and tomato-y it will taste.)

2. Roughly chop each tomato half into about 8 chunks—or if they're ripe enough, you can just pull the tomato halves apart into chunks with your fingers.

3. Place the chopped tomatoes in a large pot with a wide surface area. (If you're using the same pot you blanched the tomatoes in, be sure to cool it down—you want to start with a cold pot.) Top the tomatoes with the salt. The salt is absolutely integral to the recipe. It goes in at the beginning of the cooking process to help draw the moisture out of the tomatoes so it can evaporate. If you cut down the amount of salt, the sauce won't work.

4. Turn the heat to medium and let the tomatoes cook down at a lazy bubble, stirring occasionally to prevent sticking. This'll take 45 minutes to 1¼ hours, depending on season, ripeness, and the general quality of your tomatoes; 30 minutes for canned tomatoes. As the tomatoes cook, use a ladle to remove excess water. (The amount of excess could be anywhere from a cup to a quart, depending on how ripe the tomatoes are, but the sauce should be tomatoes and liquid, not tomatoes floating in liquid.) Smash the tomatoes with a wooden spoon as they cook so that the sauce gradually becomes smoother.

TO PREPARE THE FLAVORED OIL:

1. Cut the top off the garlic head so that the skin stays on but the tops of the cloves are exposed. Combine the garlic, olive oil, basil leaves, and red pepper flakes in a small pot over medium heat and bring to a simmer. As soon as you hear the basil leaves "crack" (the sound is almost exactly like adding milk to Rice Krispies), take the mixture off the heat and reserve.

TO FINISH THE SAUCE:

1. When the sauce is reduced by half to two thirds and is thick but still bright red, strain the oil into the pot and stir to combine.

2. Cook the sauce for about 10 more minutes at a lazy bubble. Stir occasionally to keep it from sticking. When the oil and tomatoes have completely emulsified and the sauce looks "whole," turn off the heat and stir it up a bit in the pot with a masher or a hand blender set on low.

Mix this sauce with your pasta while it's hot (don't just dump it on top!) or allow the sauce to cool before storing it in the freezer or fridge.

PESTO

Pesto is another of those Italian staples served just about everywhere, from Michelin-starred restaurants in Emilia-Romagna to the Olive Garden in Detroit. And—just like tomato sauce—everyone has a hundred opinions about it. The biggest issue? The electric blender: labor-saving device or pesto killer? I've used both the electric-blender technique and the mortar-and-pestle option many, many times, and, believe it or not, I prefer the blender. It's less work, the basil stays nice and green, and the pesto has the same flavor as the mortar-and-pestle variety—it might even be a bit fresher-tasting.

Pesto freezes really well, so you can make a big batch of it in the summer, when basil is at its best, and keep it around. (Look for plants with little leaves and no flowers: you don't want the old, bitter leaves nobody loves.) The best basil is the stuff that you grow yourself, and it's the easiest thing in the world to do; you can even grow basil on a New York City apartment windowsill. And you can't beat a midwinter pasta featuring pesto made with basil you grew, picked, and cooked in the summer.

There are lots of variations on pesto. My mom, for instance, likes to make pesto with walnuts instead of pine nuts, because pine nuts are—let's face it—really damn expensive. And believe it or not, that's a totally authentic variation: you can find lots of walnut pesto recipes from way back. In Liguria, they make a walnut pesto that has no basil whatsoever; instead, it features an herb called nepitella. You probably won't find this in your local grocery store, but my mom has pretty much an endless supply: I brought some nepitella back from Liguria ten years ago (don't tell the FDA) and planted it in my parents' front yard. The stuff grows like crazy. It's taken over the whole yard, and every year, when my dad watches his nepitella-laced grass come in, he gets mad all over again. But it makes great pesto, so isn't that worth it?

TIMING: Superfast; about 15 minutes, tops, not counting water-boiling time

MAKES 5 CUPS
(ENOUGH FOR ABOUT 2 TO 3 RECIPES)

INGREDIENTS

3 bunches basil, leaves picked
   (about 8 tightly packed cups)
3 cups extra-virgin olive oil
2 cloves garlic, peeled
2 cups pine nuts
1 cup Parmigiano-Reggiano
1 ½ teaspoons salt

METHOD

1 Put a large pot of water on to boil.

2 Remove the stems from the basil leaves. Wash the basil leaves in two changes of water, the way you would wash spinach, to get rid of the sand. Dry the leaves by placing them on a paper towel or lightly spinning them using a salad spinner, being careful not to bruise them.

3 When the water comes to a boil, blanch the basil leaves by dropping them in the boiling water for about 30 seconds, so that they soften but retain their greenness. Remove the basil from the boiling water with a slotted spoon or spider and place in a bowl of ice water to stop the cooking. When the basil is cold, remove it from the water and squeeze it with your hands to dry it (the same way you would squeeze excess water out of a sponge).

4 Combine 1 cup of the olive oil and the garlic in a blender and blend on medium-high until the mixture is smooth, about 15 seconds.

5 Add the basil and the remaining 2 cups of olive oil. Blend on medium until the basil is thoroughly chopped into small bits. Add 1 cup of warm water and blend on medium until the mixture is thoroughly emulsified. Add the pine nuts and blend on medium until everything is thoroughly mixed and the pine nuts have been chopped up a bit. Add the cheese and salt and blend briefly to combine everything. The pesto will hold in the fridge for 3 to 4 days, in the freezer for up to 6 months.

BRINE

Brine is the king in my kitchen. It's not used very often in everyday Italian cooking, but this is one of those areas where cooking outside the boot is a good idea, because brine just makes some meats better. The salt bath softens the protein strands, so pork chops and chicken are magically juicier: it's like an instant internal sunblock for meat. Brine will hold forever in the fridge, but it's so easy to make that I usually just throw it together the night before I need it.

TIMING: About as long as it takes to boil water

MAKES ENOUGH FOR 1 STANDING PORK ROAST OR 2 CHICKENS

INGREDIENTS

1½ cups kosher salt
1⅓ cups sugar
2 quarts water

METHOD

1. Combine the salt, sugar, and water in a large pot.

2. Bring the mixture to a boil.

3. Cool it down overnight in the fridge in a nonreactive container before using.

CRUMBS YO!

Toasted breadcrumbs are one of my cooking secrets: I toss them in everything. They just make stuff taste better—they give everything a little bit of crunch, from salads to pastas (yes, that's right: pastas. This ain't yer Chef Boyardee supersoft pasta, kids). My crew and I named these breadcrumbs Crumbs Yo! because we're always yelling to each other in the kitchen, "Pass me some crumbs, yo!"

This recipe is incredibly easy, but the simple move of toasting the breadcrumbs in olive oil makes them taste exponentially better than just plain old ordinary breadcrumbs. You can also flavor Crumbs Yo! with black pepper, herbs, grated citrus zest, grated cheese, bits of bacon or pancetta ... trust your instincts about the flavor profile you want to add to that extra crunch. I've given you the start-to-finish recipe here, but if you don't have day-old bread sitting around, panko breadcrumbs will work just as well.

TIMING: Superquick; no more than ½ hour if you're making homemade crumbs; about 6 minutes if you use panko crumbs

MAKES I CUP
INGREDIENTS

For the breadcrumbs:

5 slices of 1- or 2-day-old bread

For the Crumbs Yo!:

2 tablespoons extra-virgin olive oil

1 cup breadcrumbs (homemade
 or panko)

¼ teaspoon salt

¼ teaspoon pepper

Optional:

You can use any one or any combination of these ingredients (or none at all) to flavor the Crumbs Yo! I'll leave it up to the inner chef in you.

1 tablespoon chopped fresh herbs
 (thyme or rosemary)

zest of 1 lemon or orange

1 teaspoon ground fennel seed or
 other spice

¼ cup bacon or pancetta (2 slices),
 diced

a pinch of red pepper flakes

a pinch of dried oregano

METHOD
TO MAKE THE BREADCRUMBS:

1 Preheat the oven to 300°.

2 Cut the bread (including crusts) into 2-inch chunks and put the chunks on a baking tray. Bake for about 10 minutes, until the bread is thoroughly dried out.

3 Let the bread cool slightly—just enough to handle. Pulse the bread in a food processor until it is reduced to coarse crumbs.

TO MAKE THE CRUMBS YO!:

1 In a sauté pan, heat the olive oil over medium heat and toast the breadcrumbs, salt, and pepper until golden brown, about 4 minutes. If you're flavoring your crumbs, toss your flavoring(s) of choice in the pan in the last minute of cooking.

2 Spread the Crumbs Yo! on a plate to cool. They'll will keep for up to 2 days in the fridge, or for a long time in the freezer.

DRIED HERBS

Good dried herbs give great flavor to Italian cooking, but you'd never know that if you only cooked with those dried herbs you buy in the little jars at the supermarket. I know: When I started cooking at home, without that convenient restaurant-purveyor delivery at the door every morning, I tried working with the herbs in those little jars. I think I went through six brands before I gave up—I couldn't believe how flavorless they were. I think they must have been picked sometime in the '70s, dried in the desert for a decade or so, and then stored away in a hot warehouse on the side of a freeway somewhere.

But don't despair: you can beat the Man on this one if you think ahead. It's easy to make your own. Buy fresh local herbs in the middle of the summer and dry 'em out the right way, so the flavor intensifies (like grapes on the vine) rather than withering away. If you keep them in a sealed mason jar, they'll be good through the winter, and they'll give an intense herb flavor to all kinds of dishes. Sprinkle this herb mixture on fish or meat before grilling; add it to salad dressings or sauces. It's good with just about everything. Use the stuff in the little supermarket jars for the catbox.

INGREDIENTS

I'm not giving you measurements here: they'll vary significantly depending on the size of your herbs, because you're buying them on the branch, not loose. The proportions should be roughly like this:

30 percent fresh whole rosemary
30 percent fresh whole thyme
20 percent fresh whole savory
10 percent fresh whole lavender

METHOD

1 Place the herbs on a baking sheet, with spaces between bits so that the air can get to everything. Find a safe spot in your kitchen and leave the herbs there, on the baking sheet, until they dry out and become brittle and gray-green, about 3 to 5 days.

2 Run your fingers down each branch and remove the dried leaves. Mix all the herbs together and store in an airtight container. They're good for six months or so.

GARLIC DRESSING

This dressing kicks ass, and that's all about the roasted garlic. For this recipe, I do what my grandma taught me the first time we made a salad dressing together: I add a little bit of water and sugar to tone down the acidity.

This dressing is great with salads (like the Fig Salad with Arugula, Parmigiano-Reggiano, and Prosciutto, page 73), but it's also an excellent marinade—for vegetables, grilled shrimp, or broiled fish.

TIMING: After the hour it takes to roast the garlic, about 10 minutes

MAKES ¾ CUP

INGREDIENTS

For the roasted garlic:

2 heads garlic

1 teaspoon extra-virgin olive oil

a pinch of kosher salt or sea salt

a pinch of coarse-ground black pepper
   (1 crack of the pepper mill)

For the dressing:

¼ cup rice wine vinegar

¼ cup extra-virgin olive oil

¼ cup grapeseed oil (or corn oil)

2 teaspoons dried oregano, preferably
   on the branch (Sicilian or Calabrian)

¼ teaspoon Tabasco sauce

¼ teaspoon salt

¼ teaspoon coarse-ground black pepper

¼ teaspoon sugar

METHOD

TO ROAST THE GARLIC:

1 Preheat the oven to 450°.

2 Cut across the top of each head of garlic to expose some of the garlic flesh.

3 Place each garlic head cut-side up on a piece of tinfoil big enough to easily wrap it, about 3 inches by 3 inches. Sprinkle the garlic with the olive oil, salt, and pepper. Wrap the garlic up in the foil, making a Hershey's-Kiss shape.

4 Bake on a baking tray on the center rack in the oven until the cloves are soft and golden brown, about 1 hour. Cool the garlic in the fridge or freezer until it's cool to the touch. (The garlic can hold in the fridge for up to 3 days at this stage.)

TO PREPARE THE DRESSING:

1 Pick up each garlic head by the bottom and squeeze the meat into a fine sieve. With the back of a spoon, press the meat of the garlic through the sieve to get as much through as possible. Be sure to scoop the remnants from the underside of the sieve into the bowl. Discard the skins.

2 Add the dressing ingredients and 2 tablespoons of water to the bowl, whisking as you go to combine. When all the ingredients are in the bowl, whisk again to make sure the flavors are incorporated. Taste and adjust the seasonings and sweetness.

The dressing will hold in the fridge for up to a week.

HOW TO ROAST PEPPERS THE EASY WAY

People seem to think you've got to be crazy to roast peppers yourself at home. "Why not just buy them in those little jars?" they ask. Well, my friends, the vegetable matter in those little jars—they're roast peppers, but they're not *roast peppers*. The texture's not right, and the charring tastes ... uncharred. You can do much better, and it's really pretty easy—especially when you use the broiler, the single most underused oven setting in America.

TIMING: About an hour, but most of this is waiting for the peppers to roast, then waiting for them to steam

MAKES ABOUT 3 CUPS
INGREDIENTS

6 bell peppers—red, yellow, orange, or
    a mixture
¼ cup extra-virgin olive oil
a generous pinch each of salt and
    coarse-ground black pepper

METHOD

1 Turn the oven on to broil.

2 Cut the peppers in half from top to bottom, stem and all, splitting the stems in half lengthwise. With each pepper half, hook your thumb under the seeds and the stem and pull the whole thing out in one go. Pull off any remaining white pith.

3 Put the pepper halves in a bowl and pour the olive oil over the top. Mix with your hands to coat each pepper piece completely. Season with salt and pepper.

4 Lay the peppers skin-side up on a roasting rack and place them on the middle oven rack to roast. At the 5-minute mark, rotate the pan to ensure even roasting. At 10 minutes, the skins should be black and blistery; turn the peppers over and return them to the oven. At the 15-minute mark, rotate the pan again. When the peppers are thoroughly blistered and blackened in places on both sides (about 20 minutes), use a pair of tongs to remove them to a bowl.

5 Cover the bowl with aluminum foil or plastic wrap and let the peppers steam for 20 minutes. They will continue to cook without browning, and the skins will peel away from the meat.

6 Slip the skins off and discard them. At the bottom of the bowl in which the peppers have been steaming, you'll find what I call "liquid gold"—the most intense roasted-pepper flavor possible. Save it: you can use it in my Peperonata Modo Mio (page 76) or Chicken Leg Cacciatore with Sweet Peppers, Fennel, and Green Olives (page 162), and if you've got leftover roast peppers, you can store them in the fridge in the liquid gold to help them keep their flavor and texture. They'll keep for up to a week.

PASTA DOUGH FOR LONG PASTA

Everyone knows that the best pasta is made the traditional way, by hand, right? You know: you pile the flour on your pasta board, forming a small mountain; you make a well for the egg ... and so on and so forth. It helps, of course, if you do this while impersonating an old Italian woman in a housedress. I hear the pasta comes out much better that way. Also that Target sells old-Italian-women housedresses. Very reasonable. (Woven hairnets and slippers, too.)

Okay, so the traditional technique is very rustic and atmospheric and all. But it also takes forever, makes a huge mess, and is generally unreliable. I never use it—at home or at the restaurant. Me, I use a KitchenAid with a dough hook. I know this sounds like sacrilege to all those *Under the Tuscan Sun* true believers—but this, my friends, is Urban Italian, not thousand-year-old-grandma-with-an-outhouse-and-no-hot-water Italian.

This pasta is all about texture, so there's no olive oil. I use durham semolina flour—very grainy, almost like corn flour—because it's important that the strands of pasta grip the sauce a little bit. I also use "00" flour here. You can substitute regular white flour if you need to, but this stuff makes better pasta: it's very fine, but it's made from durham wheat, which is very hard, so the pasta is strong and doesn't break apart. There are a number of different brands available in the U.S.; I use Gran Mugnaio.

I get very unhappy if dinnertime is approaching and I mess up something in the pasta-making process and then discover I've run out of dough, so this recipe makes plenty of extra. Part of the craft of being a good cook is not letting your guests know about your mistakes.

TIMING: Pretty quick. You can easily do this in the morning after breakfast, let the dough rest in the fridge, and make pasta for dinner.

MAKES ABOUT 2½ POUNDS OF DOUGH

INGREDIENTS

2 cups durham semolina flour

4 cups "00" flour plus more for flouring
   work surface and dough

1 teaspoon salt

8 whole eggs

4 egg yolks

METHOD

1. Flour a board, marble slab, or countertop well.

2. Combine the two flours and the salt in a KitchenAid bowl and combine on speed 1 using the dough hook. Add the eggs and the egg yolks. Turn it up to speed 5 and mix until it looks like a rough dough, about 30 seconds.

3. Remove the dough from the machine and mix it well with your hands, first in the bowl (to scoop up and integrate the unmixed flour on the bottom) and then on the floured board or work surface to ensure that everything is very well combined.

4. Return the dough to the KitchenAid and blend on speed 3 just until the mixture comes together as a smoother, tighter dough and pulls away from the sides of the bowl, 15 seconds or so. (Remember: every KitchenAid, like every oven, is different, so use your eye to judge.)

5. Flour your work surface again and turn the dough out onto it. Sprinkle flour on the dough to keep it from sticking.

>>>

6 Roll the dough into a ball. Reach over the top of the ball, hook your fingers in, and fold it back toward you; then press the folded bit in with the heel of your hand. (You're basically turning the outside part into the inside part.) That, repeated many times, is how the dough is worked. Keep adding lots of flour, so the dough is not sticky. When the dough is nice and smooth on the outside, like a well-kneaded bread dough—this takes about 3 minutes—form it into a tight ball. Wrap it snugly in 2 layers of plastic wrap, so it's nice and tight, and put it in the fridge to rest for at least 2 hours—preferably overnight.

PASTA DOUGH FOR RAVIOLI

The method for ravioli dough is exactly the same as the method for long pasta; only the ingredients change. You want this pasta to be really light colored and smooth, so we're adding olive oil, leaving out the semolina flour, and upping the quotient of "00" flour.

INGREDIENTS

6 cups "00" flour, plus more
   for flouring work surface
   and dough

1 teaspoon salt

7 whole eggs

5 egg yolks

2 tablespoons olive oil

HOW TO ROLL OUT FETTUCCINI

INGREDIENTS

1 recipe Pasta Dough for Long Pasta
　　(page 295)

all-purpose flour for dusting

METHOD

1　Remove the pasta dough from the fridge and turn it out onto a well-floured surface. With a wooden rolling pin, roll the dough out into a square or a rectangle, so that it fits inside your pasta machine.

2　Flour the pasta to remove stickiness and roll it through the pasta machine. Cut the resulting sheet of dough in half (so the final sheet doesn't get too long). Roll the pasta through the pasta machine again, reducing the setting. Repeat until the dough is thin enough to allow you to see the outline and color of your hand through it, but not so thin that it gets fragile: it should feel like a piece of velvet. At this point, run the dough through once more without changing the setting.

3　Cut the dough into 12- to 14-inch lengths.

4　Pass each one through the fettuccini-sized attachment on your pasta maker.

5　Return the fettuccini to the floured surface, sprinkle more flour over the top, and toss with your hands so that all the strands are well floured and don't stick. Place the dough on a floured sheet tray or a plate and return to the fridge. The dough will hold in the fridge for up to 1 week.

SALSA GIALLO

Salsa Giallo—my fancy name for "yellow sauce"—is always on my menu in the summertime, when we have beautiful local peppers and tomatoes. It's super-super-easy, and great with grilled fish like tuna or seafood like shrimp.

This sauce gives great eye appeal at fancy parties, for minimum labor. Just pool it in the bottom of the plate and put your fish or shrimp on top.

TIMING: Very quick and easy; under ½ hour, including steaming time

SERVES 4 TO 6
INGREDIENTS

For the peppers:

2 tablespoons extra-virgin olive oil

1 clove garlic, sliced Goodfellas thin

1 medium-sized ripe yellow pepper, sliced

a pinch of red pepper flakes

¼ teaspoon salt

To finish the salsa:

1 very ripe medium yellow tomato, rough-chopped (skin included)

1 tablespoon extra-virgin olive oil

1 tablespoon red wine vinegar or sherry vinegar

½ teaspoon sugar

¼ teaspoon salt

METHOD
TO PREPARE THE PEPPERS:

1   Heat the olive oil in a medium pot over low heat. Add the garlic and toast until fragrant, about 30 seconds.

2   Add the yellow pepper slices, red pepper flakes, and salt. Cook very slowly, covered, stirring occasionally to keep from sticking, until the peppers are very soft, 12 to 15 minutes. If the peppers start to color or stick, add ¼ cup of water and allow them to steam-cook.

TO FINISH THE SALSA:

1   Put the peppers in the blender. Add the chopped tomato, olive oil, vinegar, sugar, and salt. Pulse until the ingredients have combined into a thick liquid. Adjust the seasoning. Every tomato is different—some are sweeter, some have more acid—so if you taste the mixture and say to yourself, "This is sour" (instead of, you know, "This is delicious"), add a little more sugar. If you find it too sweet, add vinegar. If the bits of pepper peel bother you, push the mixture through a strainer, using the back of a spoon.

Serve at room temperature.

SALSA ROSSA

This is Salsa Giallo's bad-ass cousin. I got the idea for this dish from a condiment of the same name—a chopped-up red pepper purée—that I bought at a gourmet shop in Bologna. But my version is much more than just peppers: call it a true red sauce, Urban Italian–style.

I make this with Calabrian sun-dried peppers, which I buy at Coluccio's in Brooklyn—but that can be a long shopping trip if you're not within subway distance, so I've substituted sun-dried tomatoes here.

This recipe is a great accompaniment for the Shrimp Meatballs (page 62). It's also really good with grilled shrimp or lobster, grilled chicken, or grilled or baked fish.

TIMING: About 45 minutes

SERVES 4 TO 6
INGREDIENTS

For the tomato:

1 large ripe beefsteak tomato, cored and
　　halved

a pinch each of salt and coarse-ground
　　black pepper

For the bell pepper mixture:

2 tablespoons extra-virgin olive oil

2 cloves garlic, sliced

¼ cup sliced onion

1 red bell pepper, roughly chopped

a pinch of red pepper flakes

¼ teaspoon salt

1 dried bay leaf

To finish the salsa:

4 sun-dried tomatoes, soaked in hot
　　water for ½ hour

4 Peppadew or other pickled Italian
　　peppers

2 tablespoons extra-virgin olive oil

1 tablespoon red wine vinegar

½ tablespoon dried oregano, preferably
　　on the branch (Sicilian or Calabrian)

4 drops Tabasco sauce

⅛ teaspoon sweet paprika

¼ teaspoon salt

METHOD

TO PREPARE THE TOMATO:

1　Preheat the oven to 400°.

2　Place the tomato cut-side up on a sheet tray, and sprinkle it with salt and pepper. Place the tray in the oven on the middle rack. Roast until the tomato is wrinkled and browned and juice has collected in the bottom of the pan, about 20 minutes. Remove the tray from the oven. Tip the whole thing—tomatoes and juice—into the blender.

TO PREPARE THE BELL PEPPER MIXTURE:

1　Heat the olive oil in a medium pot over medium heat. Add the garlic and onion and toast until the garlic is golden brown and the onion is slightly softened, about 1 minute.

2　Add the bell pepper, red pepper flakes, salt, and bay leaf. Cover the pot and cook until the bell pepper is very soft, about 20 minutes, stirring occasionally to keep it from sticking. (When you open the lid to stir the mixture, hold it vertically and use a wooden spoon to scrape the liquid that has condensed back into the pot, so the peppers continually steam in their own juices.)

TO FINISH THE SALSA:

1　Remove the bay leaf from the pepper mixture and add the peppers to the blender. Add the sun-dried tomatoes, Peppadews or pickled peppers, olive oil, vinegar, oregano, Tabasco, paprika, and salt. Blend on medium until smooth. Serve at room temperature.

SALSA VERDE

Not to be confused with the spicy Mexican sauce of the same name, this is an Italian classic, traditionally served with specialties like *bollito misto*. I love it with grilled beef, like the Steak Picante (page 200), but it's also great with grilled fish, or as a dressing for vegetable antipasti. I'm usually a big fan of labor-saving technology, but I like to do this one by hand, so that I can preserve the textures of the ingredients. If you're pressed for time and your knife work is less than warp speed, however, you can always throw everything in the processor.

At the restaurant, we leave the cornichons out because they sometimes color the sauce, dulling the green. If your primary concern is the beautiful bright-green color of the mixture, you might want to do the same. If, on the other hand, issues like "the tonal purity of my green sauce" don't keep you up at night, use the cornichons: they add depth, crunch, and flavor.

TIMING: Super-super-fast; maybe 20 minutes plus egg-boiling time. Also supereasy: there's not even any heat involved here.

MAKES ENOUGH TO ACCOMPANY 12 STEAKS

INGREDIENTS

1 tablespoon chopped capers

1 teaspoon Dijon mustard

3 anchovies, mashed into a paste with
    the side of a knife

1 clove garlic, minced fine

1 shallot, minced fine

¾ cup olive oil

1 cup chopped Italian parsley

¼ cup chopped basil

1 egg, hard-boiled

a pinch each of salt, coarse-ground black
    pepper, and sugar

Optional:

8 whole cornichons

METHOD

1 Combine the capers, mustard, anchovy paste, garlic, shallot, olive oil, parsley, basil, and cornichons (if using) in a bowl.

2 Press the hard-boiled egg through a fine sieve to "grate" it into the bowl. (This addition of the egg is an old, old cooking technique that gives the sauce body. Don't be tempted to use a cheese grater for this instead: you want to be sure all the egg gets into the bowl in tiny, even pieces, and with a grater bits of all sizes will fall all over the place.)

3 Add pinches of salt, pepper, and sugar to taste. Mix to combine. As the name suggests, the flavor should be very "green." Serve at room temperature. This sauce will hold in the fridge for up to a week.

{ A GUIDE TO LOCATIONS }

Here's a list of some of the places to buy and eat food that I mention in the book.
If you're in Italy—or in New York—try to stop by. You'll be happy, I promise.

I T A L Y

Antica Macelleria Cecchini
Via XX Luglio, 11
Panzano in Chianti, Firenze
055 852020

Buca di Bacco
Corso Italia, 113
Pietra Ligure, Savona
019 615307

Cascina Cornale
Corso Guglielmo Marconi, 64
Magliano Alfiori CN
www.cascinacornale.it

Dal Pescatore
Località Runate
Canneto sull'Oglio, Mantova
0376 723001
www.dalpescatore.com

Folparo (da Guido)
Piazza della Frutta
Padova

Girarrosto Francia
Corso francia, 261
Torino

Hostaria da Ivan
Via Villa, 73
Fontanelle, Parma
0521 870113
www.hostariadaivan.it

Il Ristorante Duomo
Via Capitano Bocchieri, 31
Ragusa
0932 651265
www.ristoranteduomo.it

La Dogana di Vittoriano Pierucci
Via Sarzanese, 442
Capezzano Pianore, Lucca
0584 915159

L'Antica Dolceria Bonajuto
Corso Umberto 1, n. 159
Modica, Ragusa
0932 941225
www.bonajuto.it

La Frasca
Via Matteotti, 34
Castrocaro Terme, Forlì-Cesena
0543 767471
www.lafrasca.it

Le Calandre
Via Liguria, 1
Sarmeola di Rubano, Padova
049 630303
www.calandre.com

Liugi Guffanti
Via Milano, 140
Arona, Novara
0322 242038
www.guffantiformaggi.com

Locanda nel Borgo Antico
Via Boschetti, 4
Barolo, Cuneo
017 356355
www.locandanelborgo.com

Nangalarruni
Via Alberghi, 5
Castelbuono, Palermo
0921 671428

Quattro Passi
Via A. Vespucci, 13 N
Massalubrese, Naples
081 8082800
www.ristorantequattropassi.it

Tartufi Morra
Piazza Pertinace, 3
Alba, Cuneo
www.tartufimorra.com

Tenuta Vannulo
Via S. Galilei, 10
Capaccio Scalo, Savona
0828 724765
www.vannulo.it

Terra Santa
Piazza Materdomini, 46
Nocera, Salerno
081 933562
www.osteriaterrasanta.it

Trattoria da Omer
Via Torre, 33
Modena
059 218050

Biancardi Meats

*(For baby lamb, goat, liver
sausage, and veal)*

2350 Arthur Avenue

Bronx, NY 10458

718-733-4058

**Borgatti's Ravioli and
Egg Noodles**

(For ravioli and fresh pasta)

632 East 187th Street

Bronx, NY 10458

718-367-3799

www.borgattis.com

BuonItalia

*(For Calabrian oregano, and
every other Italian specialty
you can imagine)*

75 9th Avenue

New York, NY 10011

212-633-9090

www.buonitalia.com

Calabria Pork Store

*(For sopressata and spicy
anchovies)*

2338 Arthur Avenue

Bronx, NY 10458

718-367-5145

D. Coluccio and Sons

*(For Sicilian extra-virgin olive
oil, polenta, and Calabrian
sun-dried peppers)*

1214 60th Street

Brooklyn, NY 11219

718-436-6700

www.dcoluccioandsons.com

DiPaolo's Dairy

*(For fresh ricotta and
mozzarella)*

206 Grand Street

New York, NY 10013

212-226-1033

Murray's Cheese

*(For every Italian cheese
you can imagine, and some
you can't)*

245 Bleecker Street

New York, NY 10012

212-243-3289

www.murrayscheese.com

Primizie Fine Foods

*(For various Italian goods; this
is the best place to buy fresh
Italian truffles and truffle
products)*

www.primiziefinefoods.com

Royal Crown Pastry Shop

*(For broccoli rabe bread,
sausage-and-pepper bread,
and prosciutto bread)*

6512 14th Avenue

Brooklyn, NY 11219

718-234-1002

**Villabate Pasticceria and
Bakery**

*(For cannoli, cassata, and
other southern Italian
desserts)*

7117 18th Avenue

Brooklyn, NY 11204

718-331-8430

www.villabate.net

ACKNOWLEDGMENTS

Many thanks are due to many people for this book and everything that led up to it: my awesome core group of chefs, Luke Ostrom, Joshua Gripper, Ron Rosselli, and Rich Torrisi—all of whom contributed recipes to this book; cooks Emily Iguchi, Anthony Coffee, and Jose Guermos, who did emergency extra recipe testing; from the other side of the swinging door, my longtime colleagues Ron Levine, Olivier Flosse, Joseph Scherr, and Dante Camera; the great professional cooks who have inspired and taught me over the years, including John D'Amico, Dino Baldini, Nicola Bindini, Mitchell Davis, Valentino Mercatelli, Gray Kunz, Daniel Boulud, Jean François Bruel, Eric Betoia, and Bertrand Chemel.

Big thanks to our agent, Kim Witherspoon, for shaping our ideas into a great book proposal; to Bloomsbury editor in chief Karen Rinaldi, for helping us to create a book that's exactly what we wanted; to Amy King, for her spot-on art direction; to our editor, Nick Trautwein, for heroic, generous, and pitch-perfect guidance and editing and general (and repeated) saving of the day; and to Quentin Bacon for his beautiful work.

We sent out all the recipes in this book to family and friends around the country and in Canada to get some feedback from the trenches. Our volunteer cooks were amazing, and their comments and suggestions made everything much better. So our special thanks to:

Kate Atherly and Norman Wilner, Amy and Mike Bandwen, Karen Bandwen, Tony and Heather Bentowski, Margaret Bertin, Tommy and Margo Bertin, Gee Bertolini, Paolo Burzese, Mitchell Davis, Michael John Derbecker, Nicolette Flosse, Bryna and Gerry Hyman, Emily Klein, Liz and Ron Levine, the Megesi family, Darren and Hanna Mieskowski, Devorah Miller, Jeff Morris, Dean Nole, Felice Ramela, Alan Richman, Sharla Sava, Vince Scalera, Juanita Sherba, Rachel Sherba, Becky Varner, Jeremy Varner, and Peter Waisberg.

INDEX